PRENTICE HALL LITERATURE

PENGUIN EDITION

Skills Development Workbook

Grade Seven

PEARSON

Prentice Hall

Upper Saddle River, New Jersey
Boston, Massachusetts

ISBN 0-13-250240-2

2 3 4 5 6 7 8 9 10   10 09 08 07 06

Contents

Unit 2 Short Stories

Part 1 Predicting

Part 2 Making Inferences

Unit 3 Types of Nonfiction

Part 1 Main Idea

Part 2 Fact and Opinion

Unit 4 Poetry

Part 1 Drawing Conclusions

Part 2 Paraphrasing

Unit 5 Drama

Part 1 Purpose for Reading

Part 2 Summarizing

"The Monsters Are Due on Maple Street" by Rod Serling

from *Grandpa and the Statue* by Arthur Miller

"My Head Is Full of Starshine" by Peg Kehret

Part 2 Comparison and Contrast

Richard Peck
Listening and Viewing

Segment 1: Meet Richard Peck
- From where does Richard Peck draw his inspiration to write stories about young people?
- If you were writing a story, where might you get ideas for writing?

____
____
____
____

Segment 2: Fiction and Nonfiction
- Do you agree with Richard Peck that fiction can be "truer than fact"?
- How might a work of fiction be more convincing than a work of nonfiction, such as a newspaper article?

____
____
____
____

Segment 3: The Writing Process
- Why does Richard Peck throw out the first chapter of a book once he has written the ending?
- Which one of Richard Peck's writing methods would you use? Why?

____
____
____
____

Segment 4: The Rewards of Writing
- Why does Richard Peck believe readers "have an advantage" over people who do not read?
- How has reading helped you better understand another person, a situation, or yourself? Explain.

____
____
____
____

Learning About Fiction and Nonfiction

This chart compares and contrasts **fiction** and **nonfiction**:

Fiction	Nonfiction
tells about *made-up* people or animals, called **characters:** The characters experience a series of made-up events, called the **plot;** the plot takes place at a certain real or imagined time in a certain real or imagined location, which is the **setting;** the plot also contains a problem, or **conflict,** that characters must solve	tells about *real* people, animals, places, things, events, and ideas; presents facts and discusses ideas; may reflect the **historical context** of its time by making references to current events, society, and culture
may be told from the perspective of a character in the story (**first-person point of view**) or a narrator outside the story (**third-person point of view**)	is told from the **perspective** of the author
takes the form of short stories, novellas, novels	takes the form of biographies, autobiographies, memoirs, letters, journals, diaries, essays, articles, textbooks, and documents, such as application forms and instructions
to explain, inform, persuade, or entertain	to explain, inform, persuade, or entertain

A. DIRECTIONS: *Using clues in each title, write* fiction *or* nonfiction *on the line.*

_______________________ 1. "My Family Came From Mars"

_______________________ 2. "Historic Landings on the Moon"

_______________________ 3. *The Life of Thomas Jefferson*

_______________________ 4. *Jackie Rabbit, King of the Meadow*

_______________________ 5. "How to Make Oatmeal Bread"

B. DIRECTIONS: *Read this paragraph carefully, and decide whether it is fiction or nonfiction. Indicate your choice. Then, explain what hints led you to make your choice.*

The Ramirez family set off on their summer vacation yesterday. Luis was excited. It was the first trip that his family had taken since coming to the United States last year. Luis had brought along two books to read during the trip. He'd have plenty of time to read. After all, flying to a distant galaxy would take at least a week.

Fiction / Nonfiction: ____

Explanation: ____

"The Three-Century Woman" by Richard Peck
Model Selection: Fiction

Every work of **fiction** includes made-up people or animals, called **characters,** and a made-up series of events, called the **plot.** The plot may seem realistic. For example, it may be a story about students like you. On the other hand, the plot may be a fantasy. It might, for example, feature talking cats.

The plot takes place at a certain time and in a certain location, called the **setting.** The setting may or may not be real. Every plot contains a problem, or **conflict,** that one or more characters must solve.

A speaker, called the **narrator,** tells the story from a certain perspective, or **point of view.** If the narrator is a character in the story, he or she tells it from the **first-person point of view.** If the narrator is outside the story, he or she tells it from the **third-person point of view.**

Examples of fiction include novels, novellas, and short stories.

A. Directions: *"The Three-Century Woman" is a work of fiction. Complete the following items to provide details about its characters, narrator, setting, and plot.*

1. The **characters:** ____

____

2. Is the **narrator** inside or outside the story? ___________________

3. Is the story told from the **first-person** or **third-person** point of view? _________

____

4. Clues that indicate the point of view: _______________________________

____

5. When does the story take place? ____________________________________

____

6. Where does the story take place? ___________________________________

____

7. Is the **setting** realistic or imaginary? Explain. _____________________

____

8. Is the **plot** realistic or fantastic? ___________________

9. Examples of real or fantastic **plot** elements: _______________________

____

10. What **conflict,** or problem, do the characters face?

____

____

"The Fall of the *Hindenburg*" by Michael Morrison
Model Selection: Nonfiction

Nonfiction deals with *real* people, animals, places, things, events, and ideas. It may present facts or discuss ideas.

A work of nonfiction is narrated from the **point of view,** or perspective, of the author. Often nonfiction reflects the **historical context** of its time by including references to current events, society, or culture. For example, an article about the American Revolution would contain social and cultural information about the East Coast of North America in the mid-1700s.

Works of nonfiction include biographies, autobiographies, memoirs, letters, journals, diaries, essays, articles, textbooks, and various documents, such as application forms and instructions.

A. DIRECTIONS: *Answer these questions about "The Fall of the* Hindenburg.*"*

1. What real event does the article discuss?

   ____

2. On what date, and in what location, did the event take place?

   ____

3. List three facts that the author presents.

   ____

   ____

   ____

4. What conclusions can you draw about the topic, based on your reading of the article?

   ____

   ____

5. Give an example of a detail that sets a historical context for the article.

   ____

B. DIRECTIONS: *Authors have one or more purposes for writing a piece of nonfiction. For example, an author might write to explain how to do something, to tell the story of a person's life, to inform readers about a topic, to persuade readers to share an opinion, or to share a personal experience. In your opinion, what was Michael Morrison's purpose for writing "The Fall of the Hindenburg"? Support your answer by citing facts, reasons, and examples from the article.*

____

____

____

"Papa's Parrot" by Cynthia Rylant
Reading: Use Context Clues to Unlock the Meaning

Context, the words and phrases surrounding a word, can help you understand a word you do not know. When you come across an unfamiliar word, **use context clues to unlock the meaning.** Look for a word or words that might mean the same thing or have the opposite meaning of the unfamiliar word. In addition, you may find definitions, examples, or descriptions of the unfamiliar word. For example, in this passage from "Papa's Parrot," the italicized words are clues to the meaning of *unpack:*

> *New shipments of candy and nuts* would be arriving. . . .

> ...Harry told his father that he would go to the store every day after school and <u>unpack</u> boxes. He would *sort out all the candy and nuts.*

As you read, use context clues to find possible meanings for unfamiliar words. Check the words in a dictionary after you read.

DIRECTIONS: *Read each of the following sentences or short passages from "Papa's Parrot." Look at the underlined word. Then, find other words in the passage that can be used as context clues to help you figure out the meaning of the underlined word. Write the context clue or clues on the first line. Write the meaning of the underlined word on the second line. Then, check your answer by looking up the underlined word in a dictionary.*

Hint: Sometimes the context clues appear a distance away from the unfamiliar word. For item 3, below, the context clue appears in the first paragraph of the story.

1. Harry stopped liking candy and nuts when he was around seven, but, in spite of this, he and Mr. Tillian had <u>remained</u> friends and were still friends the year Harry turned twelve.

   Context clues: ____

   Meaning of word: ____

2. At home things were different. Harry and his father joked with each other at the dinner table as they always had—Mr. Tillian <u>teasing</u> Harry about his smelly socks; Harry teasing Mr. Tillian about his blubbery stomach.

   Context clues: ____

   Meaning of word: ____

3. Though his father was fat and merely owned a candy and nut shop, Harry Tillian liked his papa. . . . Harry and his father joked with each other at the dinner table as they always had—Mr. Tillian teasing Harry about his smelly socks; Harry teasing Mr. Tillian about his <u>blubbery</u> stomach.

   Context clues: ____

   Meaning of word: ____

"Papa's Parrot" by Cynthia Rylant
Literary Analysis: Narrative Writing

Narrative writing is any type of writing that tells a story. The act or process of telling a story is also called **narration.**

- A narrative is usually told in chronological order—the order in which events occur in time.
- A narrative may be fiction, nonfiction, or poetry.

When you look at events in chronological order, you see that events that occur later in a narrative often depend on events that occurred earlier. For example, in "Papa's Parrot" the part of the story in which Harry walks by his father's store and hears him talking to Rocky must follow the part in which Mr. Tillian buys Rocky in the first place.

DIRECTIONS: *Below is a list often events from "Papa's Parrot." Put the events in chronological order by writing a number from 1 to 10 on the line before the event. The first event has been marked for you. Remember that each event has to make sense in terms of what has already occurred in the story.*

____ **A.** Harry stops going to the candy and nut shop when he sees his father talking to Rocky.

____ **B.** Harry goes to the candy and nut shop to unpack boxes and feed Rocky.

____ **C.** Harry yells at Rocky and throws peppermints at him.

____ **D.** Mr. Tillian buys a parrot, spending more money than he can afford.

____ **E.** Harry understands what Rocky means and goes to visit his father in the hospital.

____ **F.** Mr. Tillian falls ill and is taken to the hospital.

____ **G.** When they were young, Harry and his friends stopped by his father's candy and nut shop after school to buy penny candy or roasted peanuts.

____ **H.** Mr. Tillian talks to Rocky, and the two watch television together.

____ **I.** After Harry enters junior high school, he and his friends stop going to the candy and nut shop and spend more time playing video games and shopping for records.

____ **J.** The parrot says, "Hello, Rocky!" and "Where's Harry?" over and over.

"Papa's Parrot" by Cynthia Rylant
Vocabulary Builder

Word List

ignored   resumed

A. DIRECTIONS: *Read the incomplete paragraphs below. On each line, write one of the words from the Word List. You will use each word more than once. Think about the meaning of the word in the context of the paragraphs.*

When the parrot started squawking, Harry called to him to be quiet. After a few seconds, Rocky (1) _____________________ his squawking. Harry (2) _____________________ the noise for a while and then became annoyed. He called to Rocky again to hush up. Rocky was silent for a short time, and then he (3) _____________________ his squawking. So Harry (4) _____________________ his yelling. Now Rocky was flapping his wings. Harry had (5) _____________________ the problem long enough.

He went to the back of the shop. The neighborhood cat had gotten in. She was interested in Rocky. The parrot had been trying to tell Harry. Harry sent the cat on her way, and then he (6) _____________________ the parrot yet again and (7) _____________________ his video game. The parrot (8) _____________________ him, too. Rocky was busy watching a soap opera.

B. DIRECTIONS: *Think about the meaning of the italicized Word List word in each item below. Then, answer the question, and explain your answer.*

1. After his hospital stay, Mr. Tillian *resumed* his place in the candy and nut shop. Were his customers pleased?

   ____

2. While Mr. Tillian was in the hospital, Harry *ignored* his friends. Were his friends pleased?

   ____

C. DIRECTIONS: *On each line, write the letter of the word that means the* opposite *of the Word List word.*

____ 1. ignored
     A. overlooked   B. neglected   C. listened   D. missed

____ 2. resumed
     A. halted   B. continued   C. proceeded   D. went on

Unit 1 Resources: Fiction and Nonfiction

"Papa's Parrot" by Cynthia Rylant
Support for Writing a Brief Essay

Use the graphic organizer below to record details that show what Harry was like before he entered junior high school.

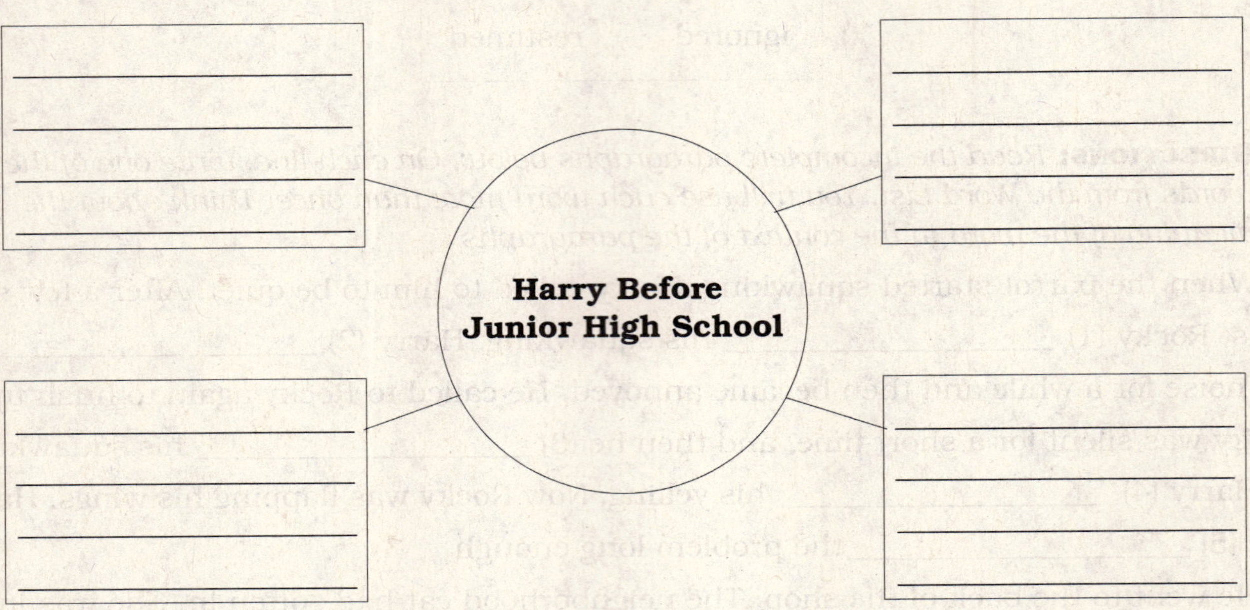

Use the graphic organizer below to record details that show Harry's behaviors and thoughts after he began junior high school. Think about Harry both before and after his father became ill.

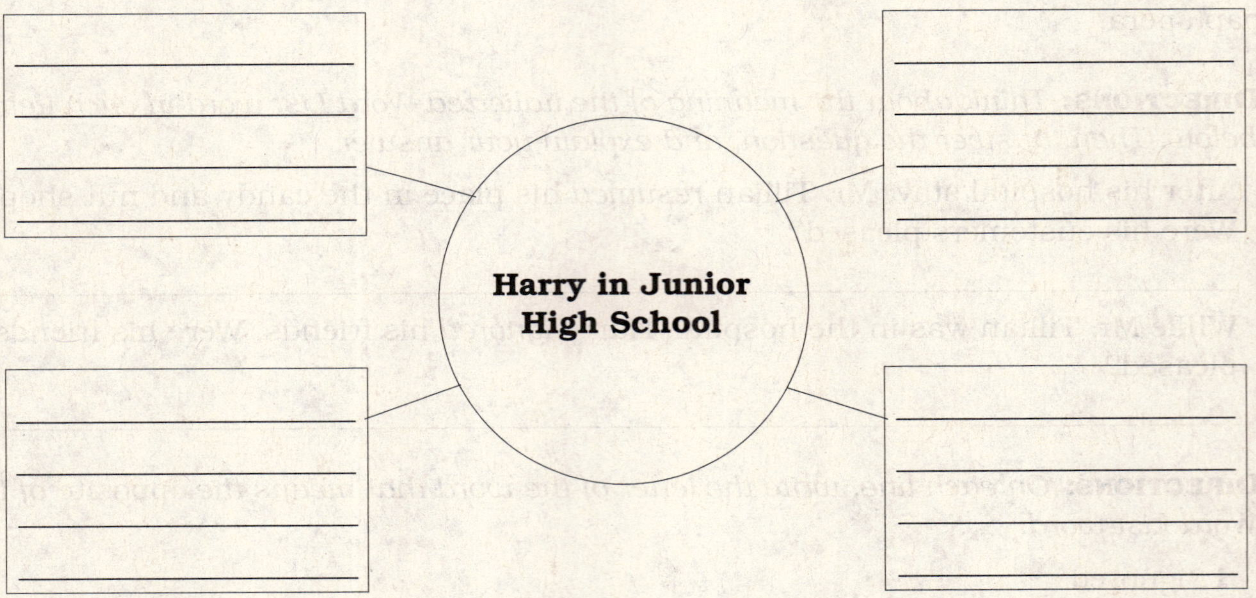

Now, use your notes to draft a brief essay comparing and contrasting Harry's behavior before and after he entered junior high school.

"MK" by Jean Fritz

Reading: Use Context Clues to Unlock the Meaning

Context, the words and phrases surrounding a word, can help you understand a word you do not know. When you come across an unfamiliar word, **use context clues to unlock the meaning.** Look for a word or words that might mean the same thing or have the opposite meaning of the unfamiliar word. In addition, you may find definitions, examples, or descriptions of the unfamiliar word. For example, in this passage from "MK," the italicized words are clues to the meaning of *protected*:

> The women and children going to Shanghai would be <u>protected</u> *from bullets by steel barriers erected around the deck.*

As you read, use context clues to find possible meanings for unfamiliar words. Check the words in a dictionary after you read.

DIRECTIONS: *Read each of the following sentences or short passages from "MK." Look at the underlined word. Then, find other words in the passage that can be used as context clues to help you figure out the meaning of the underlined word. Write the context clue or clues on the first line. Write the meaning of the underlined word on the second line. Then, check your answer by looking up the underlined word in a dictionary.*

1. I couldn't let on how I really felt. . . . "I'll be okay," I said, sniffing back fake tears. Sometimes it's necessary to <u>deceive</u> your parents if you love them, and I did love mine.

   Context clues: ____

   Meaning of word: ____

2. The girls were given what looked like dance cards and the boys were supposed to sign up for the talk sessions they wanted. Of course a girl could feel like a <u>wallflower</u> if her card wasn't filled up, but mine usually was.

   Context clues: ____

   Meaning of word: ____

3. It was a three-day trip across most of the <u>continent</u>, but it didn't seem long. Every minute America was under us and rushing past our windows—the Rocky Mountains, the Mississippi River, flat ranch land, small towns, forests, boys dragging school bags over dusty roads.

   Context clues: ____

   Meaning of word: ____

4. I decided that American children were <u>ignorant</u>. Didn't their teachers teach them anything?

   Context clues: ____

   Meaning of word: ____

"MK" by Jean Fritz
Literary Analysis: Narrative

Narrative writing is any type of writing that tells a story. The act or process of telling a story is also called **narration.**

- A narrative is usually told in chronological order—the order in which events occur in time.
- A narrative may be fiction, nonfiction, or poetry.

When you look at events in chronological order, you see that events that occur later in a narrative often depend on events that occurred earlier. In "MK," for example, the part of the story in which Jean takes her first steps on American soil must follow the part in which Jean and her family cross the Pacific Ocean to reach America.

DIRECTIONS: *Below is a list of ten events from "MK." Put the events in chronological order by writing a number from 1 to 10 on the line before the event. The first event has been marked for you. Remember that each event has to make sense in terms of what has already occurred in the story.*

_____ A. Paula, Jean's roommate at the Shanghai American School, cuts Jean's hair in a bob, the latest American style.

_____ B. Jean and most of the other passengers are seasick as they cross the Pacific Ocean on a steamer.

_____ C. Fletcher Barrett tells Jean that he is in love with her.

_____ D. In America, Jean wonders why her classmates are ignorant.

_____ E. Jean's mother enrolls Jean in the Shanghai American School.

_____ F. When Jean is almost ready to fall in love, her parents appear and tell her that the family is leaving China for America.

_____ G. When Jean meets her aunts and uncles and grandmother, she is thrilled to be part of a real family.

_____ H. Jean's mother learns that all of the American women and children in Wuhan must leave for Shanghai.

_____ I. In college, Jean reads about "real" Americans and makes a decision to write about them someday.

_____ J. When Jean first enters the Shanghai American School, she wonders why people make a fuss about football.

"MK" by Jean Fritz
Vocabulary Builder

Word List

quest	adequate	deceive	transformation	ignorant

A. DIRECTIONS: *Read the incomplete paragraph below. On each line, write one of the words from the Word List. Think about the meaning of each word in the context of the paragraph.*

I was watching a quiz show one night. I tried to answer a series of questions about China. I realized I didn't know as much as I thought I did. In fact, I was (1) ___________________ about the country and its people. I decided to begin a search for information. My (2) ___________________ began at the library, where I found many books on China. Some of them were (3) ___________________, but others did not provide enough information to suit my purposes. Next I checked out the Internet. There I learned about the country's topography and its rivers. A month later, I had read ten books, consulted a dozen Web sites, and watched three documentaries. I had undergone a (4) ___________________. I had changed from someone who knew little about China to someone who knew a great deal. I would not try to (5) ___________________ myself again by thinking that I was educated when I was, in fact, uneducated.

B. DIRECTIONS: *On each line, write the letter of the word whose meaning is the same as that of the Word List word.*

____ 1. quest
    A. trial   B. story   C. search   D. query

____ 2. adequate
    A. absent   B. enough   C. insufficient   D. compassionate

____ 3. deceive
    A. promise   B. yell   C. educate   D. mislead

____ 4. transformation
    A. alteration   B. selection   C. substitution   D. application

____ 5. ignorant
    A. skilled   B. uninformed   C. questioning   D. hopeful

"**MK**" by Jean Fritz

Support for Writing a Brief Essay

Use this graphic organizer to record details that show Jean's feelings about America before she arrives in the United States.

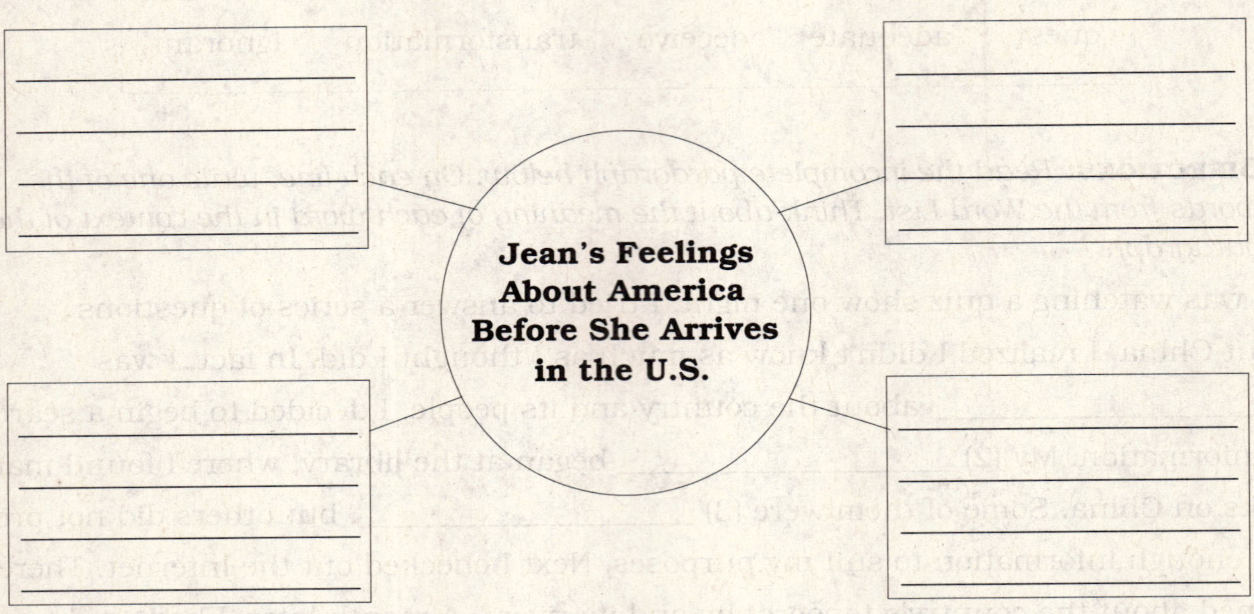

Use this graphic organizer to record details that show Jean's feelings about America after she arrives in the United States.

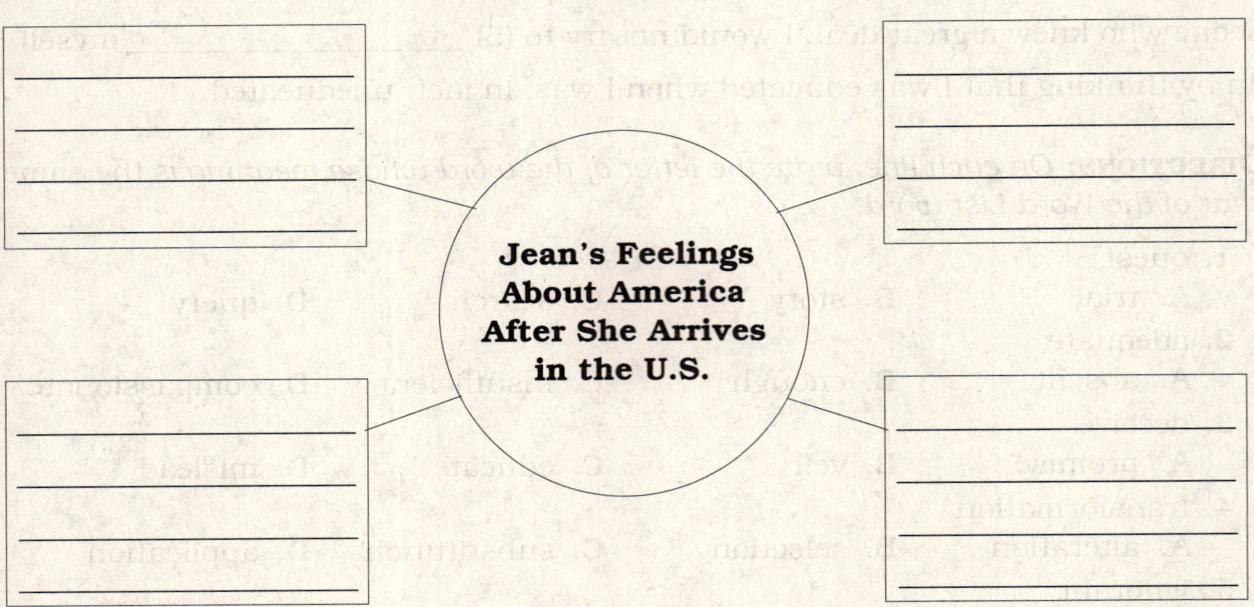

Now, use your notes to draft a brief essay comparing and contrasting Jean's feelings about America before and after she arrives in the United States.

12

"Papa's Parrot" by Cynthia Rylant
"MK" by Jean Fritz

Build Language Skills: Vocabulary

Word Origins

When you learn the *significance* of something, you can *reveal* its deepest meaning. You can start by learning about the word *significance*. It comes from the Latin word *significans*. Knowing that *significance* is related to *signify*, you can look up the origin of *signify*. The words *signify* and *significance* share a common Latin origin—*signum*, which means "sign." The significance of something is its meaning or importance.

The teacher explained the <u>significance</u> of the symbol in the poem.

The word *reveal* comes from the Latin word *revelare*, which means "to draw back the veil." This word origin is helpful in visualizing what the word *reveal* means. *Reveal* means "to make known" or "show."

The curtain was drawn back to <u>reveal</u> a stunning mountain view.

A. DIRECTIONS: *Write sentences using words that come from the Latin* signum *or* revelare.

1. Use *signal* in a sentence about a secret plan.

   ____

2. Use *significant* in a sentence about an important event.

   ____

3. Use *revelation* in a sentence about a discovery that came as a surprise to you.

   ____

Academic Vocabulary Practice

B. DIRECTIONS: *Answer each of the following questions by paying attention to the academic vocabulary word. Then, explain each answer.*

1. Does the author of a murder mystery usually *reveal* the name of the murderer in the first chapter?

   Yes/No: ______ **Why or why not?** ____

2. If someone asked you to *clarify* an idea, would you give a three-word response?

   Yes/No: ______ **Why or why not?** ____

3. If a politician is quoted out of *context*, is he or she likely to be annoyed?

   Yes/No: ______ **Why or why not?** ____

4. If you wanted to *verify* the date the Civil War began, would you look in a dictionary?

   Yes/No: ______ **Why or why not?** ____

"Papa's Parrot" by Cynthia Rylant
"MK" by Jean Fritz
Build Language Skills: Grammar

Common and Proper Nouns

All nouns can be classified as either **common nouns** or **proper nouns.** A **common noun** names a person, place or thing—such as a feeling or an idea. Common nouns are not capitalized unless they begin a sentence or are an important word in a title. In the following sentence, the common nouns are underlined.

Harry had always stopped in to see his <u>father</u> at <u>work</u>.

In that sentence, the words *father* and *work* are general names for a person and a place.

A **proper noun** names a specific person, place, or thing. Proper nouns are always capitalized. In the following sentence, the proper noun is underlined.

<u>Harry Tillian</u> liked his papa.

Harry Tillian is a proper noun because it names a specific person.

A. PRACTICE: *The following sentences are from or based on "Papa's Parrot" or "MK." Circle each proper noun, and underline each common noun.*

1. "Rocky was good company for Mr. Tillian."
2. "New shipments of candy and nuts would be arriving. Rocky would be hungry."
3. "Harry told his father that he would go to the store every day after school and unpack boxes."
4. Jean had just finished sixth grade at the British School in Wuhan.
5. "All American women and children had to catch the . . . boat to Shanghai."
6. "Mr. Barrett met us in Shanghai and drove us to their home, where his wife was on the front porch."

B. Writing Application: *Rewrite each of the following sentences. Replace as many of the common nouns as you can with a proper noun to make the information more specific.*

1. The author lived in another country when she was young.

   ____

2. The boy was disappointed when his father bought a parrot.

   ____

3. The author moved to another country.

   ____

4. The parrot showed by his speech that the father missed his son.

   ____

from *An American Childhood* by Annie Dillard
Reading: Reread and Read Ahead to Confirm Meaning

Context clues are the examples, descriptions, and other details in the text around an unfamiliar or unusual word or expression. Sometimes these clues can help you figure out what the word or expression means. When you come across an unfamiliar word, use the context clues to figure out what the word probably means. **Reread and read ahead to confirm the meaning.**

Read this example from *An American Childhood:*

> But if you flung yourself <u>wholeheartedly</u> at the back of his knees—if you gathered and joined body and soul and pointed them diving fearlessly . . .

Which context clues tell you what *wholeheartedly* means? If you look for clues before and after the word, you find the phrases "flung yourself," "joined body and soul," and "pointed them diving fearlessly." These suggest that *wholeheartedly* probably means something like "completely" or "fully"—which it does.

DIRECTIONS: *Read each quotation from* An American Childhood. *Figure out the meaning of the underlined word by looking for context clues. Write the context clue or clues on the first line. Write the meaning of the word on the second line. Then, check your definitions in a dictionary.*

1. I started making an iceball—a perfect iceball, from perfectly white snow, perfectly spherical, . . . I had just <u>embarked</u> on the iceball project when we heard tire chains come clanking from afar.

   Context clues: ____

   Meaning of word: ____

2. Wordless, we split up. We were on our turf; we could lose ourselves in the neighborhood backyards, everyone for himself. I paused and considered. Everyone had <u>vanished</u> except Mikey Fahey, who was just rounding the corner of a yellow brick house.

   Context clues: ____

   ____

   Meaning of word: ____

3. You have to <u>fling</u> yourself at what you're doing, you have to point yourself, forget yourself, aim, dive.

   Context clues: ____

   Meaning of word: ____

4. Mikey and I unzipped our jackets. I pulled off my <u>sopping</u> mittens. . . . The man's lower pants legs were wet, his cuffs were full of snow.

   Context clues: ____

   Meaning of word: ____

Unit 1 Resources: Fiction and Nonfiction

from *An American Childhood* by Annie Dillard
Literary Analysis: Point of View

Point of view is the perspective from which a narrative is told. Point of view affects the kinds of details that are revealed to the reader.

- **First-person point of view:** The narrator is a character who participates in the action of the story and tells the story using the words *I* and *me*. The narrator can reveal only his or her own observations, thoughts, and feelings.
- **Third-person point of view:** The narrator is not a character in the story and uses third-person pronouns such as *he, she,* and *they* to refer to the characters. The narrator may know and reveal the observations, thoughts, and feelings of more than one person or character in the narrative.

Read this example from *An American Childhood:*

It was a long time before he could speak. I had some difficulty at first recalling why we were there. My lips felt swollen; I couldn't see out of the sides of my eyes; I kept coughing.

You can see from the pronouns *I, we,* and *my* that the event is being told from the first-person point of view. The speaker is there—her lips are swollen; her eyes are clouded; she is coughing.

DIRECTIONS: *Read each quotation from* An American Childhood. *Underline each pronoun that shows that the event is told from the first-person point of view. Then, on the lines that follow, briefly describe what you learned from or about the speaker.*

1. Boys welcomed me at baseball, too, for I had, through enthusiastic practice, what was weirdly known as a boy's arm.

   What I learned: ____

   ____

2. He ran after us, and we ran away from him, up the snowy Reynolds sidewalk. At the corner, I looked back; incredibly, he was still after us. . . . All of a sudden, we were running for our lives.

   What I learned: ____

   ____

3. He chased us silently over picket fences, through thorny hedges, between houses, around garbage cans, and across streets. Every time I glanced back, choking for breath, I expected he would have quit. He must have been as breathless as we were.

   What I learned: ____

   ____

from *An American Childhood* by Annie Dillard
Vocabulary Builder

Word List

strategy   compelled   improvising

A. DIRECTIONS: *Think about the meaning of the underlined Word List word in each sentence. Then, answer the question.*

1. The children came up with a <u>strategy</u> for throwing snowballs at passing vehicles. Did the children have a plan? How do you know?

   ____

   ____

2. The man <u>compelled</u> Dillard to run through the neighborhood. Did she have a choice? How do you know?

   ____

   ____

3. Dillard and Mikey were <u>improvising</u> their escape route as they went along. Had they planned an escape route? How do you know?

   ____

   ____

B. DIRECTIONS: *On each line, write the letter of the word or phrase that means* the same *as the Word List word.*

____ 1. strategy
   A. battle   C. plan
   B. fort   D. game

____ 2. compelled
   A. discouraged   C. released
   B. forced   D. thrown

____ 3. improvising
   A. inventing on the spur of the   C. telling jokes before a live
      moment   audience
   B. making better as you go along   D. bringing goods into the country

from *An American Childhood* by Annie Dillard
Support for Writing a Description That Includes Hyperbole

To prepare to write **descriptions** that include **hyperbole,** complete the following chart, making notes about three experiences.

Questions About the Circumstance or Situation	First Circumstance or Situation	Second Circumstance or Situation	Third Circumstance or Situation
What was the experience?			
When and where did it take place?			
Was I alone? If not, who was with me?			
What happened?			
What part can I exaggerate?			

Now, for each circumstance or situation, use your notes to write a description that includes hyperbole.

"**The Luckiest Time of All**" by Lucille Clifton
Reading: Reread and Read Ahead to Confirm Meaning

Context clues are the examples, descriptions, and other details in the text around an unfamiliar or unusual word or expression. Sometimes these clues can help you figure out what the word or expression means. When you come across an unfamiliar word or expression, use the context clues to figure out what the word probably means. **Reread and read ahead to confirm the meaning.**

In "The Luckiest Time of All," the writer sometimes uses words and phrases that may mean something different from the meanings of the individual words. Look at this example:

"Somethin like the circus. Me and Ovella wanted to join that thing and see the world. Nothin wrong at home or nothin, we just wanted to travel and see new things and have <u>high</u> times."

In another context, you would probably decide that *high* means "tall" or "rising above." In this context, notice the words and phrases around the word *high:* "somethin like the circus," "see the world," and "wanted to travel and see new things." These context clues tell you that in this selection, *high* means "exciting."

DIRECTIONS: *Read each quotation from "The Luckiest Time of All." Figure out the meaning of the underlined word or expression by looking for context clues. Write the context clue or clues on the first line. Write the meaning of the word or expression on the second line.*

1. We got there after a good little walk and it was the <u>world</u>, Baby, such music and wonders as we never had seen! They had everything there, or seemed like it.

   Context clues: ____

   ____

   Meaning of word: ____

2. But the stone was gone from my hand and Lord, it hit that dancin dog right on his nose! Well, he <u>lit out</u> after me, poor thing. He <u>lit out</u> after me and I flew! Round and round the Silas Greene we run.

   Context clues: ____

   ____

   Meaning of word: ____

3. I stopped then and walked slow and shy to where he had picked up that poor dog to see if he was hurt, <u>cradlin</u> him and talkin to him soft and sweet.

   Context clues: ____

   Meaning of word: ____

4. He . . . helped me find my stone. . . . We search and searched and at last he <u>spied</u> it!

   Context clues: ____

   ____

   Meaning of word: ____

Unit 1 Resources: Fiction and Nonfiction
© Pearson Education, Inc., publishing as Pearson Prentice Hall. All rights reserved.

19

"The Luckiest Time of All" by Lucille Clifton
Literary Analysis: Point of View

Point of view is the perspective from which a narrative is told. Point of view affects the kinds of details that are revealed to the reader.

- **First-person point of view:** The narrator is a character who participates in the action of the story and tells the story using the words *I* and *me*. The narrator can reveal only his or her own observations, thoughts, and feelings.
- **Third-person point of view:** The narrator is not a character in the story and uses third-person pronouns such as *he, she,* and *they* to refer to the characters. The narrator may know and reveal the observations, thoughts, and feelings of more than one person or character in the narrative.

Read this example from the beginning of "The Luckiest Time of All":

Mrs. Elzie F. Pickens was rocking slowly on the porch one afternoon when her Great-granddaughter, Tee, brought her a big bunch of dogwood blooms, and that was the beginning of a story.

"Ahh, now that dogwood reminds me of the day I met your Great-granddaddy, Mr. Pickens, Sweet Tee."

The story begins by introducing two characters, Mrs. Elzie F. Pickens and her great-granddaughter, Tee. The pronoun *her* tells you that the narrative is told from the third-person point of view. In the first paragraph of dialogue, Elzie is telling her story using the pronoun *I*, but that does not mean the story is a first-person account. It is not a first-person account because Elzie is not the narrator. The narrator is quoting Elzie as she tells her story to Tee.

DIRECTIONS: *Read each numbered passage. (Two passages are from "The Luckiest Time of All," and two are about Lucille Clifton.) Underline each pronoun that tells that the passage is told from the third-person point of view. Then, on the lines that follow, briefly describe what you learned from the passage.*

1. Tee's Great-grandmother shook her head and laughed out loud.

   What I learned: ____

2. And they rocked a little longer and smiled together.

   What I learned: ____

3. Lucille Sayles Clifton was born into a large, working-class family in New York State. Although her parents were not formally educated, she learned from their example to appreciate books and poetry.

   What I learned: ____

   ____

"The Luckiest Time of All" by Lucille Clifton
Vocabulary Builder

Word List

twine   acquainted

A. DIRECTIONS: *Think about the meaning of the underlined Word List word in each sentence. Then, answer the question.*

1. Are mountain climbers likely to use <u>twine</u> to attach themselves to each other while crossing a dangerous crevice? Why or why not?

   ____

   ____

2. If you are <u>acquainted</u> with someone, are you likely to know where he or she lives? Why or why not?

   ____

   ____

B. DIRECTIONS: *On each line, write the letter of the word or phrase that means* the same *as the Word List word.*

____ 1. twine
    A. complaint   C. twist
    B. sparkle   D. string

____ 2. acquainted
    A. lightly colored   C. familiar with
    B. related to   D. well-known

Name ____ Date _______________________

"The Luckiest Time of All" by Lucille Clifton
Support for Writing a Description That Includes Hyperbole

To prepare to write **descriptions** that include **hyperbole,** complete the following chart, making notes about three qualities or skills a person might have.

Questions About the Quality or Skill	First Quality or Skill	Second Quality or Skill	Third Quality or Skill
What is the quality or skill?			
Who or what might have this quality or skill?			
What is exceptional about this quality or skill?			
How can I exaggerate this quality or skill?			

Now, choose one quality or skill, and use your notes to write a description of it that includes hyperbole.

from *An American Childhood* by Annie Dillard
"The Luckiest Time of All" by Lucille Clifton
Build Language Skills: Vocabulary

Word Origins

The word *context* comes from the Latin *com-*, meaning "together," and *texere*, meaning "to weave." *Context* is the connection, or weaving together, of the words and phrases surrounding a word to construct meaning.

The <u>context</u> of her remarks made all the difference to our reactions.

The word *verify* comes from the Latin word *verus*, meaning "true." If you verify something, you prove whether or not it is true or correct.

By checking the dictionary, we were able to <u>verify</u> the spelling of *millennium*.

A. DIRECTIONS: *Read each question that contains a word with the Latin prefix* com- *or comes from the Latin word* verus. *Then, answer the question, using a dictionary if needed. Include the word in your answer.*

1. If someone accused you of telling a lie, how would you <u>contest</u> the accusation?

   ____

2. Why is the <u>veracity</u> of an advertiser's claims important?

   ____

Academic Vocabulary Practice

B. DIRECTIONS: *Revise each sentence so that the academic vocabulary word is used logically. Be sure to use the vocabulary word in your revised sentence.*

Example: The detective thought the footprints near the crime scene were of no <u>significance</u>.

                The detective thought the footprints near the crime scene were of <u>great significance</u>.

1. I looked in my science book to <u>verify</u> the birth date of George Washington.

   ____

2. I used lizards and worms as <u>context</u> clues to the meaning of *mammals*.

   ____

3. The teacher said that she would use complicated language to <u>clarify</u> the test directions.

   ____

4. When the time came to <u>reveal</u> his new painting, the artist threw a drapery over it.

   ____

5. The discovery was so <u>significant</u> that no newspaper published an article about it.

   ____

Unit 1 Resources: Fiction and Nonfiction

23

from *An American Childhood* by Annie Dillard
"The Luckiest Time of All" by Lucille Clifton
Build Language Skills: Grammar

Possessive Nouns

A **possessive noun** is a noun that shows ownership. Ownership is indicated by the use of the apostrophe.

- To form the possessive to a singular noun, add an apostrophe and *-s:*
  The black <u>car's</u> tires left tracks.
- To form the possessive of a plural noun that ends in *-s*, add only an apostrophe:
  All of the <u>cars'</u> tires left tracks.
- To form the possessive of a plural noun that does not end in *-s*, add an apostrophe and *-s:*
  The <u>children's</u> game had unexpected consequences.

A. PRACTICE: *Each of the following sentences is based an* An American Childhood *or* "The Luckiest Time of All." *On the line, rewrite each underlined noun as a possessive. Be sure to place the apostrophe correctly to indicate that the possessive is singular or plural.*

1. The <u>boys</u> games were more exciting to Dillard than the <u>girls</u> activities.

   _________________   _________________

2. The <u>snowball</u> *splat* led the <u>car</u> driver to jump out and chase the children.

   _________________   _________________

3. The <u>boy</u> path took him through the <u>neighbors</u> front yard.

   _________________   _________________

4. Many years later the young <u>women</u> adventure would be the subject of the <u>girl</u> curiosity.

   _________________   _________________

B. Writing Application: *On the line after each description in brackets, write a possessive noun that matches the description. Make sure the possessives you choose make sense in the sentence.*

1. The [*belonging to the singular female adult*] ___________________ stone hit the [*belonging to the singular animal*] ___________________ nose.
2. The [*belonging to the plural male children*] ___________________ games included throwing snowballs at the [*belonging to the plural vehicle*] ___________________ windows.
3. The [*belonging to the singular adult male*] ___________________ breath came in gasps and his [*belonging to the legs of his clothing*] ___________________ cuffs were full of snow.

24

***from* Barrio Boy** by Ernesto Galarza
"A Day's Wait" by Ernest Hemingway
Literary Analysis: Comparing Fiction and Nonfiction

Fiction is prose writing that tells about imaginary characters and events. Novels, novellas, and short stories are types of fiction. **Nonfiction** is prose writing that presents and explains ideas or tells about real people, places, objects, or events. News articles, essays, and historical accounts are types of nonfiction.

In the excerpt from *Barrio Boy,* the writer tells about an actual event in his life. In contrast, the writer of "A Day's Wait" created a narrator who tells about an imagined event in the lives of an imagined father and son.

DIRECTIONS: *Complete the following chart by answering the questions about the excerpt from* Barrio Boy *and "A Day's Wait."*

Question	from *Barrio Boy*	"A Day's Wait"
1. Who tells the story?		
2. Who are the main characters?		
3. Is there important dialogue? If so, summarize it.		
4. What important events make up the action of the story?		
5. What feelings does the main character have as events unfold?		
6. How is the main character's problem resolved?		

from **Barrio Boy** by Ernesto Galarza
"A Day's Wait" by Ernest Hemingway
Vocabulary Builder

Word List

reassuring	contraption	formidable	epidemic	flushed	evidently

A. DIRECTIONS: *Think about the meaning of the italicized word in each question. Then, answer the question.*

1. When there is an *epidemic*, why are infected people kept away from healthy people?

   ____

2. What is an example of a *formidable* school project?

   ____

3. Why might someone call a typewriter a *contraption*?

   ____

4. If Elizabeth is *evidently* healthy, how do you know that she is healthy?

   ____

5. What is a *reassuring* gesture?

   ____

6. When a hunting dog has *flushed* quail from the bushes, what has the dog done?

   ____

B. DIRECTIONS: *For each pair of related words in capital letters, write the letter of the pair of words that best expresses a* similar *relationship.*

____ 1. EPIDEMIC : DOCTORS ::
    A. hospital : nurses   C. sick : well
    B. war : soldier   D. medicine : science

____ 2. FORMIDABLE : UNIMPORTANT ::
    A. dangerous : great   C. difficult : simple
    B. square : rectangular   D. large : huge

____ 3. EVIDENTLY : SEEMINGLY ::
    A. evidence : trial   C. suddenly : sudden
    B. slowly : quickly   D. certainly : surely

***from* Barrio Boy** by Ernesto Galarza
"A Day's Wait" by Ernest Hemingway
Support for Writing to Compare Literary Works

To prepare to write an essay that compares and contrasts the narrators of *Barrio Boy* and "A Day's Wait," use this graphic organizer. Respond to each question by jotting down ideas about how the narrators present their stories.

Question	from *Barrio Boy*	"A Day's Wait"
Who is the narrator? What is the point of view?		
What details about the narrator are revealed?		
How is dialogue used in each work?		
How are the narrator's feelings involved in the work?		
What theme do the narrator's thoughts and actions suggest?		
How do other characters affect the narrator?		
How does the narrator bring the story to a close?		

Now, use your notes to write an essay comparing and contrasting the narrators of *Barrio Boy* and "A Day's Wait."

"All Summer in a Day" by Ray Bradbury

Reading: Recognize Details That Indicate
the Author's Purpose

Fiction writers write for a variety of **purposes.** They may wish to entertain, to teach, to call to action, or to reflect on experiences. They may also wish to inform, to persuade, or to create a mood. **Recognizing details that indicate the author's purpose** can give you a richer understanding of a selection. For example, in this passage from "All Summer in a Day," Bradbury creates a mood:

> Margot stood alone. She was a very frail girl who looked as if she had been lost in the rain for years and the rain had washed out the blue from her eyes and the red from her mouth and the yellow from her hair. She was an old photograph dusted from an album.

DIRECTIONS: *Read these passages from "All Summer in a Day." Then, write the purpose or purposes you think the author had for writing that passage. Choose from these purposes:* to entertain, to inform, to create a mood. *A passage may have more than one purpose.*

1. It had been raining for seven years; thousands upon thousands of days compounded and filled from one end to the other with rain, with the drum and gush of water, with the sweet crystal fall of showers and the concussion of storms so heavy they were tidal waves come over the islands.

   Author's purpose: ____

2. There was talk that her father and mother were taking her back to Earth next year; it seemed vital to her that they do so, though it would mean the loss of thousands of dollars to her family.

   Author's purpose: ____

3. But they were running and turning their faces up to the sky and feeling the sun on their cheeks like a warm iron; they were taking off their jackets and letting the sun burn their arms.

   Author's purpose: ____

4. They walked slowly down the hall in the sound of cold rain. They turned through the doorway to the room in the sound of the storm and thunder, lightning on their faces, blue and terrible. They walked over to the closet door slowly and stood by it.

   Behind the closet door was only silence.

   They unlocked the door, even more slowly, and let Margot out.

   Author's purpose: ____

28

"All Summer in a Day" by Ray Bradbury
Literary Analysis: Setting

The **setting** of a story is the time and place of the action. In this example from "All Summer in a Day," the underlined details help establish the story's setting.

> The sun came out.
>
> It was <u>the color of flaming bronze</u> and it was <u>very large</u>. And the sky around it was <u>a blazing blue tile color</u>. And <u>the jungle burned with sunlight</u> as the children, released from their spell, rushed out, yelling, into the springtime.

- In some stories, setting is just a backdrop. The same story events might take place in a completely different setting.
- In other stories, setting is very important. It develops a specific atmosphere or mood in the story, as in the example above. There, the children joyfully rush outside to feel the sun in the springtime after seven years of constant rain. The setting may even relate directly to the story's central conflict or problem.

DIRECTIONS: *Read the name of the character or characters from "All Summer in a Day" and the passage that follows. Then, on the lines, identify the setting described in the passage and the way the character or characters feel about it. Write your response in a short sentence or two.*

1. Margot: "And once, a month ago, she had refused to shower in the school shower rooms, had clutched her hands to her ears and over her head, screaming the water mustn't touch her head."

   Setting and character's feeling about it: ____

   ____

2. Margot: "They surged about her, caught her up and bore her, protesting, and then pleading, and then crying, back into a tunnel, a room, a closet, where they slammed and locked the door. They stood looking at the door and saw it tremble from her beating and throwing herself against it."

   Setting and character's feeling about it: ____

   ____

3. The children: "The children lay out, laughing, on the jungle mattress, and heard it sigh and squeak under them, resilient and alive. They ran among the trees, they slipped and fell, they pushed each other, . . . but most of all they squinted at the sun until tears ran down their faces, they put their hands up to that yellowness and that amazing blueness and they breathed of the fresh, fresh air."

   Setting and character's feeling about it: ____

   ____

"All Summer in a Day" by Ray Bradbury
Vocabulary Builder

Word List

slackening   vital   tumultuously   resilient

A. DIRECTIONS: *For each item below, think about the meaning of the italicized Word List word, and then answer the question.*

1. If rain were *slackening*, would you expect better weather? Why or why not?

   ____

   ____

2. If someone tells you something *vital*, are you likely to pay attention? Why or why not?

   ____

   ____

3. If a stream is moving *tumultuously*, is it safe to wade across? Why or why not?

   ____

   ____

4. Is concrete a *resilient* material? Why or why not?

   ____

   ____

B. DIRECTIONS: *Read each sentence. If the italicized word is used correctly, write* Correct *on the line. If it is not used correctly, rewrite the sentence to correct it.*

1. The speed of the rocket was *slackening* as it prepared to land on Earth.

   ____

2. It is said that water is *vital* to life; you can live without it.

   ____

3. During the calm before the storm, the wind blew *tumultuously*.

   ____

4. Because Margot was *resilient*, she could not get used to the conditions on Venus.

   ____

"All Summer in a Day" by Ray Bradbury
Support for Writing a News Report

In preparation for your **news report** that tells about the day the sun appeared on Venus, complete the chart on this page. Answer the questions with information in "All Summer in a Day."

Questions for News Report on the Day the Sun Shone on Venus

Question	Information in "All Summer in a Day"
Who sees the sun, and who does not see it?	
What happens in the story when the sun is shining?	
When does the sun shine, and for how long?	
Where do the events take place?	
Why do the characters in the story respond to the sun the way they do?	

Now, use your notes to write a news report that tells about the day the sun appeared on Venus. Present your most important information in the first paragraph.

"Suzy and Leah" by Jane Yolen

Reading: Recognize Details That Indicate the Author's Purpose

Fiction writers may write for a variety of **purposes.** They may wish to entertain, to teach, to call to action, or to reflect on experiences. They may also wish to inform, to persuade, or to create a mood. **Recognizing details that indicate the author's purpose** can give you a richer understanding of a selection. For example, the following passage from "Suzy and Leah" is written to teach readers about the background of some Eastern European Jews:

> I have a little English. But Ruth and Zipporah and the others, though they speak Yiddish and Russian and German, they have no English at all.

DIRECTIONS: *Read these passages from "Suzy and Leah." On the line that follows each passage, write the purpose or purposes you think the author had for writing that passage. Choose from these purposes:* to entertain, to inform, to create a mood. *A passage may have more than one purpose.*

1. Leah: "Today we got cereal in a box. At first I did not know what it was. Before the war we ate such lovely porridge with milk straight from our cows. And eggs fresh from the hen's nest."

   Author's purpose: ____

2. Leah: "But they made us wear tags with our names printed on them. That made me afraid. What next? Yellow stars? I tore mine off and threw it behind a bush before we went in [to the school]."

   Author's purpose: ____

3. Suzy: "Mr. Forest . . . gave me the girl with the dark braids. . . . Gee, she's as prickly as a porcupine. I asked if I could have a different kid. . . . He wants her to learn as fast as possible so she can help the others. As if she would, Miss Porcupine."

   Author's purpose: ____

4. Leah: "One day this Suzy and her people will stop being nice to us. They will remember we are not just refugees but Jews, and they will turn on us. Just as the Germans did. Of this I am sure."

   Author's purpose: ____

5. Suzy: "[Leah's] English has gotten so good. Except for some words, like victory, which she pronounces 'wick-toe-ree.' I try not to laugh. . . . She can't dance at all. She doesn't know the words to any of the top songs."

   Author's purpose: ____

"Suzy and Leah" by Jane Yolen
Literary Analysis: Setting

The **setting** of a story is the time and place of the action. In this example from "Suzy and Leah," the underlined details help establish the story's setting:

August 5, 1944

Dear Diary,

   Today I walked past *that* place. . . . Gosh, is it <u>ugly</u>! A line of <u>rickety wooden buildings</u> just like in the army. And <u>a fence lots higher than my head</u>. <u>With barbed wire</u> on top.

- In some stories, setting is just a backdrop. The same story events might take place in a completely different setting.
- In other stories, setting is very important. It develops a specific atmosphere or mood in the story, as in the example above. There, the reader is introduced to the refugee camp through the eyes of Suzy, who has lived a privileged life. The setting may even relate directly to the story's central conflict or problem.

DIRECTIONS: *Read the name of the character from "Suzy and Leah" and the passage that follows. Then, on the lines, identify the setting described in the passage and the way the character feels about it. Write your response in a short sentence.*

1. Suzy: "With barbed wire on top. How can anyone—even a refugee—live there?"

   Setting and character's feeling about it: _________________________________

   ____

2. Leah: "But I say no place is safe for us. Did not the Germans say that we were safe in their camps?"

   Setting and character's feeling about it: _________________________________

   ____

3. Leah: "Zipporah braided my hair, but I had no mirror until we got to the school and they showed us the toilets. They call it a bathroom, but there is no bath in it at all, which is strange."

   Setting and character's feeling about it: _________________________________

   ____

4. Suzy: "[Mom] said the Nazis killed people, mothers and children as well as men. In places called concentration camps. . . . It was so awful I could hardly believe it, but Mom said it was true."

   Setting and character's feeling about it: _________________________________

   ____

Unit 1 Resources: Fiction and Nonfiction

"Suzy and Leah" by Jane Yolen
Vocabulary Builder

Word List

refugee   porridge   permanent

A. DIRECTIONS: *For each item below, think about the meaning of the italicized Word List word, and then answer the question.*

1. Would a *refugee* remain in his or her country during a war? Why or why not?

____

____

2. If you were making dinner for someone, would you likely serve *porridge*? Why or why not?

____

3. Is a *permanent* scar one that will eventually go away? Why or why not?

____

B. DIRECTIONS: *Read each sentence. If the italicized word is used correctly, write* Correct *on the line. If it is not used correctly, rewrite the sentence to correct it.*

1. The *refugee* fled across the border.

____

2. The *porridge* made a wonderful dessert.

____

3. The *permanent* frown on Leah's face disappeared when Suzy offered candy.

____

C. DIRECTIONS: *For each item, write the letter of the word that means the same as the Word List word.*

_____ 1. refugee
    A. warlord   B. exile   C. ancestor   D. sailor

_____ 2. porridge
    A. stew   B. soup   C. dessert   D. cereal

_____ 3. permanent
    A. lasting   B. temporary   C. changing   D. realistic

Name ____ Date ___________________________

Support for Writing a News Report

In preparation for your **news report** that tells about the refugee camp where Leah is living, complete the chart on this page. Answer the questions with information in "Suzy and Leah."

Questions for News Report on Leah's Refugee Camp

Question	Information in "Suzy and Leah"
Who is living in the camp that Suzy visits?	
What has brought Suzy to the camp?	
When are the events taking place?	
Where (in what country) is the camp?	
Why has the camp been set up?	

Now, use your notes to write a news report that tells about the refugee camp where Leah is living. Present your most important information in the first paragraph.

"Suzy and Leah" by Jane Yolen
"All Summer in a Day" by Ray Bradbury

Build Language Skills: Vocabulary

The Prefix *re-*

The prefix ***re-*** means "again" or "back." To *recall* means "to call back" or "to remember."

The manufacturer *recalled* the cars because of faulty gas tanks.

Do you *recall* the name of the man who saved those people from the fire?

A. DIRECTIONS: *Use what you know about prefixes to match each italicized word below with its definition.*

___ 1. The searchers will *retrace* their
route to find the missing campers.

___ 2. We can *reheat* the leftovers for
dinner tonight.

___ 3. The writer will *review* the film
before she writes a criticism.

___ 4. Run the *replay* so we can see the
end of the game.

A. take a second look at
B. show the same sequence again
C. go back over the same route
D. warm up

Academic Vocabulary Practice

previous	recall	background	establish	prior

B. DIRECTIONS: *Read each sentence and pay attention to the underlined word. Find a vocabulary word from the box that means the same or about the same as the underlined word. Write the vocabulary word on the line. Two of the vocabulary words are interchangeable.*

1. The detective tried to <u>determine</u> where the suspect had been at the time of the robbery.

   ____

2. Your <u>experience</u> is important when you apply for a job.

   ____

3. In her <u>earlier</u> games, this athlete has proved herself an able goalie.

   ____

4. Jenny could not <u>remember</u> whether she had taken her warm jacket to the game.

   ____

5. At his <u>former</u> school, Mark was in the orchestra.

   ____

"Suzy and Leah" by Jane Yolen
"All Summer in a Day" by Ray Bradbury

Build Language Skills: Grammar

A **pronoun** is a word that takes the place of a noun or a group of words acting as a noun. A **nominative pronoun** is a pronoun used as a subject. An **objective pronoun** is a pronoun used as an object.

Suzy met Leah at the camp.	**She** met Leah at the camp.	Nominative pronoun
Suzy met **Leah** at the camp.	Suzy met **her** at the camp.	Objective pronoun

Some important nominative and objective pronouns:

Nominative	Objective
I	me
he	him
she	her
we	us
they	them

A. PRACTICE: *Read each sentence based on sentences in "Suzy and Leah" or "All Summer in a Day." Underline each nominative pronoun. Circle each objective pronoun.*

1. When I looked back, she was gone, and I didn't see her again until the next day.

2. They didn't know how to peel oranges, so I taught them.

3. She loves Avi and tries to protect him.

4. They hated her because she had seen the sun.

5. He gave her a shove, but she did not move away from him.

6. The thunder and rain chased them back inside, where they let her out of the closet.

B. Writing Application: *Rewrite each sentence by replacing each underlined noun with a pronoun. Be sure to see the difference between a nominative pronoun and an objective pronoun.*

1. The students wanted to see the sun, so the teacher let the students go outside.

____

2. Margot hoped to see the sun, but the students locked Margot in the closet.

____

3. William said Margot was a liar, but Margot stuck to Margot's story.

____

"My First Free Summer" by Julia Alvarez

Reading: Use Background Information to Determine the Author's Purpose

One way to determine the **author's purpose,** or reason, for writing a nonfiction work is to **use background information** that you already know about the author and topic. For example, knowing that an author grew up outside the United States might help you determine that she wrote an essay to inform readers about the country where she spent her childhood.

Although she was born in the United States, Julia Alvarez spent much of her childhood in the Dominican Republic. Near the beginning of her essay, she writes,

> That was the problem. English. My mother had decided to send her children to the American school so we could learn the language of the nation that would soon be liberating us.

The author's purpose for providing this background information is to inform readers of her reasons for studying English and attending an American school. Authors provide background information for other purposes as well—for example, to entertain or to create a mood.

DIRECTIONS: *Read each of these passages from "My First Free Summer." Decide whether the author's purpose is to inform, to create a mood, or to entertain. Write the purpose on the line following the passage. A passage may have more than one purpose.*

1. For thirty years, the Dominican Republic had endured a bloody and repressive dictatorship. From my father, who was involved in an underground plot, my mother knew that *los américanos* had promised to help bring democracy to the island.

   Author's purpose(s): ____

2. Meanwhile, I had to learn about the pilgrims with their funny witch hats, about the 50 states and where they were on the map, about Dick and Jane and their tame little pets, Puff and Spot, about freedom and liberty and justice for all—while being imprisoned in a hot classroom with a picture of a man wearing a silly wig hanging above the blackboard.

   Author's purpose(s): ____

3. The grounds on which the American school stood had been donated by my grandfather. . . . The bulk of the student body was made up of the sons and daughters of American diplomats and business people, but a few Dominicans—most of them friends or members of my family—were allowed to attend.

   Author's purpose(s): ____

"My First Free Summer" by Julia Alvarez
Literary Analysis: Historical Context

When a literary work is based on real events, the historical context can help you understand the action. **Historical context**—the actual political and social events and trends of the time—can explain why characters act and think the way they do. Read the following passage from "My First Free Summer." Think about what it tells you about the historical context of the selection.

For thirty years, the Dominican Republic had endured a bloody and repressive dictatorship. From my father, who was involved in an underground plot, my mother knew that *los americanos* had promised to help bring democracy to the island.

DIRECTIONS: *Read each of these passages from "My First Free Summer." On the lines that follow, write a sentence telling how the historical context affects the action.*

1. I didn't know about my father's activities. I didn't know the dictator was bad. All I knew was that my friends who were attending Dominican schools were often on holiday to honor the dictator's birthday, the dictator's saint day, the day the dictator became the dictator, the day the dictator's oldest son was born, and so on.

   How context affects action: ___________________________________

   ____

2. But the yard replete with cousins and friends that I had dreamed about all year was deserted. Family members were leaving for the United States, using whatever connections they could drum up. The plot had unraveled. Every day there were massive arrests. The United States had closed its embassy and was advising Americans to return home.

   How context affects action: ___________________________________

   ____

3. I was about to tell her that I didn't want to go to the United States, where . . . everyone spoke English. But my mother lifted a hand for silence. "We're leaving in a few hours. I want you all to go get ready! I'll be in to pack soon." The desperate look in her eyes did not allow for contradiction. We raced off, wondering how to fit the contents of our Dominican lives into four small suitcases.

   How context affects action: ___________________________________

   ____

4. Next morning, we are standing inside a large, echoing hall as a stern American official reviews our documents. What if he doesn't let us in? What if we have to go back? I am holding my breath. My parents' terror has become mine.

   How context affects action: ___________________________________

   ____

"My First Free Summer" by Julia Alvarez
Vocabulary Builder

Word List

| vowed   diplomats   summoned   interrogation |

A. DIRECTIONS: *For each item below, think about the meaning of the italicized Word List word, and then answer the question.*

1. Was Julia laughing when she *vowed* to learn her fractions? Why or why not?

   ____

2. If the children of *diplomats* attend your school, would you expect their parents to talk about medicine on career day? Why or why not?

   ____

3. If the principal *summoned* Julia and her mother to his office, would they leave the school? Why or why not?

   ____

4. If the airport officials subjected Julia's family to an *interrogation*, would the questioning be friendly? Why or why not?

   ____

B. DIRECTIONS: *Something is wrong with the following sentences. Revise each one, using the Word List word in a way that makes the sentence logical.*

1. After her first free summer, Julia *vowed* to pass all her subjects.

   Revision: ____

2. The mission of the *diplomats* was to negotiate the terms of the new car's warranty.

   Revision: ____

3. When Julia's mother *summoned* her daughters, Julia and her sister left for the beach.

   Revision: ____

4. The suspect put the detectives through a night-long *interrogation*.

   Revision: ____

"My First Free Summer" by Julia Alvarez

Support for Writing a Letter to Young Julia Alvarez

Before you write your **letter** to ten-year-old Julia Alvarez describing what it is like to go to school in the United States, gather your ideas. Use the graphic organizer below to record information about your school day.

Going to School in the United States

Topics for Letter	My Ideas About These Topics
School hours, holidays, and the school year	
Subjects	
Homework	
After-school activities	
The best things about school	
The worst things about school	

When you write your letter, include the date, a greeting, a closing, and your signature.

41

"My Furthest-Back Person" by Alex Haley

Reading: Use Background Information to Determine the Author's Purpose

One way to determine the **author's purpose,** or reason, for writing a nonfiction work is to **use background information** that you already know about the author and topic. For example, knowing that an author is descended from a slave might help you realize how important it would be to him to find out about his African ancestors.

Alex Haley describes his seemingly abrupt decision to research his family history in the National Archives:

> After about a dozen microfilmed rolls, I was beginning to tire, when in utter astonishment I looked upon the names of Grandma's parents: Tom Murray, Irene Murray . . . older sisters of Grandma's as well—every one of them a name that I'd heard countless times on her front porch.

The author's purpose for providing this information is to inform readers of what he learned at the beginning of his long search for his African ancestors. Authors provide background information for other purposes as well—for example, to entertain or to create a mood.

DIRECTIONS: *Read each of these passages from "My Furthest-Back Person." Decide whether the author's purpose is* to inform *or* to create a mood. *Write the purpose on the line following the passage. A passage may have more than one purpose.*

1. Dr. Vansina, his manner very serious, finally said, The sounds your family has kept sound very probably of the tongue called "Mandinka."

   I'd never heard of any "Mandinka." Grandma just told of the African saying . . . "*Kamby Bolong*" for a Virginia river. . . .

   "*Bolong*," he said, was clearly Mandinka for "river." Preceded by "*Kamby*," it very likely meant "Gambia River."

   Author's purpose(s): ____

2. Then the interpreters went to him, as the villagers thronged around me.

   And it hit me like a gale wind: every one of them, the whole crowd, was *jet black.* An enormous sense of guilt swept me—a sense of being some kind of hybrid . . . a sense of being impure among the pure. It was an awful sensation.

   Author's purpose(s): ____

3. "About the time the king's soldiers came, the eldest of these four sons, Kunta, when he had about 16 rains, went away from his village, to chop wood to make a drum . . . and he was never seen again . . ."

   Goose-pimples the size of lemons seemed to pop all over me. . . . My Grandma, Cousin Georgia and the others told of the African "*Kin-tay*" who always said he was kidnapped near his village—while chopping wood to make a drum . . .

   Author's purpose(s): ____

"**My Furthest-Back Person**" by Alex Haley
Literary Analysis: Historical Context

When a literary work is based on real events, the historical context can help you understand the action. **Historical context**—the actual political and social events and trends of the time—can explain why characters act and think the way they do. Read the following passage from "My Furthest-Back Person." What does it tell you about the historical context of the selection?

> After about two hours, we put in at James Island, for me to see the ruins of the once British-operated James Fort. Here two centuries of slave ships had loaded thousands of cargoes of Gambian tribespeople.

DIRECTIONS: *Read each of these passages from "My Furthest-Back Person." Then, write a short sentence telling how the historical context affects the action.*

1. And when a main reading room desk attendant asked if he could help me, I wouldn't have dreamed of admitting to him some curiosity hanging on from boyhood about my slave forebears. I kind of bumbled that I was interested in census records of Alamance County, North Carolina, just after the Civil War.

   How context affects action: ____

   ____

2. I was on a jet returning to New York when a thought hit me. Those strange, unknown-tongue sounds, always part of our family's old story . . . they were obviously bits of our original African "*Kin-tay's*" native tongue. What specific tongue? Could I somehow find out?

   How context affects action: ____

   ____

3. It is embarrassing to me now, but despite Grandma's stories, I'd never been concerned much with Africa, and I had the routine images of African people living mostly in exotic jungles. But a compulsion now laid hold of me to learn all I could, and I began devouring books about Africa, especially about the slave trade.

   How context affects action: ____

   ____

4. If you really knew the odyssey of us millions of black Americans, if you really knew how we came in the seeds of our forefathers, captured, driven, beaten, inspected, bought, branded, chained in foul ships, if you really knew, you needed weeping . . .

   Back home, I knew that what I must write, really, was our black saga, where any individual's past is the essence of the millions.

   How context affects action: ____

   ____

"My Furthest-Back Person" by Alex Haley
Vocabulary Builder

Word List

intrigue   uncanny   eminent   destination

A. DIRECTIONS: *For each item below, think about the meaning of the italicized Word List word, and then answer the question.*

1. A friend has lent you a copy of *Roots* and tells you that it is filled with *intrigue*. Are you eager to read it? Why or why not?

   ____

2. Haley finds an *uncanny* resemblance between his grandmother's story and the *griot*'s. Does he find it eerie? Why or why not?

   ____

3. Haley visits an *eminent* professor of African languages. Is the man distinguished? How do you know?

   ____

4. The African's *destination* is Annapolis. Is he happy about that? Why or why not?

   ____

B. DIRECTIONS: *Something is wrong with the following sentences. Revise each one, using the Word List word, in a way that makes the sentence logical.*

1. The *intrigue* of his family history led Haley to end his research.

   Revision: ____

2. Dr. Vansina did not think it was *uncanny* that Haley's grandmother's utterances sounded like the Mandinka language.

   Revision: ____

3. No one recognized the name of the *eminent* scholar.

   Revision: ____

4. Kunta Kinte's *destination* was the Gambia River.

   Revision: ____

"My Furthest-Back Person" by Alex Haley
Support for Writing a Letter of Proposal

Before you write a letter proposing the publication of Haley's book, gather your ideas. Use the graphic organizer below to record information about the project as it has been revealed in "My Furthest-Back Person."

Alex Haley's Proposal for *Roots*

Information to Include	My Ideas About the Information
Haley's reasons for writing the book	
Research Haley has carried out to date	
Work on the book that remains to be done	
Haley's requests from the publisher	

Now, use your notes to write a **letter of proposal** that Haley might have written to a publisher. Follow the format of a business letter.

"**My First Free Summer**" by Julia Alvarez
"**My Furthest-Back Person**" by Alex Haley
Build Language Skills: Vocabulary

The Prefix *pre-*

The prefix **pre-** means "before." The word *previous* contains the prefix *pre-*, meaning "before," and a form of the Latin word *via*, meaning "road." The original meaning meant going before someone else down a road. The word *previous* today means "occurring before in time or order."

A. DIRECTIONS: *Use what you know about prefixes to match each italicized word below to its definition.*

___ 1. Jason was a *premature* baby, but he is fine now.

___ 2. You have to *prepay* for this video before they will send it.

___ 3. Don't *prejudge* the defendant until you have heard his story.

___ 4. The dinosaurs are *prehistoric* animals.

A. give payment ahead of time
B. form an opinion before knowing all the facts
C. occurring before recorded history
D. born before the proper time

Academic Vocabulary Practice

previous	recall	background	establish	prior

B. DIRECTIONS: *Write a complete sentence to answer each question. For each item, use an Academic Vocabulary word in place of the underlined word or phrase.*

1. What kind of <u>experience</u> should a student have to babysit?

   ____

2. What is a good way to <u>remember</u> the way to your friend's home?

   ____

3. Has this singer made any recordings <u>before</u> now?

   ____

4. How can you <u>make sure</u> that your math answers are correct?

   ____

5. What did you do <u>earlier</u> today to get ready for the party?

   ____

"My First Free Summer" by Julia Alvarez
"My Furthest-Back Person" by Alex Haley
Build Language Skills: Grammar

A **possessive pronoun** is a pronoun that shows ownership.

The football that belongs to **me**	**my** football
The video that belongs to **you**	**your** video
The idea that belongs to **her**	**her** idea
The answer that belongs to **him**	**his** answer
The house that belongs to **them**	**their** house
The decision that belongs to **us**	**our** decision

A. Practice: *Underline each possessive pronoun in the sentences below.*

1. Alvarez vowed she would learn her English.
2. My mother decided to send her children to the American school.
3. I had to learn about the pilgrims with their funny witch hats.
4. The soldiers go seat by seat, looking at our faces.
5. Alex Haley looked for his family's ancestors, proof of their history.
6. His grandmother's stories told him she cared about her family's background.

B. Writing Application: *For each sentence below, change the underlined pronoun into a possessive pronoun.*

1. Alvarez learned <u>she</u> subjects, so she could play with <u>she</u> family that summer.

   ____

2. But, she says, "<u>I</u> family were packing <u>they</u> clothing to move to America."

   ____

3. Haley took <u>he</u> search for <u>he</u> roots across the Atlantic.

   ____

4. Grandma Murray would have been happy to know he had found <u>they</u> family's roots.

   ____

"Melting Pot" by Anna Quindlen
"Was Tarzan a Three-Bandage Man?" by Bill Cosby
Literary Analysis: Comparing Author's Purpose

The **author's purpose** is his or her main reason for writing. For example, an author may want to entertain, inform, or persuade the reader. Other times, an author may be trying to teach a lesson or reflect on an experience. An author can convey his or her purpose through word choice, types of detail, and tone. These can all support and develop the essay's central idea.

"Melting Pot" and "Was Tarzan a Three-Bandage Man?" are similar in that both are autobiographical essays. They are different, however, in their authors' purposes for writing. You can discover an author's purpose by asking yourself questions as you read.

DIRECTIONS: *Answer the following questions about each essay.*

1. What is the author's subject?

   "Melting Pot": ____

   "Was Tarzan a Three-Bandage Man?": _______________________________

2. What details support the author's points?

   "Melting Pot": ____

   ____

   "Was Tarzan a Three-Bandage Man?": _______________________________

   ____

3. What is the nature of the details? For example, are they factual or imagined, serious or humorous, unbiased or biased?

   "Melting Pot": ____

   ____

   "Was Tarzan a Three-Bandage Man?": _______________________________

   ____

4. What is the author's tone? For example, is it playful or serious, formal or informal?

   "Melting Pot": ____

   "Was Tarzan a Three-Bandage Man?": _______________________________

5. What is the author's purpose? Is it to persuade, to entertain, to provide information, to teach something, or to reflect on an experience? Is it a combination of purposes?

   "Melting Pot": ____

   "Was Tarzan a Three-Bandage Man?": _______________________________

Unit 1 Resources: Fiction and Nonfiction

"Melting Pot" by Anna Quindlen
"Was Tarzan a Three-Bandage Man?" by Bill Cosby
Vocabulary Builder

> fluent   bigots   emulate   dejectedly

A. DIRECTIONS: *For each item below, think about the meaning of the italicized Word List word. Then answer the question.*

1. If your neighbor is *fluent* in English and Spanish, how is he or she able to communicate?

____

2. How would *bigots* treat people who are different from them?

____

3. If a teenager were trying to *emulate* a pop star, how might he or she dress, talk, or act?

____

4. If a boy acts *dejectedly* because he has not gotten his way, how might he act? Describe his attitude or behavior.

____

B. DIRECTIONS: *Indicate whether each sentence is* True *or* False. *Then, explain your answer.*

1. A person who is *fluent* in a language speaks the language haltingly.

   True/False: ____________________ **Explanation:** ____________________

   ____

2. *Bigots* are likely to be hostile to neighbors whose ethnic background differs from theirs.

   True/False: ____________________ **Explanation:** ____________________

   ____

3. You are likely to *emulate* a person you disrespect.

   True/False: ____________________ **Explanation:** ____________________

   ____

4. A person whose work has been praised will most likely respond *dejectedly*.

   True/False: ____________________ **Explanation:** ____________________

   ____

"**Melting Pot**" by Anna Quindlen
"**Was Tarzan a Three-Bandage Man?**" by Bill Cosby
Support for Writing to Compare Literary Works

Use this graphic organizer as you prepare to write an essay comparing the purpose and tone of "Melting Pot" with the purpose and tone of "Was Tarzan a Three-Bandage Man?"

<table>
<tr><td align="center">**"Melting Pot"**</td><td align="center">**"Was Tarzan a Three-Bandage Man?"**</td></tr>
<tr><td>

Author's purpose:
____
____
____
____
____

</td><td>

Author's purpose:
____
____
____
____
____

</td></tr>
<tr><td>

Author's tone:
____
____
____
____
____

</td><td>

Author's tone:
____
____
____
____
____

</td></tr>
<tr><td>

Details from essay that create tone:
____
____
____
____
____
____
____
____
____
____

</td><td>

Details from essay that create tone:
____
____
____
____
____
____
____
____
____
____

</td></tr>
</table>

Now, use your notes to compare Quindlen's purpose and tone in "Melting Pot" with Cosby's purpose and tone in "Was Tarzan a Three-Bandage Man?" Be sure to consider how each writer's tone is suited to his or her purpose and which essay better communicates the writer's ideas.

Walter Dean Myers
Listening and Viewing

Segment 1: Meet Walter Dean Myers
- Why was it important for Walter Dean Myers to write about his community?
- What would you write about your community?

____

____

____

____

Segment 2: The Short Story
- Why would a scrapbook be a good basis for a short story?
- In what ways might Myers's short stories serve as his own scrapbook?

____

____

____

____

Segment 3: The Writing Process
- What does Myers use for inspiration for his characters?
- Would that method help you develop characters? Why or why not?

____

____

____

____

Segment 4: The Rewards of Writing
- What does Walter Dean Myers mean when he says, "Reading can make you more"?
- How has reading made you "more"?

____

____

____

____

Unit 2
Learning About Short Stories

The **short story** is a form of fiction. Certain elements are common to short stories. For example, all short stories contain **characters,** the people or animals in the story. The reasons that explain why characters act as they do are called their **motivation.** The way in which a writer reveals a character's personality and qualities is called **characterization.** There are two kinds of characterization:

- Through **direct characterization,** the writer *tells* what the character is like.
- Through **indirect characterization,** the writer *shows* what the character is like. That is, the reader must draw conclusions about the character's personality and qualities based on the character's appearance, words, and actions and what other characters say about him or her.

The **plot** is the series of events in a short story. A plot usually has five parts:

1. The **exposition** introduces the **setting** (the time and place of the story), the characters, and the basic situation.
2. The **rising action** introduces, develops, and deepens the **conflict,** or problem.
3. The **climax** is the point of highest tension, the turning point. During the climax, the characters confront the conflict.
4. During the **falling action,** the characters solve the problem, and the tension eases.
5. The **resolution** is the conclusion, when the conflict is settled and the outcome of the story is revealed.

The **theme** is a central message about life. A **universal theme** is one that is expressed in many cultures and time periods. It reflects basic human values. An example is "Crime does not pay."

A. DIRECTIONS: *On the line, write the letter of the short story element that each sentence illustrates.*

_____ 1. "Experience is a great teacher."
    A. conflict   B. theme

_____ 2. "He was a clever man."
    A. direct characterization   B. indirect characterization

_____ 3. "It was a cold winter's night."
    A. setting   B. plot

_____ 4. "Jake couldn't hold on to the rocky ledge any longer. He started to fall."
    A. resolution   B. climax

_____ 5. "Once the fire was out, we found a safe place to lie down and rest."
    A. rising action   B. falling action

B. DIRECTIONS: *On a separate sheet of paper, write the exposition of a short story. In your exposition, introduce the setting, a main character, and a basic situation. Use indirect characterization to show what your main character is like.*

52

"The Treasure of Lemon Brown" by Walter Dean Myers
Model Selection: Short Story

The characters in short stories are driven by **motivations**—reasons, needs, and feelings that cause them to act the way they do.

Characterization is the way in which a writer reveals a character's traits, or personal qualities. Through **direct characterization,** the writer *tells* what the character is like. Through **indirect characterization,** the writer *shows* what the character is like. With indirect characterization, the reader must draw conclusions about the character based on the character's appearance, words, and actions, as well as what other characters say about him or her.

A. DIRECTIONS: *Answer these questions about the plot, characters, characterization, and setting of "The Treasure of Lemon Brown."*

1. In the exposition, Greg is angry. What basic situation has caused his anger?

   ____

2. Describe the traits, or personal qualities, of Lemon Brown.

   ____

   ____

3. Lemon Brown says, "Hard times caught up with me." What does he mean? Is this an example of direct or indirect characterization? Explain your answer.

   ____

   ____

4. What conflict do Greg and Lemon Brown face?

   ____

   ____

5. How do Greg and Lemon Brown behave at the climax of the story?

   ____

B. DIRECTIONS: *The **theme** of a story is its message about life. A **universal theme** reflects basic human values in many cultures. An example is "Hard work pays off." Answer these questions about the theme of "The Treasure of Lemon Brown."*

1. What might be the theme of "The Treasure of Lemon Brown"? Support your answer by citing details from the story.

   ____

   ____

2. Is the theme you stated universal? Explain why or why not.

   ____

   ____

"The Bear Boy" by Joseph Bruchac
Reading: Use Prior Knowledge to Make Predictions

Predicting means making an intelligent guess about what will happen next in a story based on details in the text. You can also **use prior knowledge to make predictions.** For example, if a character in a story notices animal tracks in the snow, you can predict that the animal will play a part in the story because you know from prior knowledge that animal tracks mean that the animal is nearby.

DIRECTIONS: *Fill in the following chart with predictions as you read "The Bear Boy." Use clues from the story and your prior knowledge to make predictions. Then, compare your predictions with what actually happens. An example is shown.*

Story Details and Prior Knowledge	What I Predict Will Happen	What Actually Happens
People said that someone who followed a bear's tracks might never come back, but Kuo-Haya had never been told that. I know that if people are not warned of a danger, they may do something dangerous.	Kuo-Haya will see and follow a bear's tracks.	Kuo-Haya sees and follows a bear's tracks and finds some bear cubs.

"The Bear Boy" by Joseph Bruchac
Literary Analysis: Plot

Plot is the related sequence of events in a short story and other works of fiction. A plot has the following elements:

- **Exposition:** introduction of the setting (the time and place), the characters, and the basic situation
- **Rising Action:** events that introduce a **conflict,** or struggle, and increase the tension
- **Climax:** the story's high point, at which the eventual outcome becomes clear
- **Falling Action:** events that follow the climax
- **Resolution:** the final outcome and tying up of loose ends, when the reader learns how the conflict is resolved

In a story about a race, for example, the exposition would probably introduce the runners. The rising action might include a description of a conflict between two of the runners and some information about the start of the race. The climax might be the winning of the race by one of the runners. The falling action might include a meeting between the two runners, and the resolution might describe the end of their conflict.

DIRECTIONS: *Answer the following questions about the plot elements of "The Bear Boy."*

1. The exposition of "The Bear Boy" introduces characters and describes a setting. Who are the characters, and what is the setting?

   ____

   ____

2. How do you know that the father's neglect of Huo-Kaya is part of the rising action?

   ____

   ____

3. What happens in the climax of "The Bear Boy"?

   ____

   ____

4. Describe one event in the falling action of the story.

   ____

   ____

5. What happens in the resolution of "The Bear Boy"?

   ____

   ____

"The Bear Boy" by Joseph Bruchac
Vocabulary Builder

Word List

timid	initiation	neglected

A. DIRECTIONS: *Use each vocabulary word by following the instructions below. Use the words in the same way they are used in "The Bear Boy," and write sentences that show you understand the meaning of the word.*

1. Use the word *timid* in a sentence about a rabbit.

   ____

   ____

2. Use the word *initiation* in a sentence about a ceremony.

   ____

   ____

3. Use the word *neglected* in a sentence about a garden.

   ____

   ____

B. DIRECTIONS: *On each line, write the letter of the word that is a synonym for the vocabulary word.*

____ 1. initiation
   A. question
   B. performance
   C. ceremony
   D. hunt

____ 2. neglected
   A. tended
   B. afraid
   C. hurt
   D. ignored

____ 3. timid
   A. shy
   B. helpless
   C. restless
   D. worried

Name ____ Date _______________

Support for Writing an Informative Article

Use the graphic organizer below to record details from each section of "The Bear Boy." Your details should tell *when, how much, how often,* or *to what extent.*

Introduction

Details:

Body

Details:

Conclusion

Details:

Now, use your notes to write an informative article telling how mother bears care for their cubs. Write for an audience of third-graders.

"Rikki-tikki-tavi" by Rudyard Kipling
Reading: Use Prior Knowledge to Make Predictions

Predicting means making an intelligent guess about what will happen next in a story based on details in the text. You can also **use prior knowledge to make predictions.** For example, if a story introduces a mongoose and a snake and you know that mongooses and snakes are natural enemies, you can predict that the story will involve a conflict between the two animals.

DIRECTIONS: *Fill in the following chart with predictions as you read "Rikki-tikki-tavi." Use clues from the story and your prior knowledge to make predictions. Then, compare your predictions with what actually happens. An example is shown.*

Story Details and Prior Knowledge	What I Predict Will Happen	What Actually Happens
Teddy's mother says, "Perhaps he isn't really dead." I know that Rikki-tikki is the hero of the story, and heroes rarely die during a story.	The mongoose will live.	The mongoose lives.

"Rikki-tikki-tavi" by Rudyard Kipling
Literary Analysis: Plot

Plot is the related sequence of events in a short story and other works of fiction. A plot has the following elements:

- **Exposition:** introduction of the setting (the time and place), the characters, and the basic situation
- **Rising Action:** events that introduce a **conflict,** or struggle, and increase the tension
- **Climax:** the story's high point, at which the eventual outcome becomes clear
- **Falling Action:** events that follow the climax
- **Resolution:** the final outcome and tying up of loose ends, when the reader learns how the conflict is resolved

For example, in a story about a battle, the exposition would introduce the contestants. The rising action might explain the conflict between the contestants and describe events leading up to the battle. The climax might be the winning of the battle by one of the contestants. The falling action could include a celebration of the victory, and the resolution might tell about events that took place in the years following the battle.

DIRECTIONS: *Answer the following questions about the plot elements of "Rikki-tikki-tavi."*

1. Who are the characters, and what is the setting described in the exposition?

   ____

   ____

2. How do you know that the appearance of Nag is part of the rising action?

   ____

   ____

3. What happens in the climax of "Rikki-tikki-tavi"?

   ____

   ____

4. Describe one event in the falling action of the story.

   ____

   ____

5. What happens in the resolution of "Rikki-tikki-tavi"?

   ____

   ____

"Rikki-tikki-tavi" by Rudyard Kipling
Vocabulary Builder

Word List

revived   immensely   consolation

A. DIRECTIONS: *Use each vocabulary word by following the instructions below. Use the words in the same way they are used in "Rikki-tikki-tavi," and write sentences that show you understand the meaning of the word.*

1. Use the word *revived* in a sentence about a bird.

   ____

   ____

2. Use the word *consolation* in a sentence about a race.

   ____

   ____

3. Use the word *immensely* in a sentence about an activity.

   ____

   ____

B. DIRECTIONS: *On each line, write the letter of the word or phrase that is a synonym for the vocabulary word.*

____ 1. immensely
   A. mildly   C. immediately
   B. greatly   D. loudly

____ 2. revived
   A. continued to live   C. returned to consciousness
   B. relaxed in a reclining position   D. fell asleep again

____ 3. consolation
   A. confusion about a loss   C. confidence in victory
   B. assurance of victory   D. comfort after a disappointment

"Rikki-tikki-tavi" by Rudyard Kipling

Support for Writing an Informative Article

Use the graphic organizer below to record details from each section of "Rikki-tikki-tavi." Your details should tell *when, how much, how often,* or *to what extent.*

Introduction

Details:

↓

Body

Details:

↓

Conclusion

Details:

Now, use your notes to write a short informative article about mongooses. Write for an audience of third-graders.

"**The Bear Boy**" by Joseph Bruchac
"**Rikki-tikki-tavi**" by Rudyard Kipling
Build Language Skills: Vocabulary

The Root *-dict-*

The word *predict* comes from the root *-dict-*, meaning "to speak," and the prefix *pre-*, meaning "before" or "in front of." When you *predict* something, you *speak* about what might happen *before* you know for sure what will happen.

A. DIRECTIONS: *Look up each word in a dictionary, and write its meaning on the line following the word. Then, explain how the meaning of the root -dict- ("to speak") is contained in the word's meaning.*

1. *diction:* ____

   Explanation: ____

2. *dictionary:* ____

   Explanation: ____

Academic Vocabulary Practice

anticipate   indicate   plot   predict   verify

B. DIRECTIONS: *Use an Academic Vocabulary word from the box in your answer to each question. Answer the question in a full sentence, and use each word only once.*

1. A friend has told you that a movie is very good. Do you consider seeing it? Why or why not?

   ____

2. Think of a story or movie you liked. What did you like about its sequence of events?

   ____

3. You are reading a suspenseful story. Before it is over, do you say or think about what is going to happen? Why or why not?

   ____

4. You are shopping for something that is in a display case, and you would like to take a closer look at it. How do you tell the salesperson which item you would like to see?

   ____

5. Your friend insists that your favorite movie was made in 1992, but you are sure it was made in 1994. How do you find out which date is correct?

   ____

"The Bear Boy" by Joseph Bruchac
"Rikki-tikki-tavi" by Rudyard Kipling
Build Language Skills: Grammar

Action Verbs and Linking Verbs

Verbs are words that express an action (for example, *swim* and *throw*) or a state of being (for example, *am, is, was,* and *seemed*). The verbs that express an action are called *action verbs.*

> Jessica *climbed* a mountain.

The verbs that express a state of being are called *linking verbs.* Linking verbs join the subject of a sentence with a word or expression that describes or renames the subject.

> Jessica *seems* strong.

> Jessica *is* a mountain climber.

Besides forms of *be* and *seem,* other verbs that can describe or rename a subject are *appear, look,* and *sound.*

A. PRACTICE: *Underline the verbs in each sentence. On the line, identify each verb as an* action verb *or a* linking verb.

1. Rikki-tikki-tavi is a brave little mongoose. _____________________

2. Mongooses seem harmless, but they fight bravely. _____________________, _____________________

3. Rikki-tikki lives with a human family, and they love him. _____________________, _____________________

4. A snake threatens the family, and Rikki-tikki is furious. _____________________, _____________________

5. Rikki-tikki defeats the snake, and the family is very happy. _____________________, _____________________

B. Writing Application: *Write a paragraph about a time when you or someone you know was in danger. Use at least three action verbs and three linking verbs. Underline each action verb once and each linking verb twice.*

____

____

____

____

____

____

____

from *Letters from Rifka* by Karen Hesse
Reading: Read Ahead to Verify Predictions and Reread to Look for Details

A **prediction** is an informed guess about what will happen. Use details in the text and your own knowledge and experience to make predictions as you read. Then, **read ahead to verify predictions,** to check whether your predictions are correct.

- As you read, ask yourself whether new details support your predictions. If they do not, revise your predictions based on the new information.
- If the predictions you make turn out to be wrong, **reread to look for details** you might have missed that would have helped you make a more accurate prediction.

If it had not been for your father, though, I think my family would all be dead now: Mama, Papa, Nathan, Saul, and me.

Details in this passage can help you predict that the narrator will reveal that Rifka has escaped a dangerous situation. You can read further in the excerpt from *Letters from Rifka* to check this prediction.

DIRECTIONS: *Complete the following chart. If a prediction in the second column is correct, write* Correct *in the third column. If a prediction is wrong, write* Incorrect *in the third column. Then, in the fourth column, describe what does happen, and include a detail that would have allowed an accurate prediction. The first item has been completed as an example.*

Detail in *Letters from Rifka*	Prediction	Verification of Prediction	Event in Selection and Additional Detail
1. Tovah's father helps Rifka's family.	Tovah's father is in danger.	Incorrect	Tovah's father makes it home safely: "I am sure you and Cousin Hannah were glad to see Uncle Avrum come home today."
2. Rifka is not sure she will be able to distract the guards.	Rifka will not succeed.		
3. Nathan deserts the army.	Soldiers will look for Nathan.		
4. Rifka says, "Don't we need papers?"	Papa will find the papers.		

from *Letters from Rifka* by Karen Hesse
Literary Analysis: Character

A **character** is a person or an animal that takes part in the action of a literary work.

- A **character's motives** are the emotions or goals that drive him or her to act one way or another. Some powerful motives are love, anger, and hope.
- **Character traits** are the individual qualities that make each character unique. These may be things such as stubbornness, sense of humor, or intelligence.

Characters' motives and qualities are important because they influence what characters do and how they interact with other characters. As you read, think about what the characters are like and why they do what they do. For example, consider this passage:

> I am sure you and Cousin Hannah were glad to see Uncle Avrum come home today. How worried his daughters must have been after the locked doors and whisperings of last night.

This passage illustrates Rifka's character traits: her caring nature and concern for others. It also suggests a motive for her actions: She wants her family to be safe.

A. DIRECTIONS: *After each character's name, write as many adjectives as you can think of that describe that character's traits.*

1. **Rifka:** ____

   ____

   ____

2. **Papa:** ____

   ____

   ____

B. DIRECTIONS: *Each quotation on the right states or hints at a motive for one of the actions on the left. On the line before each action, write the letter of the quotation that provides the motive.*

___ 1. Rifka writes to Tovah.

___ 2. Nathan deserts the army.

___ 3. Rifka distracts guards.

___ 4. Mama insists on taking candlesticks.

___ 5. Avrum helps the family escape.

A. "I've come," he said, "to warn Saul."

B. "Soon enough they will sweep down like vultures to pick our house bare."

C. "We made it!"

D. "If it had not been for your father, . . . my family would all be dead now."

E. "I knew, no matter how frightened I was, I must not let them find Nathan."

Unit 2 Resources: Short Stories

from *Letters from Rifka* by Karen Hesse
Vocabulary Builder

Word List

distract	emerged	huddled

A. DIRECTIONS: *Think about the meaning of the underlined word in each of these sentences. Then, answer the question.*

1. What might Rifka have done to <u>distract</u> the guards?

   ____

2. If Nathan had <u>emerged</u> from under the burlap bags, what might have happened?

   ____

3. Why had the family <u>huddled</u> in Tovah's cellar through the night?

   ____

   ____

B. DIRECTIONS: *Write the letter of the word or phrase that can replace the Word List word in each sentence.*

____ 1. Rifka tried to <u>distract</u> the guards from finding Nathan by talking to them about Pushkin.
   A. play a trick on
   B. frighten
   C. draw attention away from
   D. entertain

____ 2. The travelers <u>emerged</u> from the train looking tired and pale.
   A. ran away
   B. got onto
   C. fell
   D. came into view

____ 3. To keep warm, the family <u>huddled</u> together.
   A. crowded
   B. fought
   C. slept
   D. hid

from *Letters from Rifka* by Karen Hesse
Support for Writing a Journal Entry

For your **journal entry,** put yourself in the place of the character you have chosen. Write that character's name on the line. Then, imagine what you see and what you feel on the night of the escape, and record those ideas on this chart.

My character: ____

Event	Details from My Point of View	My Feelings About the Escape
Nathan's arrival home		
The plan to escape		
Hiding on the train		
Rifka's distraction		

Now, use your notes to write a journal entry about the night of the escape.

Unit 2 Resources: Short Stories

"Two Kinds" by Amy Tan

Reading: Read Ahead to Verify Predictions
and Reread to Look for Details

A **prediction** is an informed guess about what will happen. Use details in the text and your own knowledge and experience to make predictions as you read. Then, **read ahead to verify predictions,** to check whether your predictions are correct.

- As you read, ask yourself whether new details support your predictions. If they do not, revise your predictions based on the new information.
- If the predictions you make turn out to be wrong, **reread to look for details** you might have missed that would have helped you make a more accurate prediction.

"Of course you can be prodigy, too," my mother told me when I was nine. "You can be best anything."

Details in this passage can help you predict that the narrator's mother will encourage her to become a prodigy. You can read further in "Two Kinds" to check this prediction.

DIRECTIONS: *Complete the following chart. If a prediction in the second column is correct, write* Correct *in the third column. If a prediction is wrong, write* Incorrect *in the third column. Then, in the fourth column, describe what does happen, and include a detail that would have allowed an accurate prediction. The first item has been completed as an example.*

Details in "Two Kinds"	Prediction	Verification of Prediction	Event in Selection and Additional Detail
1. The mother wants her daughter to be "a Chinese Shirley Temple."	The daughter will become the Chinese Shirley Temple.	Incorrect	The narrator fails at being Shirley Temple. "We didn't immediately pick the right kind of prodigy."
2. The daughter begins to think thoughts with "won'ts."	The daughter will rebel against her mother.		
3. The narrator must perform a simple piece "that sounded more difficult than it was."	She will perform well.		
4. The daughter sees her mother's offers of the piano "as a sign of forgiveness."	The daughter will take the piano.		

"**Two Kinds**" by Amy Tan
Literary Analysis: Character

A **character** is a person or an animal that takes part in the action of a literary work.

- A **character's motives** are the emotions or goals that drive him or her to act one way or another. Some powerful motives are love, anger, and hope.
- **Character traits** are the individual qualities that make each character unique. These may be things such as stubbornness, sense of humor, or intelligence.

Characters' motives and qualities are important because they influence what characters do and how they interact with other characters. As you read, think about what the characters are like and why they do what they do. For example, consider this passage:

> She had come here in 1949 after losing everything in China: her mother and father, her family home, her first husband, and two daughters, twin baby girls. But she never looked back with regret. There were so many ways for things to get better.

This passage illustrates the mother's character traits: her strength and courage. It also suggests a motive for her actions: She wants things to get better.

A. DIRECTIONS: *After each character's name, write as many adjectives as you can think of that describe that character's traits.*

1. **The daughter:** ____

____

____

2. **The mother:** ____

____

____

B. DIRECTIONS: *Each quotation on the right states or hints at a motive for one of the actions on the left. On the line before each action, write the letter of the quotation that provides the motive.*

____ 1. Daughter wants to become a prodigy.

____ 2. Mother pushes her daughter to be a prodigy.

____ 3. Daughter refuses to play the piano.

____ 4. Mother offers her daughter the piano.

____ 5. Daughter begins to resist her mother's efforts to make her a prodigy.

A. I could sense her anger rising to its breaking point. I wanted to see it spill over.

B. I was filled with a sense that I would soon become *perfect*. My mother and father would adore me.

C. I saw the offer as a sign of forgiveness, a tremendous burden removed.

D. I won't let her change me, I promised myself. I won't be what I'm not.

E. "Only ask you be your best. For your sake."

"Two Kinds" by Amy Tan
Vocabulary Builder

Word List

reproach   conspired   devastated

A. DIRECTIONS: *Think about the meaning of the underlined word in each of these sentences. Then, answer the question.*

1. Would the daughter have been beyond <u>reproach</u> if she had become a prodigy? Why or why not?

   ____

   ____

2. How would the daughter have felt when her mother's expression <u>devastated</u> her?

   ____

   ____

3. If the mother and Old Chong <u>conspired</u> to hold a talent show, whose idea was it? How do you know?

   ____

   ____

B. DIRECTIONS: *Write the letter of the word or phrase that can replace the Word List word in each sentence.*

____ 1. The parents <u>conspired</u> to show off their children's talents.
   A. talked eagerly
   B. made contacts
   C. worked together
   D. revealed the plans

____ 2. The conflict between mother and daughter might have <u>devastated</u> their relationship for good.
   A. renewed
   B. destroyed
   C. eliminated
   D. restored

____ 3. The daughter knew that her attitude toward practicing for the recital was worthy of <u>reproach</u>.
   A. praise
   B. perfection
   C. enthusiasm
   D. blame

"Two Kinds" by Amy Tan

Support for Writing a Journal Entry

For your **journal entry,** put yourself in the narrator's place after the piano recital. Imagine your thoughts and your feelings, and record them on this chart.

Event	Details from My Point of View	My Feelings About the Piano Recital
Members of the Joy Luck Club comment on the recital.		
I travel home on the bus with my parents.		
My mother says nothing and goes to her bedroom.		
I think about the day.		

Now, use your notes to write a journal entry describing the narrator's thoughts and feelings at the end of the day of the piano recital.

from *Letters from Rifka* by Karen Hesse
"Two Kinds" by Amy Tan
Build Language Skills: Vocabulary

The Roots *-dict-* and *-ver-*

The word *predict* comes from the root *dict-*, meaning "to speak," and the prefix *pre-*, meaning "before" or "in front of." When you *predict* something, you *speak* about what might happen *before* you know for sure what will happen.

The word *verify* contains the root *-ver-*, meaning "true." When you read ahead to *verify* a prediction, you check to see whether the prediction will turn out to be *true*.

A. DIRECTIONS: *Rewrite each sentence, replacing the italicized word or phrase with one of these words:* predict, verify, verdict.

1. The meteorologists *say that in the future* it will rain heavily.

   ____

2. The scientists conducted a study to *find out whether* their theory *was true*.

   ____

3. The jurors delivered their *judgment* solemnly.

   ____

Academic Vocabulary Practice

anticipate	indicate	plot	predict	verify

B. DIRECTIONS: *Follow the instructions to write sentences using each Academic Vocabulary word.*

1. Use *indicate* in a sentence about getting lost.

   ____

2. Use *anticipate* in a sentence about tryouts for a play.

   ____

3. Use *plot* in a sentence about a movie.

   ____

4. Use *predict* in a sentence about taking a test.

   ____

5. Use *verify* in a sentence about a science experiment.

   ____

from *Letters from Rifka* by Karen Hesse
"Two Kinds" by Amy Tan
Build Language Skills: Grammar

Regular and Irregular Verbs

Most verbs are *regular;* that is, they form their tenses in a predictable way.

I *climb* that mountain every day.

Last month Michael *climbed* that mountain.

Jessica *has* often *climbed* that mountain.

Verbs that are *irregular* do not follow a predictable pattern.

I *am* a mountain climber.

Michael *was* a mountain climber before he broke his leg.

Jessica *has been* a mountain climber since she learned to walk.

There are four main forms of every verb, called the principal parts. Each principal part indicates when something happens. The principal parts are **present, present participle, past,** and **past participle.**

A. PRACTICE: *Underline the verbs in each sentence. On the line, identify each verb as* regular *or* irregular. *Then, identify the principal part of each verb. The principal part* will be present, present participle, past, *or* past participle.

1. Her brother ran away from the army.

   Regular/Irregular: _____________________; **Principal part:** ___________________________

2. The whole family fled from their home and is starting a new life.

   Regular/Irregular: _____________________; **Principal part:** ___________________________

   Regular/Irregular: _____________________; **Principal part:** ___________________________

3. Rifka was courageous, and she saved her family.

   Regular/Irregular: _____________________; **Principal part:** ___________________________

   Regular/Irregular: _____________________; **Principal part:** ___________________________

B. Writing Application: *Write a paragraph about a time when you or someone you know faced a frightening situation. Use at least three regular verbs and three irregular verbs. Underline each regular verb once and each irregular verb twice.*

____

____

____

____

____

"Seventh Grade" by Gary Soto
"Stolen Day" by Sherwood Anderson

Literary Analysis: Comparing Characters

A **character** is a person or an animal that takes part in the action of a literary work. In literature, you will find characters with a range of personalities and attitudes. For example, a character might be dependable and intelligent but also stubborn. One character might hold traditional values, while another might rebel against them. The individual qualities that make each character unique are called **character traits.**

Writers use the process of **characterization** to create and develop characters. There are two types of characterization:

- **Direct characterization:** The writer directly states or describes the character's traits.
- **Indirect characterization:** The writer reveals a character's personality through his or her words and actions, and through the thoughts, words, and actions of other characters.

DIRECTIONS: *To analyze the use of characterization in "Seventh Grade" and "Stolen Day," complete the following chart. Answer each question with a brief example from the story. Write* not applicable *if you cannot answer a question about one of the characters.*

Character	Words that describe the character directly	What the character says and does	How other characters talk about or act toward the character
Victor in "Seventh Grade"			
Teresa in "Seventh Grade"			
The narrator of "Stolen Day"			
The mother in "Stolen Day"			

"Seventh Grade" by Gary Soto
"Stolen Day" by Sherwood Anderson
Vocabulary Builder

Word List

elective	scowl	conviction	solemn	affects

A. DIRECTIONS: *Think about the meaning of the italicized word in each sentence. Then, answer the question.*

1. Victor might have hoped that math would be an *elective* for seventh-graders. Why? Explain your answer.

   ____

2. Michael has a *conviction* about the benefits of scowling. What does this mean?

   ____

3. The boy was *solemn* after he heard the bad news. How did the boy behave?

   ____

4. A week of rainy weather often *affects* a person's mood. What does the weather have to do with the person's mood?

   ____

5. Mr. Bueller is likely to *scowl* the next time a student speaks nonsense instead of French. How will Mr. Bueller look?

   ____

B. DIRECTIONS: *Write the letter of the word or phrase that is most* similar *in meaning to each Word Bank word.*

____ 1. solemn
    A. joyful   C. serious
    B. silent   D. cheerful

____ 2. scowl
    A. frown   C. shovel
    B. smile   D. boat

____ 3. conviction
    A. prison sentence   C. doctrine
    B. strong belief   D. term

____ 4. elective
    A. optional course   C. dismissal
    B. political process   D. requirement

"Seventh Grade" by Gary Soto
"Stolen Day" by Sherwood Anderson
Support for Writing to Compare Literary Works

Before you **write an essay comparing and contrasting** Victor in "Seventh Grade" with the narrator of "Stolen Day," jot down your ideas in this graphic organizer. In the overlapping section of each set of boxes, write details that are true of both characters. In the sections on the left, write details that describe Victor, and in the sections on the right, write details that describe the boy in "Stolen Day."

What are some of each boy's character traits?

Victor:	Both:	The boy:

What problems does each boy face? How much responsibility does each boy have in creating his problem?

Victor:	Both:	The boy:

What does the character learn from his situation? Which character learns more?

Victor:	Both:	The boy:

Now, use your notes to write an essay that compares and contrasts the two characters.

"The Third Wish" by Joan Aiken
Reading: Make Inferences by Recognizing Details

Short story writers do not directly tell you everything there is to know about the characters, setting, and events. Instead, they leave it to you to **make inferences,** or logical guesses, about unstated information.

To form inferences, you must **recognize details** in the story and consider their importance. For example, in "The Third Wish," Mr. Peters finds a swan tangled up in thorns. When he moves closer and tries to free the swan, the swan hisses at him, pecks at him, and flaps its wings in a threatening way. You can use those clues to infer that the swan does not like or trust Mr. Peters.

DIRECTIONS: *The sentences in the left-hand column of this chart offer details about characters in "The Third Wish." (Some of the items are quotations from the story; some are based on the story.) In the right-hand column, describe what the details tell you about the character.*

Detail About a Character	Inference About the Character
1. Presently, the swan, when it was satisfied with its appearance, floated in to the bank once more, and in a moment, instead of the great white bird, there was a little man all in green.	
2. Mr. Peters wishes for a wife "as beautiful as the forest." A woman appears who is "the most beautiful creature he had ever seen, with eyes as blue-green as the canal, hair as dusky as the bushes, and skin as white as the feathers of swans."	
3. But as time went by Mr. Peters began to feel that [Leita] was not happy. She seemed restless, wandered much in the garden, and sometimes when he came back from the fields he would find the house empty. She would return after half an hour with no explanation of where she had been.	
4. After Leita was returned to the form of a swan, she "rested her head lightly against [Mr. Peters's] hand. . . . Next day he saw two swans swimming at the bottom of the garden, and one of them wore the gold chain he had given Leita after their marriage; she came up and rubbed her head against his hand."	

"The Third Wish" by Joan Aiken
Literary Analysis: Conflict

Most fictional stories center on a **conflict**—a struggle between opposing forces. There are two kinds of conflict:

- When there is an **external conflict,** a character struggles with an outside force, such as another character or nature.
- When there is an **internal conflict,** a character struggles with himself or herself to overcome opposing feelings, beliefs, needs, or desires. An internal conflict takes place in a character's mind.

The **resolution,** or outcome of the conflict, often comes toward the end of the story, when the problem is settled in some way.

A story can have additional, smaller conflicts that develop the main conflict. For example, in "The Third Wish," a small external conflict occurs between Mr. Peters and the swan that is tangled up in the thorns. As Mr. Peters tries to free the bird, the swan looks at him "with hate in its yellow eyes" and struggles with him. In addition, a minor internal conflict that helps to develop the main conflict is Mr. Peters's difficulty in deciding what to do with his three wishes.

DIRECTIONS: *Based on details in each of the following passages from "The Third Wish," identify the conflict as* External *or* Internal. *Then, explain your answer.*

1. [Leita] was weeping, and as he came nearer he saw that tears were rolling, too, from the swan's eyes.

   "Leita, what is it?" he asked, very troubled.

   "This is my sister," she answered. "I can't bear being separated from her."

   Type of conflict: _________________________

   Explanation: ____

2. "Don't you love me at all, Leita?"

   "Yes, I do, I do love you," she said, and there were tears in her eyes again. "But I miss the old life in the forest."

   Type of conflict: _________________________

   Explanation: ____

3. She shook her head. "No, I could not be as unkind to you as that. I am partly a swan, but I am also partly a human being now."

   Type of conflict: _________________________

   Explanation: ____

"The Third Wish" by Joan Aiken
Vocabulary Builder

Word List

presumptuous   rash   remote   malicious

A. DIRECTIONS: *Think about the meaning of the italicized word in each sentence. Then, in your own words, answer the question that follows, and briefly explain your answer.*

1. The old King knows that most humans make *rash* decisions when they are given permission to make three magical wishes. How much thought do most humans put into their choice of wishes?

   ____

2. The old King is *presumptuous* in believing that Mr. Peters will make three foolish wishes. Is the old King overconfident? How do you know?

   ____

   ____

3. The old King is a *malicious* character. How does he act toward Mr. Peters?

   ____

4. Mr. Peters lives in a *remote* valley. Is it close to town? How do you know?

   ____

   ____

B. DIRECTIONS: *On the line, write the letter of the word whose meaning is* opposite *that of the Word List word.*

____ 1. malicious
   A. wicked   B. tangled   C. sour   D. kind

____ 2. presumptuous
   A. curious   B. modest   C. missing   D. hungry

____ 3. rash
   A. cautious   B. itchy   C. impure   D. hasty

____ 4. remote
   A. casual   B. close   C. faraway   D. controlled

"The Third Wish" by Joan Aiken
Support for Writing an Anecdote

Before writing an **anecdote** using the pattern of three wishes that "The Third Wish" follows, use this graphic organizer. In the first rectangle, briefly describe a wish that a character makes. In the oval below it, describe a problem that the wish might cause. In the square below the oval, describe a way in which your character might solve the problem. Then do the same for the second wish. Finally, complete the information for the third wish.

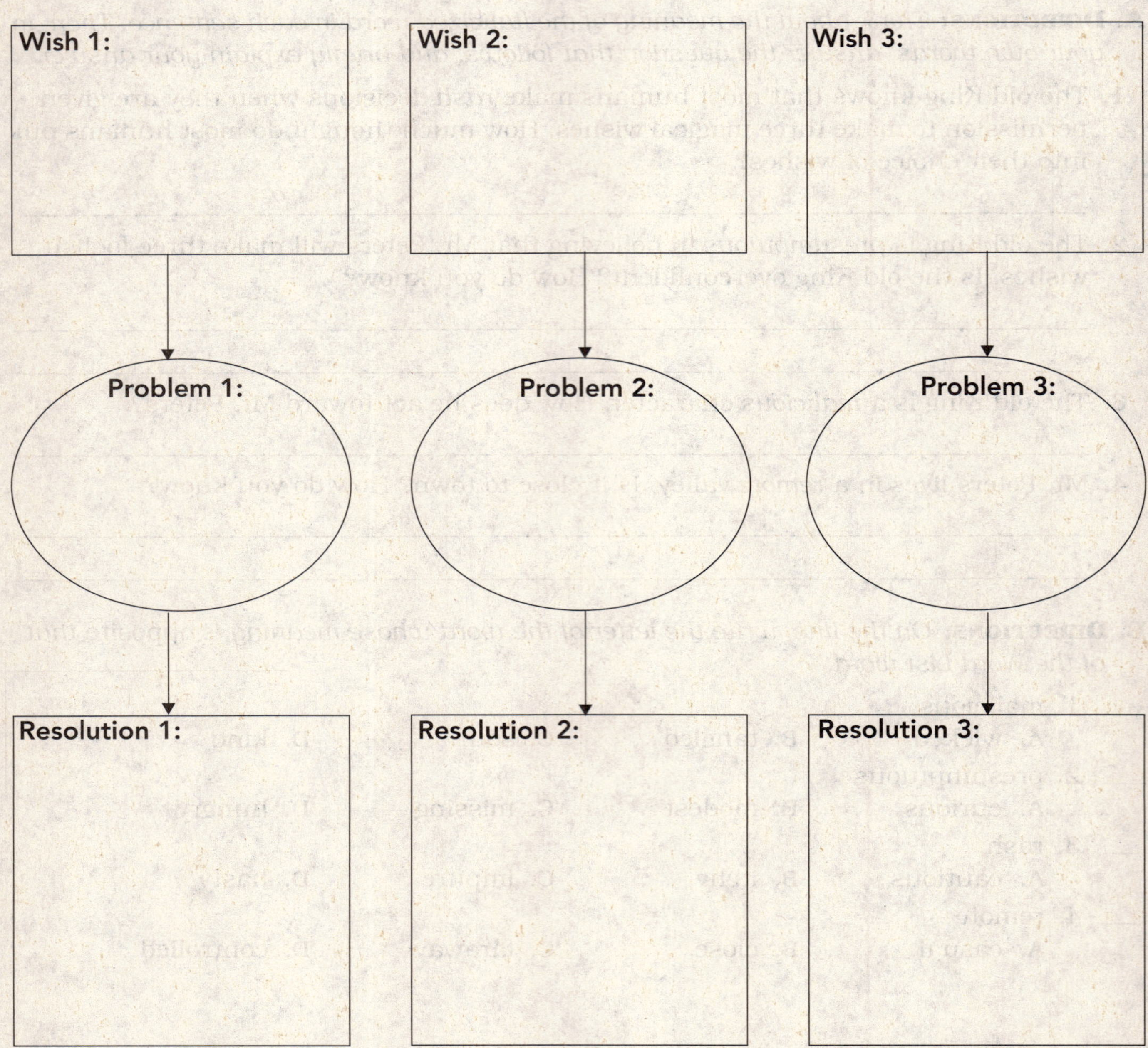

Now, use your notes to write an anecdote using the pattern of three wishes.

"Amigo Brothers" by Piri Thomas
Reading: Make Inferences by Recognizing Details

Short story writers do not directly tell you everything there is to know about the characters, setting, and events. Instead, they leave it to you to **make inferences,** or logical guesses, about unstated information.

To form inferences, you must **recognize details** in the story and consider their importance. For example, in "Amigo Brothers," the narrator says, "While some youngsters were into street negatives, Antonio and Felix slept, ate, rapped, and dreamt positive." You can use that clue to infer that Felix and Antonio stayed out of trouble.

DIRECTIONS: *The sentences in the left-hand column of this chart offer details about the amigo brothers. In the right-hand column, describe what the details tell you about one or both of these characters.*

Detail About a Character	Inference About the Character
1. "If it's fair, *hermano,* I'm for it." Antonio admired the courage of a tugboat pulling a barge five times its welterweight size.	
2. Tony jogged away. Felix watched his friend disappear from view, throwing rights and lefts. Both fighters had a lot of psyching up to do before the big fight.	
3. Felix did a fast shuffle, bobbing and weaving, while letting loose a torrent of blows that would demolish whatever got in its way. It seemed to impress the brothers, who went about their own business.	
4. [Felix] fought off a series of rights and lefts and came back with a strong right that taught Antonio respect.	
5. The announcer turned to point to the winner and found himself alone. Arm in arm the champions had already left the ring.	

Unit 2 Resources: Short Stories

81

"**Amigo Brothers**" by Piri Thomas
Literary Analysis: Conflict

Most fictional stories center on a **conflict**—a struggle between opposing forces. There are two kinds of conflict:

- When there is an **external conflict,** a character struggles with an outside force such as another character or nature.
- When there is an **internal conflict,** a character struggles with himself or herself to overcome opposing feelings, beliefs, needs, or desires. An internal conflict takes place in a character's mind.

The **resolution,** or outcome of the conflict, often comes toward the end of the story, when the problem is settled in some way.

A story can have additional, smaller conflicts that develop the main conflict. In "Amigo Brothers," for example, a small external conflict occurs one morning as Felix and Antonio work out. There is tension between them, and Felix says, "Let's stop a while, bro. I think we both got something to say to each other." A minor internal conflict occurs when Felix mentions that he has stayed awake at night, "pulling punches" on Antonio. Felix struggles with the conflict between his wish not to harm his friend and his desire to win the fight.

DIRECTIONS: *Based on details in each of the following passages from "Amigo Brothers," identify the conflict as* External *or* Internal. *Then, explain your answer.*

1. He tried not to think of Felix, feeling he had succeeded in psyching his mind. But only in the ring would he really know.

   Type of conflict: ______________________

   Explanation: ____

2. He walked up some dark streets, deserted except for small pockets of wary-looking kids wearing gang colors. Despite the fact that he was Puerto Rican like them, they eyed him as a stranger to their turf.

   Type of conflict: ______________________

   Explanation: ____

3. Antonio was passing some heavy time on his rooftop. How would the fight tomorrow affect his relationship with Felix? After all, fighting was like any other profession. Friendship had nothing to do with it. A gnawing doubt crept in.

   Type of conflict: ______________________

   Explanation: ____

4. Felix and Antonio turned and faced each other squarely in a fighting pose. Felix wasted no time. He came fast, head low, half hunched toward his right shoulder, and lashed out with a straight left.

   Type of conflict: ______________________

   Explanation: ____

"Amigo Brothers" by Piri Thomas
Vocabulary Builder

Word List

devastating	perpetual	dispelled	evading

A. DIRECTIONS: *Think about the meaning of the italicized word in each sentence. Then, in your own words, answer the question that follows and briefly explain your answer.*

1. The hurricane was *devastating* to the island of Puerto Rico. How did the hurricane affect the island?

   ____

2. When in training, the boxer worked out all day long, her body in *perpetual* motion. How would you describe the boxer when she is in training?

   ____

3. The huge audience that crowded onto the bleachers *dispelled* the rumor that there was little interest in the fight. What happened to the rumor?

   ____

4. The challenger ducked and bobbed, *evading* his opponent's punches. What did the challenger's moves allow him to do?

   ____

B. DIRECTIONS: *On the line, write the letter of the word whose meaning is* opposite *that of the Word List word.*

____ **1.** perpetual
   A. permanent   B. temporary   C. strong   D. wide

____ **2.** devastating
   A. confusing   B. appearing   C. harmful   D. helpful

____ **3.** dispelled
   A. dispersed   B. crumbled   C. gathered   D. hypnotized

____ **4.** evading
   A. confronting   B. watching   C. escaping   D. explaining

"Amigo Brothers" by Piri Thomas
Support for Writing an Anecdote

Before writing an **anecdote** that tells what might have happened if one of the "amigo brothers" had been knocked out during the fight, use this graphic organizer. In the rectangle, list details about the fight that you imagine. In the two ovals below it, describe how each boy would feel about the knockout. Then, in the squares below the ovals, describe one way in which the character might act to resolve the conflict.

The fight and the knockout (who knocks out whom?):

Feelings of the boy who lands the punch:

Feelings of the boy who is knocked out (after he comes to):

Resolution:

Resolution:

Now use your notes to write an anecdote telling what might have happened if Antonio or Felix had been knocked out. Be sure to tell whether the boys' friendship lasts beyond the fight. How do they act afterward?

"The Third Wish" by Joan Aiken
"Amigo Brothers" by Piri Thomas

Build Language Skills: Vocabulary

The Prefix *ob-*

The prefix *ob-* generally means "against" or "blocking." The word *object*, which can mean "speak against," begins with the prefix *ob-*. *Ob-* also appears at the beginning of *obstruction, obstacle,* and *obstructive,* which all have meanings related to being blocked, or "not able to continue."

A. DIRECTIONS: *Read the definition of each word that begins with the prefix* ob-. *Then, complete each sentence with the word from the list that makes the best sense. Use each word only once.*

obstacle:	something that stands in the way
obstinate:	sticking to a belief no matter what
obstruct:	to block by putting something in the way
obstructive:	blocking by putting something in the way

1. The jogger had to go around an ____________________ in the form of a tree that had fallen across her path.

2. That huge satellite dish will ____________________ my view of the mountain.

3. She was ____________________ in her views, refusing to change her mind no matter what she read.

4. In the negotiations, one side added so many requirements and was generally so ____________________ that no settlement could be reached.

Academic Vocabulary Practice

B. DIRECTIONS: *Indicate whether the following sentences make sense if the italicized Academic Vocabulary words are used in the way they are defined in your textbook. Then, explain why each sentence does or does not make sense.*

1. Emily ignored the evidence, relying on her feelings to *conclude* that the man was guilty.

   Yes/No: ______ **Explanation:** ____

2. The witness swore that he had seen the man put an *object* in his pocket.

   Yes/No: ______ **Explanation:** ____

3. The student's paper is well written even though it does not have a *subject*.

   Yes/No: ______ **Explanation:** ____

4. The jurors decided that the woman with a reputation for lying was a *credible* witness.

   Yes/No: ______ **Explanation:** ____

5. A person's *perspective* may be influenced by place of birth, education, and other factors.

   Yes/No: ______ **Explanation:** ____

"The Third Wish" by Joan Aiken
"Amigo Brothers" by Piri Thomas
Build Language Skills: Grammar

Adjectives

An **adjective** modifies or describes a noun or pronoun. An adjective may answer the questions *what kind? how many? which one?* or *whose?*

In this sentence, *beautiful* modifies *woman.* It tells what kind of woman appeared.

A *beautiful* <u>woman</u> suddenly appeared.

In this sentence, *two* modifies *boys.* It tells which boys continued to run together.

The *two* <u>boys</u> continued to run together.

A. DIRECTIONS: *Underline the adjective or adjectives in each sentence.*

1. Mr. Peters drove along a straight, empty stretch of road.
2. He heard strange cries coming from a distant bush.
3. A great white swan suddenly changed into a little man.
4. The grateful stranger granted Mr. Peters several wishes.
5. Mr. Peters soon had a gorgeous wife with pretty blue-green eyes.
6. Antonio was fair, lean, and lanky, while Felix was dark, short, and husky.
7. Antonio's lean form and long reach made him the better boxer.
8. Felix's short and muscular frame made him the better slugger.
9. Large posters were plastered on the walls of local shops.
10. The fighters changed from their street clothes into fighting gear.

B. Writing Application: *Write a sentence in response to each set of instructions.*

1. Write a sentence about Leita, using the adjective *attractive.*

   ____

   ____

2. Write a sentence about the forest, using the adjectives *dark* and *remote.*

   ____

   ____

3. Write a sentence about Antonio Cruz, using the adjectives *lean* and *talented.*

   ____

   ____

4. Write a sentence about Felix Vargas, using the adjectives *short* and *powerful.*

   ____

   ____

Unit 2 Resources: Short Stories

86

"**Zoo**" by Edward D. Hoch

Reading: Make Inferences by Reading Between the Lines and Asking Questions

An **inference** is an intelligent guess, based on what the text tells you, about things *not* stated directly in the text. Suppose a story opens with crowds forming to wait for the arrival of an interplanetary zoo. You can infer from those details that the zoo will soon arrive.

One way to make inferences is to **read between the lines by asking questions,** such as, "Why does the writer include these details?" and "Why does the writer leave out certain information?" In the opening sentence of "Zoo," for example, we learn that "the children were always good during the month of August." The next thing we learn is that the Interplanetary Zoo comes to Chicago every year around August 23. Why does the writer open his story with these details? What conclusion can be drawn about why the children are always good in August? From these details you can infer that the children are good in August because they want their parents to take them to the interplanetary zoo.

DIRECTIONS: *Read the following passages from "Zoo," and answer the questions that follow.*

1. In the following passage, what inference can you draw from the detail that the people are clutching dollars?

   Before daybreak the crowds would form, long lines of children and adults both, each one clutching his or her dollar and waiting with wonderment to see what race of strange creatures the Professor had brought this year.

   ____

   ____

2. In the following passage, what inference can you draw about the Professor from the description of his clothing?

   Soon the good Professor himself made an appearance, wearing his many-colored rainbow cape and top hat.

   ____

3. In the following passage, what inference can you draw about the horse spiders from the way they file out of their cages, listen to Hugo's parting words, and then scurry away?

   The odd horse-spider creatures filed quickly out of their cages. Professor Hugo was there to say a few parting words, and then they scurried away in a hundred different directions, seeking their homes among the rocks.

   ____

4. In the following passage, what inference can you draw from the she-creature's reaction to her mate and offspring's arrival?

   In one house, the she-creature was happy to see the return of her mate and offspring. She babbled a greeting in the strange tongue and hurried to embrace them.

   ____

"Zoo" by Edward D. Hoch
Literary Analysis: Theme

A story's **theme** is its central idea, message, or insight into life. Occasionally, the author states the theme directly. More often, however, the theme is implied.

A theme is *not* the same as the subject of a work. For example, if the subject, or topic, of a story is similarities and differences, the theme will be a message about that subject, such as "differences between groups of people can keep people from seeing the ways in which they are similar."

As you read, look at what characters say and do, where the story takes place, and objects that seem important in order to determine the theme—what the author wants to teach you about life.

DIRECTIONS: *Answer the following questions about "Zoo."*

1. What is the setting? If there is more than one setting, name and briefly describe each one.

   ____

   ____

2. What do the main characters say? Summarize the words spoken by Hugo, one of the people from Earth, the female horse spider, the male horse spider, and the little one.

   Hugo: ____

   Person from Earth: ____

   She-creature: ____

   He-creature: ____

   Little creature: ____

3. How do the characters act? Describe the actions of the people in Chicago and the actions of the horse-spider people.

   People in Chicago: ____

   ____

   Horse spiders: ____

   ____

4. What object or objects seem important?

   ____

5. What is the subject, or topic, of "Zoo"?

   ____

6. Based on these details, what would you say is the theme of "Zoo"?

   ____

"Zoo" by Edward D. Hoch
Vocabulary Builder

Word List

interplanetary   awe   expense

A. DIRECTIONS: *Complete each sentence with a word from the Word List.*

1. The ___________________ of interplanetary travel was high, but Professor Hugo earned the money back by charging admission to his zoo.
2. The crowd gazed in ___________________ at the terrifying yet unusual creatures.
3. Professor Hugo's ___________________ zoo visited Earth, Mars, Kaan, and many other planets.

B. DIRECTIONS: *Revise each sentence so that the Word List word is used logically.*

1. The *interplanetary* mission involved travel from Rome to Tokyo.

   ____

   ____

2. The spectators at the zoo were *awed* by the cute rabbits.

   ____

3. The *expense* of the zoo allowed the promoter to make a great profit.

   ____

   ____

C. DIRECTIONS: *Write the letter of the word or phrase that is most* similar *in meaning to the Word List word.*

____ 1. awe
    A. arrogance and hatred   C. amazement and fear
    B. terror and fear   D. compassion and love

____ 2. expense
    A. cost   C. total
    B. amount   D. budget

____ 3. interplanetary
    A. between galaxies   C. universal
    B. between planets   D. worldwide

"Zoo" by Edward D. Hoch

Support for Writing a Letter to the Editor

Before you write your **letter to the editor,** think about whether zoo animals should live in natural habitats or cages. Then, on this graphic organizer, write down advantages and disadvantages of each environment.

Zoo Animals

Natural Habitats

Advantages: _______________________

____

____

____

____

____

____

____

____

Disadvantages: ____________________

____

____

____

____

____

____

____

Cages

Advantages: _______________________

____

____

____

____

____

____

____

____

Disadvantages: ____________________

____

____

____

____

____

____

____

Decide which position you want to take and draft a letter to the editor of a local newspaper in support of your position. Use your notes to back up your opinion with reasons and details that will persuade readers to take your side.

"Ribbons" by Laurence Yep

Reading: Make Inferences by Reading Between the Lines and Asking Questions

An **inference** is an intelligent guess, based on what the text tells you, about things *not* stated directly in the text. One way to make inferences is to **read between the lines by asking questions,** such as, "Why does the writer include these details?" and "Why does the writer leave out certain information?" For example, "Ribbons" opens as Stacy and Ian's grandmother arrives from Hong Kong. The narrator, Stacy, says,

> Because Grandmother's . . . expenses had been so high, there wasn't room in the family budget for Madame Oblomov's ballet school. I'd had to stop my daily lessons.

Why does the writer begin with those details? What conclusion can be drawn? From these details you can infer that Stacy feels some resentment because she has had to give up her ballet lessons so that her grandmother can come from Hong Kong.

DIRECTIONS: *Read the following passages from "Ribbons," and answer the questions.*

1. What inference can you draw from Grandmother's reaction to Stacy's hug?
   When I tried to put my arms around her and kiss her, she stiffened in surprise. "Nice children don't drool on people," she snapped at me.

   ____

2. What can you infer about Grandmother's feelings about her daughter's home?
   Grandmother was sitting in the big recliner in the living room. She stared uneasily out the window as if she were gazing not upon the broad, green lawn of the square but upon a Martian desert.

   ____

3. In the following passage, what inference can you draw from those words, spoken by Stacy's mother, about Grandmother?
   [The girls' feet] were usually bound up in silk ribbons. . . . Because they were a symbol of the old days, Paw-paw undid the ribbons as soon as we were free in Hong Kong—even though they kept back the pain.

   ____

4. In the following passage, what inference about Grandmother can you draw from this attempt to show her affection for Stacy?
   She took my hand and patted it clumsily. I think it was the first time she had showed me any sign of affection.

   ____

5. What inference can you draw from Stacy's description of the invisible ribbon?
   Suddenly I felt as if there were an invisible ribbon binding us tougher than silk and satin, stronger than steel; and it joined her to Mom and me.

   ____

"**Ribbons**" by Laurence Yep
Literary Analysis: Theme

A story's **theme** is its central idea, message, or insight into life. Occasionally, the author states the theme directly. More often, however, the theme is implied.

A theme is *not* the same as the subject of a work. For example, if the subject or topic of a story is cultural differences, the theme will be a message about that, such as "cultural differences can be overcome by communication."

As you read, look at what characters say and do, where the story takes place, and objects that seem important in order to determine the theme—what the author wants to teach you about life.

DIRECTIONS: *Answer the following questions about "Ribbons."*

1. What is the setting? Briefly describe it.

   ____

2. What do the main characters say? Summarize the important statements made by Grandmother, Mom, and Stacy.

   Grandmother: ____

   ____

   Mom: ____

   ____

   Stacy: ____

   ____

3. How do the characters act? Describe the important actions of Grandmother and Stacy.

   Grandmother: ____

   ____

   Stacy: ____

   ____

   ____

4. What objects seem important?

   ____

5. What is the subject, or topic, of "Ribbons"?

   ____

6. Based on your answers above, what would you say is the theme of "Ribbons"?

   ____

"Ribbons" by Laurence Yep
Vocabulary Builder

Word List

sensitive   meek   coax   laborious   exertion

A. DIRECTIONS: *Complete each sentence with a word from the Word List.*

1. Because Grandmother's feet had been bound when she was young, she found walking and climbing stairs ___________________ activities.
2. Stacy loved ballet so much that she hardly realized that it was ___________________—until she collapsed from exhaustion after each lesson.
3. Because the binding of her feet was painful physically and emotionally, Grandmother was ___________________ about her feet.
4. Stacy hoped that she could ___________________ Grandmother into paying attention to her by explaining her love of ballet.
5. In many cultures it is expected that a daughter will be ___________________ and never challenge her parents' requests.

B. DIRECTIONS: *Write the letter of the word or phrase that is most* similar *in meaning to the Word List word.*

_____ 1. coax
    A. intimidate   C. relax into
    B. sweet-talk   D. mock

_____ 2. exertion
    A. relaxation   C. idleness
    B. mental strain   D. hard work

_____ 3. laborious
    A. difficult   C. effortless
    B. easy   D. intrusive

_____ 4. meek
    A. arrogant   C. shy
    B. bullying   D. spirited

_____ 5. sensitive
    A. emotional   C. unstable
    B. sharp   D. unfeeling

Name ____ Date _____________________

Support for Writing a Letter to the Editor

Before you write your **letter to the editor,** think about whether young people should participate in extra schooling by taking art classes, for example, or by participating in sports. Then, on this graphic organizer, write down advantages and disadvantages of each position.

**Young People's
Extra Schooling**

Art Classes	**Sports**
Advantages: ___________	**Advantages:** ___________
Disadvantages: ___________	**Disadvantages:** ___________

Decide which position you want to take and draft a letter to the editor of a local newspaper in support of your position. Use your notes to back up your opinion with reasons and details that will persuade readers to take your side.

"Zoo" by Edward Hoch
"Ribbons" by Laurence Yep

Build Language Skills: Vocabulary

The Prefixes *con-* and *sub-*

The prefix *con-* means "together" or "the same." The word *conclude*, which contains the prefix *con-*, means "to pull together details to reach an opinion or come up with an idea."

The prefix *sub-* means "under" or "below." It is the prefix in the word *subject*. One meaning of *subject* is "a topic under study or discussion."

A. DIRECTIONS: *Write a definition of the italicized word in each sentence. Base your definition on your knowledge of the prefix and the context clues in the sentence. Then, check your definition in a dictionary and revise it, if necessary.*

1. Two major stores announced that they would *consolidate* to form a single company.

   ____

2. He signed a *contract* agreeing to work as a consultant for one year for a fee of $6,000.

   ____

3. After the hurricane, water had to be pumped out of the partially *submerged* boats.

   ____

Academic Vocabulary Practice

B. DIRECTIONS: *Indicate whether the statement is* true *or* false, *and explain your answer.*

1. From the details in "Zoo," one can *conclude* that the events are imagined.

   True/False: ___________ Explanation: ___________________________________

   ____

2. From the horse spiders' *perspective*, they were the creatures on display in the zoo.

   True/False: ___________ Explanation: ___________________________________

   ____

3. The horse spiders are *credible*—one can easily believe that such creatures exist.

   True/False: ___________ Explanation: ___________________________________

   ____

4. The *subject* of "Ribbons" is understanding and communication.

   True/False: ___________ Explanation: ___________________________________

   ____

5. A significant *object* in "Ribbons" is the message that differences can be resolved by communication.

   True/False: ___________ Explanation: ___________________________________

   ____

Unit 2 Resources: Short Stories

"Zoo" by Edward Hoch
"Ribbons" by Laurence Yep

Build Language Skills: Grammar

Adverbs

An **adverb** is a word that modifies or describes a verb, an adjective, or another adverb. Adverbs provide information by answering the question *how? when? where? how often?* or *to what extent?* Many adverbs end in the suffix *-ly.*

In the first sentence, the adverb, *always,* tells how often the children are good. In the second sentence, the adverb, *outside,* tells where the car stops:

> The children were *always* <u>good</u> during the month of August.

> A car <u>stopped</u> *outside.*

A. DIRECTIONS: *Underline the adverb in each sentence once, and underline the word it modifies twice.*

1. The sides slowly slid up to reveal the familiar barred cages.
2. The citizens of Earth clustered around as Professor Hugo's crew quickly collected the waiting dollars.
3. The odd horse-spider creatures filed quickly out of their cages.
4. The little one enjoyed it especially.
5. Mom bowed formally as Grandmother reached the porch.
6. I'd been practicing my ballet privately in the room I now shared with Ian.
7. I clutched the ribbons tightly against my stomach.
8. Suddenly I felt as if there were an invisible ribbon binding us.

B. Writing Application: *Write a sentence in response to each set of instructions. Underline the word or phrase that the adverb you use modifies.*

1. Use *quickly* in a sentence about catching a school bus.

   ____

2. Use *never* in a sentence about a food you dislike.

   ____

3. Use *gently* in a sentence about something you do.

   ____

4. Use *always* in a sentence about something else you do.

   ____

5. Use *finally* in a sentence about a process that involves several steps.

   ____

"**After Twenty Years**" by O. Henry
"**He—y, Come On Ou—t!**" by Shinichi Hoshi

Literary Analysis: Irony

Irony involves a contradiction or contrast of some kind. In **situational irony** (or **irony of situation**), something takes place that a character or reader does not expect to happen. For example, a student voted Most Likely to Succeed ends up going to prison.

In **verbal irony,** a writer, speaker, or character says something that deliberately contradicts or blurs what he or she actually means. Think of a man who has been dreading a reunion with his best friend from twenty years before. When they meet, he says, "I've been *so* looking forwarding to seeing you." That is verbal irony.

In **dramatic irony,** the reader or audience knows or understands something that a character or speaker does not. For example, readers know that the apple Snow White is about to bite into is poisoned, but Snow White does not know it. That is dramatic irony.

As you read "After Twenty Years" and "He—y, Come On Ou—t!" look for situational irony in particular.

DIRECTIONS: *Answer the following questions.*

1. What is the general situation, or the plot? Describe it briefly.

   "After Twenty Years": ____
   ____

   "He—y, Come On Ou—t!": _______________________________________
   ____

2. What outcome do you expect?

   "After Twenty Years": ____

   "He—y, Come On Ou—t!": _______________________________________

3. What happens? How does the story end?

   "After Twenty Years": ____

   "He—y, Come On Ou—t!": _______________________________________

4. What details in the story lead you to expect a certain outcome? Describe one or two details, and state what they lead you to expect.

   "After Twenty Years": ____
   ____

   "He—y, Come On Ou—t!": _______________________________________
   ____

5. What is ironic about the ending of the story?

   "After Twenty Years": ____

   "He—y, Come On Ou—t!": _______________________________________

"After Twenty Years" by O. Henry
"He—y, Come On Ou—t!" by Shinichi Hoshi
Vocabulary Builder

Word List

spectators intricate destiny simultaneously apparent plausible proposal

A. DIRECTIONS: *Revise each sentence so that the italicized vocabulary word is used logically. Be sure to use the vocabulary word in your new sentence.*

1. The plot of the short story was so *intricate* that we followed it easily.

____

2. The *destiny* of a criminal is likely to include time spent as a police officer.

____

3. The two men arrived *simultaneously,* one reaching the doorway an hour after the other.

____

4. Because there were many *spectators* when the crime was committed, no eyewitnesses could testify at the trial.

____

____

5. The *apparent* smile on the face of the scientist was not visible to anyone.

____

6. The *plausible* explanation made sense to no one.

____

7. Because he offered no solution, everyone accepted the concessionaire's *proposal.*

____

B. DIRECTIONS: *Write the letter of the word whose meaning is most similar to that of the Word Bank word.*

____ 1. intricate
   A. complicated   B. tiny   C. simple   D. intelligent

____ 2. simultaneously
   A. genuinely   B. apart   C. together   D. separately

____ 3. apparent
   A. obvious   B. hidden   C. deceptive   D. similar

"After Twenty Years" by O. Henry
"He—y, Come On Ou—t!" by Shinichi Hoshi
Support for Writing to Compare Literary Works

Before you write an essay that compares your reaction to "After Twenty Years" with your reaction to "He—y, Come On Ou—t!" use this graphic organizer to consider how irony is used in the two stories.

What details make the story believable or realistic?

"After Twenty Years":	**"Hey—y, Come On Ou—t!":**

How does the believability or the realism of the story affect your response? Do you prefer a believable story to a fantasy one? Why or why not?

"After Twenty Years":	**"Hey—y, Come On Ou—t!":**

What is the story's message? Is the message easy to understand? Why or why not?

"After Twenty Years":	**"Hey—y, Come On Ou—t!":**

When you respond to a story, are you influenced by the difficulty of understanding its message? Why or why not?

"After Twenty Years":	**"Hey—y, Come On Ou—t!":**

Now, use your notes to write an essay in which you compare your reactions to the use of irony in "After Twenty Years" and "He—y, Come On Ou—t!"

Unit 2 Resources: Short Stories

Richard Mühlberger
Listening and Viewing

Segment 1: Meet Richard Mühlberger
- Why do you think Richard Mühlberger chose to write art history books?
- Do you agree with the writing advice given to Mühlberger by a fellow writer "to stick to the masters"?

____

____

____

Segment 2: The Essay
- According to Richard Mühlberger, what are some characteristics of essays?
- When would you write an essay, and why?

____

____

____

Segment 3: The Writing Process
- Why is it very important to Richard Mühlberger to write in precise, detailed language when writing about a painting?
- Why do you think Richard Mühlberger chooses to write his books in a "conversational tone"?

____

____

____

Segment 4: The Rewards of Writing
- What does Richard Mühlberger hope that his readers will gain by reading books about art?
- Why do you think books about art are important?

____

____

____

Learning About Nonfiction

An author has a specific **purpose for writing** an essay or article. Often, that purpose is to explain, to entertain, to inform, or to persuade. An essay or an article uses one or more of these **formats:**

- Expository writing: presents facts, discusses ideas, or explains a process
- Persuasive writing: attempts to persuade the reader to adopt a particular point of view or take a particular course of action
- Reflective writing: addresses an event or experience and gives the writer's insights about its importance
- Humorous writing: entertains the audience by evoking laughter
- Narrative writing: tells about real-life experiences
- Descriptive writing: appeals to the reader's senses of sight, hearing, taste, smell, and touch
- Analytical writing: breaks a large idea into parts to help the reader see how they work together as a whole

A. DIRECTIONS: *The following are titles of nonfiction essays or articles. Circle the letter of the answer choice that shows the best format for each title. Then, circle the letter of the answer choice that shows the purpose that the author probably had for writing the article.*

1. "How to Build a Doghouse"
   Format: A. persuasive   B. expository   C. narrative   D. reflective
   Purpose: A. to explain   B. to entertain

2. "Don't Throw That Cardboard and Paper in the Trash!"
   Format: A. persuasive   B. analytical   C. narrative   D. humorous
   Purpose: A. to entertain   B. to persuade

3. "Moving to Tucson Changed My Life"
   Format: A. persuasive   B. expository   C. analytical   D. reflective
   Purpose: A. to persuade   B. to share insights

B. DIRECTIONS: *Below are essay topics and their purpose. Write the format that you would use to write each essay. Explain your choice. Refer to the bulleted list above as needed for help.*

Topic: how to draw a face   Purpose: to explain
Format choice/reason: <u>expository; it explains a process</u>.

1. Topic: a strange animal   Purpose: to entertain
   Format choice/reason: _______________________________

2. Topic: vote for a certain candidate   Purpose: to persuade
   Format choice/reason: _______________________________

3. Topic: The Civil War   Purpose: to present ideas
   Format choice/reason: _______________________________

"What Makes a Rembrandt a Rembrandt?" by Richard Mühlberger
Model Selection: Nonfiction

Nonfiction writing is about real people, places, objects, ideas, and experiences. Here are some common types:

Type of Nonfiction	Description
Biography	the life story of a real person, written by another person
Autobiography	the author's account of his or her own life
Media Accounts	true stories written for newspapers, magazines, television, or radio
Essays and Articles	short nonfiction works about a particular subject

Nonfiction writing must be organized to present information logically and clearly. Writers use **chronological organization** (they present details in time order); **comparison-and-contrast organization** (they show similarities and differences); **cause-and-effect organization** (they show relationships among events); and **problem-and-solution organization** (they identify a problem and present a solution).

DIRECTIONS: *On the lines below, answer these questions about "What Makes a Rembrandt a Rembrandt?"*

1. What type of nonfiction writing is "What Makes a Rembrandt a Rembrandt?" Explain.

   ____

2. How is the first paragraph in "Two Handsome Soldiers" organized? Explain.

   ____

   ____

3. What two real people are the most important in this article?

   ____

4. Why does Richard Mühlberger use an expository format for sections of "What Makes a Rembrandt a Rembrandt?"

   ____

5. Often, nonfiction writers have more than one purpose for writing an article or essay. Which *two* purposes did Richard Mühlberger have for writing this article? Check your choices.

   _______ A. to persuade his city to form a militia company as a social club

   _______ B. to entertain readers with a humorous event

   _______ C. to explain Rembrandt's painting techniques

   _______ D. to explain why Banning Cocq was a great Dutch soldier

   _______ E. to inform readers with facts about the painting *Night watch*

"Life Without Gravity" by Robert Zimmerman

Reading: Adjust Your Reading Rate to Recognize Main Ideas and Key Points

The **main idea** is the central point of a passage or text. Most articles and essays have a main idea. Each paragraph or passage in the work also has a main idea, or **key point.**

The main idea of a paragraph is usually stated in a **topic sentence.** The paragraph then supplies **supporting details** that give examples, explanations, or reasons.

When reading nonfiction, **adjust your reading rate to recognize main ideas and key points.**

- **Skim** the article to get a sense of the main idea before you begin reading. Look over the text quickly, looking for text organization, topic sentences, and repeated words.
- **Scan** the text when you need to find answers to questions or to clarify or find supporting details. Run your eyes over the text, looking for a particular word or idea.
- **Read closely** to learn what the main ideas are and to identify the key points and supporting details.

A. DIRECTIONS: *Scan each paragraph below to find answers to the questions that follow.*

Our bodies are adapted to Earth's gravity. Our muscles are strong in order to overcome gravity as we walk and run. Our inner ears use gravity to keep us upright. And because gravity wants to pull all our blood down into our legs, our hearts are designed to pump hard to get blood up to our brains.

1. What parts of the body are discussed in this paragraph?

   ____

In microgravity, you have to learn new ways to eat. Don't pour a bowl of cornflakes. Not only will the flakes float all over the place, the milk won't pour. Instead, big balls of milk will form. You can drink these by taking big bites out of them, but you'd better finish them before they slam into a wall, splattering apart and covering everything with little tiny milk globules.

2. What foods are mentioned in this paragraph?

   ____

B. DIRECTIONS: *Now, read the paragraphs closely. Answer these questions.*

1. What is the main idea of the first paragraph?

   ____

2. What are two details that support that main idea?

   ____

3. What is the main idea of the second paragraph?

   ____

4. What are two details that support that main idea?

   ____

"Life Without Gravity" by Robert Zimmerman
Literary Analysis: Expository Essay

An **expository essay** is a short piece of nonfiction that explains, defines, or interprets ideas, events, or processes. The way in which the information is organized and presented depends on the specific topic of the essay. Writers organize the main points of their essays logically, to aid readers' comprehension. They may organize information in one of these ways or in a combination of ways:

- Comparison and contrast
- Cause and effect
- Chronological order
- Problem and solution

"Life Without Gravity" is an expository essay that explains an idea. It uses cause and effect to make the explanation clear. In the paragraph below, the details help readers understand some of the effects of weightlessness.

> Worse, weightlessness can sometimes be downright unpleasant. Your body gets upset and confused. Your face puffs up, your nose gets stuffy, your back hurts, your stomach gets upset, and you throw up.

DIRECTIONS: *The left-hand column of the following chart names parts of the human body that are affected by weightlessness. In the right-hand column, write the effect—in your own words—as it is described in "Life Without Gravity." If one effect causes yet another effect, describe the second effect as well.*

Body Part	Effects of Weightlessness
The blood	Weightlessness causes ________________________
The spine	Weightlessness causes ________________________
The bones	Weightlessness causes ________________________
The muscles	Weightlessness causes ________________________
The stomach	Weightlessness causes ________________________

"Life Without Gravity" by Robert Zimmerman
Vocabulary Builder

Word List

spines	feeble	blander

A. DIRECTIONS: *Think about the meaning of the italicized word in each sentence. Then, answer the question.*

1. If patients complain of aching *spines*, what might a physical therapist suggest they do to ease the pain? What part of the body will the therapist suggest they treat?

____

____

2. What would you think of a team whose players made only a *feeble* attempt to compete? Why?

____

____

3. If an astronaut prefers food that is *blander* than oatmeal, would you expect him or her to be happy with the food on a space mission? Why or why not?

____

____

B. DIRECTIONS: *On the short line, write* T *if the following statement is true and* F *if it is false. Then, explain your answer in a complete sentence.*

____ 1. Animals' *spines* are very strong.

____

____ 2. A *feeble* voice is one that can be heard across a room.

____

____ 3. Foods made without pepper are *blander* than the same foods prepared with pepper.

____

C. DIRECTIONS: *On the line, write the letter of the word whose meaning is most nearly opposite that of the Word List word.*

____ 1. feeble
    A. calm   **B.** strong   **C.** clingy   **D.** weak

____ 2. blander
    A. cooler   **B.** warmer   **C.** paler   **D.** spicier

"Life Without Gravity" by Robert Zimmerman

Support for Writing a Problem-and-Solution Essay

Before you write a **problem-and-solution essay** in which you assess, or evaluate, the difficulties of being an astronaut in space, complete the following graphic organizer. In each of the top boxes, write a problem or challenge that an astronaut might face. Then, use the article as a basis from which to write two solutions and examples that can help solve the problems.

First Problem	**Second Problem**

Solution A	Examples	Solution A	Examples

Solution B	Examples	Solution B	Examples

Now, use a separate sheet of paper to write a problem-and-solution essay in which you assess, or evaluate, the difficulties of being an astronaut in space. Use your notes to help you organize your thoughts. Use transitions to connect ideas.

"Conversational Ballgames" by Nancy Masterson Sakamoto
Reading: Adjust Your Reading Rate to Recognize Main Ideas and Key Points

The **main idea** is the central point of a passage or text. Most articles and essays have a main idea. Each paragraph or passage in the work also has a main idea, or **key point.**

The main idea of a paragraph is usually stated in a **topic sentence**—a sentence that identifies the key point. The paragraph then supplies **supporting details** that give examples, explanations, or reasons.

When reading nonfiction, **adjust your reading rate to recognize main ideas and key points.**

- **Skim** the article to get a sense of the main idea before you begin reading. Look over the text quickly, looking for text organization, topic sentences, and repeated words.
- **Scan** the text when you need to find answers to questions or to clarify or find supporting details. Run your eyes over the text, looking for a particular word or idea.
- **Read closely** to learn what the main ideas are and to identify the key points and supporting details.

A. DIRECTIONS: *Scan each paragraph below to find answers to the questions that follow.*

A western-style conversation between two people is like a game of tennis. If I introduce a topic, a conversational ball, I expect you to hit it back. If you agree with me, I don't expect you simply to agree and do nothing more. I expect you to add something—a reason for agreeing, another example, or an elaboration to carry the idea further. But I don't expect you always to agree. I am just as happy if you question me, or challenge me, or completely disagree with me. Whether you agree or disagree, your response will return the ball to me.

1. What game does the author discuss in this paragraph? ______________________________

A Japanese-style conversation, however, is not at all like tennis or volleyball. It's like bowling. You wait for your turn. And you always know your place in line. It depends on such things as whether you are older or younger, a close friend or a relative stranger to the previous speaker, in a senior or junior position, and so on.

2. What game does the author discuss in this paragraph? ______________________________

B. DIRECTIONS: *Now, read the paragraphs closely for main ideas and supporting details.*

1. What is the main idea of the first paragraph?

____

2. What are two details that support that main idea?

____

3. What is the main idea of the second paragraph?

____

4. What are two details that support that main idea?

____

"Conversational Ballgames" by Nancy Masterson Sakamoto
Literary Analysis: Expository Essay

An **expository essay** is a short piece of nonfiction that explains, defines, or interprets ideas, events, or processes. The way in which the information is organized and presented depends on the specific topic of the essay. Writers organize the main points of their essays logically, to aid readers' comprehension. They may organize information in one of these ways or in a combination of ways:

- Comparison and contrast
- Cause and effect
- Chronological order
- Problem and solution

"Conversational Ballgames" is an expository essay that explains two processes. It uses comparison and contrast to make the explanation clear. In the paragraph below, the details set up the differences between Japanese and western styles of conversation.

> Japanese-style conversations develop quite differently from western-style conversations. And the difference isn't only in the languages. I realized that just as I kept trying to hold western-style conversations even when I was speaking Japanese, so my English students kept trying to hold Japanese-style conversations even when they were speaking English.

DIRECTIONS: *Use this chart to compare and contrast Japanese-style conversation and western-style conversation. In the left-hand column, write five characteristics of western-style conversations as those conversations are described in "Conversational Ballgames." In the right-hand column, describe how the Japanese style differs from, or is similar to, each characteristic described on the left.*

Western-Style Conversation	Japanese-Style Conversation
1.	
2.	
3.	
4.	
5.	

"Conversational Ballgames" by Nancy Masterson Sakamoto
Vocabulary Builder

Word List

elaboration   murmuring   parallel   indispensable

A. DIRECTIONS: *Think about the meaning of the italicized word in each sentence. Then, answer the question.*

1. If two lines run *parallel* to each other, what do you know about them?
   ____

2. If a speaker is *murmuring,* what might he or she be asked to do?
   ____

3. Why might someone who is learning Japanese say that a dictionary is *indispensable?*
   ____

4. If you were engaged in a conversation about cultural differences, and someone asked you for *elaboration,* what would you do?
   ____

B. DIRECTIONS: *On the short line, write T if the statement is true, and F if it is false. Then, explain your answer in a complete sentence.*

____ 1. If something is explained thoroughly, it needs further <u>elaboration</u>.
   ____
   ____

____ 2. <u>Parallel</u> roads will intersect at a curve.
   ____
   ____

C. DIRECTIONS: *On the line, write the letter of the word whose meaning is most nearly opposite that of the Word List word.*

____ 1. murmuring
    A. mumbling   **B.** shouting   **C.** talking   **D.** whispering

____ 2. indispensable
    A. unnecessary   **B.** required   **C.** wasteful   **D.** needed

"Conversational Ballgames" by Nancy Masterson Sakamoto
Support for Writing a Problem-and-Solution Essay

Before you write a **problem-and-solution essay** about the challenges faced by Japanese and Westerners when they converse, or talk, with one another, complete the following graphic organizer. Write two problems in the first column. Then, using Sakamoto's essay as a starting point, offer solutions as well as evidence that suggests why each solution will solve the problem.

First Problem →	Solution A	Solution B
	Evidence:	Evidence:

Second Problem →	Solution A	Solution B
	Evidence:	Evidence:

On a separate page, use your notes to write a problem-and-solution essay about the difficulties Japanese and Westerners have in conversing with each other. Remember to pair each problem with a solution.

"Life Without Gravity" by Robert Zimmerman
"Conversational Ballgames" by Nancy Masterson Sakamoto
Build Language Skills: Vocabulary Skill

The Prefix *ir-*

You can create the opposite of some adjectives by placing the prefix *ir-* before them. The prefix *ir-* means "not."

ir- + regular = irregular

A. DIRECTIONS: *Turn each word in italics into its opposite, or antonym, by adding the prefix* ir-*. Then, rewrite the sentence using the new word. Make sure your sentence makes sense.*

1. The babysitter came to us highly recommended and proved to be *responsible.*

   Antonym: __________________ **Sentence:** ________________________________

   ____

2. The news article was *relevant* to our class discussion so we referred to it frequently.

   Antonym: __________________ **Sentence:** ________________________________

   ____

Academic Vocabulary Practice

B. DIRECTIONS: *Write the letter of the word whose meaning is most nearly* opposite *that of the Academic Vocabulary word. Then use the vocabulary word in a sentence.*

____ 1. insignificant
    A. unimportant   C. unrecognizable
    B. needy   D. important

Sentence: ____

____

____ 2. irrelevant
    A. unconnected   C. inappropriate
    B. related   D. reasonable

Sentence: ____

____

____ 3. identify
    A. recognize   C. overlook
    B. recall   D. imagine

Sentence: ____

____

Name ____ Date ____________________

"Life Without Gravity" by Robert Zimmerman
"Conversational Ballgames" by Nancy Masterson Sakamoto

Build Language Skills: Grammar

Conjunctions

Conjunctions connect words or groups of words. **Coordinating conjunctions,** such as *but, and, nor, for, so, yet,* and *or,* connect words or groups of words that have a similar function in a sentence. They might connect two or more nouns, adjectives, adverbs, groups of words, or sentences. In the following examples, the coordinating conjunctions are in bold type. The words they connect are underlined.

Connecting nouns:	Bones **and** muscles become weak in outer space.
Connecting verbs:	How can people talk **and** eat at the same time?
Connecting adjectives:	A conversation can be interesting, exciting, **or** boring.
Connecting sentences:	Becoming an astronaut is difficult, **but** it is also rewarding.

A. PRACTICE: *Circle the coordinating conjunction in each sentence. Then, underline the words, groups of words, or sentences that the conjunction connects.*

1. Some astronauts adjust well to living without gravity, but others have problems.
2. Zero gravity is hard on the bones and the muscles.
3. Astronauts are not surprised by zero gravity, for they are trained to expect it.
4. Sakamoto had mastered Japanese, yet she was having trouble communicating.
5. In western conversations, someone may agree, question, or challenge.
6. Sakamoto learned the art of Japanese conversation, so she was able to participate fully.

B. Writing Application: *Complete the following instructions by writing sentences about "Life Without Gravity" or "Conversational Ballgames." In each sentence that you write, use the coordinating conjunction in the way described.*

1. Join two nouns with the conjunction *and.* ________________________________

____

2. Join two verbs with the conjunction *or.* _________________________________

____

3. Join two sentences with the conjunction *but.* ____________________________

____

4. Join two groups of words with the conjunction *or.* _______________________

____

5. Join two adjectives with the conjunction *yet.* ___________________________

____

"I Am a Native of North America" by Chief Dan George

Reading: Make Connections Between Key Points
and Supporting Details to Understand the Main Idea

The **main idea** is the most important thought or concept in a work or a passage of text. Sometimes the author directly states the main idea of a work and then provides key points that support it. These key points are supported in turn by details such as examples and descriptions. Other times the main idea is unstated. The author gives you *only* the key points or supporting details that add up to a main idea. To understand the main idea, **make connections between key points and supporting details.** Notice how the writer groups details. Look for sentences that pull details together.

In this passage from "I Am a Native of North America," Chief George states key points and provides details that support the main idea of the essay:

> I am afraid my culture has little to offer yours. But my culture did prize friendship and companionship. It did not look on privacy as a thing to be clung to, for privacy builds up walls and walls promote distrust. My culture lived in big family communities, and from infancy people learned to live with others.

DIRECTIONS: *Write the main idea of Chief George's essay on the line below. Then, read each passage, and write its key point and the details that support it.*

Main idea: ____

And beyond this acceptance of one another there was a deep respect for everything in nature that surrounded them. My father loved the earth and all its creatures. The earth was his second mother. The earth and everything it contained was a gift from See-see-am . . . and the way to thank this great spirit was to use his gifts with respect.

1. **Key point:** ____

2. **Details:** ____

____

Love is something you and I must have. We must have it because our spirit feeds upon it. We must have it because without it we become weak and faint. Without love our self-esteem weakens. Without it our courage fails. Without love we can no longer look out confidently at the world. Instead we turn inwardly and begin to feed upon our own personalities and little by little we destroy ourselves.

3. **Key point:** ____

4. **Details:** ____

____

"I Am a Native of North America" by Chief Dan George
Literary Analysis: Reflective Essay

A **reflective essay** is a brief prose work that presents a writer's feelings and thoughts, or reflections, about an experience or idea. The purpose is to communicate these thoughts and feelings so that readers will respond with thoughts and feelings of their own. As you read a reflective essay, think about the ideas the writer is sharing. Think about whether your responses to the experience or idea are similar to or different from the writer's.

In this passage from "I Am a Native of North America," Chief George reflects on life in apartment buildings:

> I see people living in smoke houses hundreds of times bigger than the one I knew. But the people in one apartment do not even know the people in the next and care less about them.

Chief George thinks about how neighbors do not know one another and concludes that they do not care about one another.

A. DIRECTIONS: *In the second column of the chart, summarize Chief George's thoughts about each experience described in the first column. Then, in the third column, write your response. That is, describe your own thoughts on the subject.*

Experience	Author's Thoughts	My Thoughts
1. Chief George describes his grandfather's smoke house.		
2. Chief George's father finds him killing fish "for the fun of it."		
3. Chief George sees his culture disappearing.		

B. DIRECTIONS: *Write the first paragraph of a reflective essay of your own. Include a description of an experience and your thoughts about it. Write on one of these topics:*

- the role of nature in your life
- the importance of tradition in your life
- the meaning of family in your life

____

____

____

____

"I Am a Native of North America" by Chief Dan George
Vocabulary Builder

Word List

distinct   communal   justifies   promote

A. DIRECTIONS: *Use the italicized word in each sentence in a sentence of your own.*

1. Chief George seeks to *promote* a greater understanding of Native American culture.

____

____

2. Chief George suggests that *communal* living teaches people to respect one another.

____

____

3. A critical situation sometimes *justifies* a drastic solution.

____

____

4. Social scientists can identify many *distinct* cultures in North America.

____

____

B. DIRECTIONS: *Write the letter of the word that is* closest *in meaning to the Word List* word.

____ 1. communal
    A. separate   B. shared   C. apart   D. old-fashioned

____ 2. justifies
    A. excuses   B. criticizes   C. judges   D. reports

____ 3. promote
    A. prevent   B. refuse   C. argue   D. encourage

"**I Am a Native of North America**" by Chief Dan George

Support for Writing an Outline

To prepare to write an **outline** of "I Am a Native of North America," create a word web. Write the main idea in the center circle. In each of the circles around it, write a key point. In the circles around each key point, write details that support the key point.

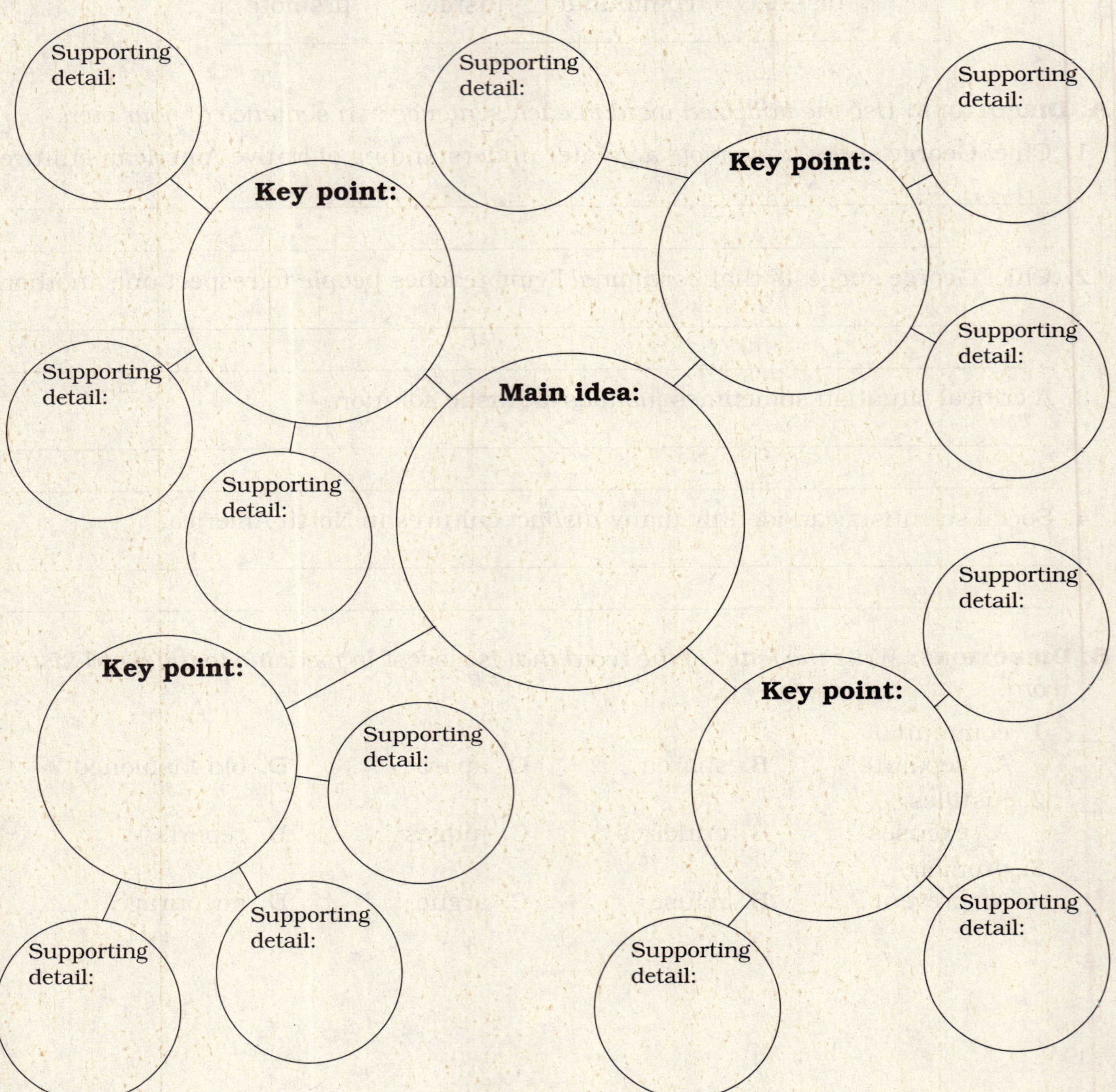

Now, use your word web to make an outline of the essay.

from **"In Search of Our Mothers' Gardens"** by Alice Walker

Reading: Make Connections Between Key Points
and Supporting Details to Understand the Main Idea

The **main idea** is the most important thought or concept in a work or a passage of text. Sometimes the author directly states the main idea of a work and then provides key points that support it. These key points are supported in turn by details such as examples and descriptions. Other times the main idea is unstated. The author gives you *only* the key points or supporting details that add up to a main idea. To understand the main idea, **make connections between key points and supporting details.** Notice how the writer groups details. Look for sentences that pull details together.

In this passage from "In Search of Our Mothers' Gardens," Alice Walker states key points and provides details that support the main idea of the essay.

> For her, so hindered and intruded upon in so many ways, being an artist has still been a daily part of her life. This ability to hold on, even in very simple ways, is work black women have done for a very long time.

DIRECTIONS: *Write the main idea of Alice Walker's essay on the line below. Then, read each passage, and write its key point and the details that support it.*

Main idea: ____

My mother made all the clothes we wore, even my brothers' overalls. She made all the towels and sheets we used. She spent the summers canning vegetables and fruit. She spent the winter evenings making quilts enough to cover our beds.

1. **Key point:** ____

____

2. **Details:** ____

____

And perhaps in Africa over two hundred years ago, there was just such a mother; perhaps she painted vivid and daring decorations in oranges and yellows and greens on the walls of her hut; perhaps she sang . . . *sweetly* over the compounds of her village; perhaps she wove the most stunning mats or told the most ingenious stories of all the village storytellers. Perhaps she was herself a poet—though only her daughter's name is signed to the poems that we know.

3. **Key point:** ____

____

4. **Details:** ____

____

from "In Search of Our Mothers' Gardens" by Alice Walker
Literary Analysis: Reflective Essay

A **reflective essay** is a brief prose work that presents a writer's feelings and thoughts, or reflections, about an experience or idea. The purpose is to communicate these thoughts and feelings so that readers will respond with thoughts and feelings of their own. As you read a reflective essay, think about the ideas the writer is sharing. Think about whether your responses to the experience or idea are similar to or different from the writer's.

In this passage from "In Search of Our Mothers' Gardens," Alice Walker reflects on the legacy of her ancestors:

> And so our mothers and grandmothers have, more often than not anonymously, handed on the creative spark, the seed of the flower they themselves never hoped to see: or like a sealed letter they could not plainly read.

Alice Walker believes that her ancestors passed their own creativity down to her.

A. DIRECTIONS: *In the second column of the chart, summarize Alice Walker's thoughts about each experience described in the first column. Then, in the third column, write your response. That is, describe your own thoughts on the subject.*

Experience	Author's Thoughts	My Thoughts
1. Alice Walker recalls the stories her mother told.		
2. Alice Walker recalls her mother's garden.		
3. Alice Walker remembers the radiance of her mother's face.		

B. DIRECTIONS: *Write the first paragraph of a reflective essay of your own. Include a description of an experience and your thoughts about it. Write on one of these topics:*

- the role of your mother or another relative in your life
- the importance of creativity in your life
- the meaning of family in your life

____

____

____

____

____

from **"In Search of Our Mothers' Gardens"** by Alice Walker
Vocabulary Builder

Word List

anonymous	profusely	radiant	hindered

A. DIRECTIONS: *Use the italicized word in each sentence in a sentence of your own.*

1. Although *hindered* by poverty, Alice Walker's mother created beauty in her life.

____

____

2. In warm, rainy climates, plants usually grow *profusely.*

____

____

3. Walker's mother's happiness was evident in her *radiant* appearance.

____

____

4. Museums collect the folk art that has been created by *anonymous* women.

____

____

B. DIRECTIONS: *Write the letter of the word that is* closest *in meaning to the Word List word.*

____ 1. anonymous
    A. unknown   **B.** popular   **C.** respected   **D.** agreeing

____ 2. radiant
    A. circular   **B.** round   **C.** yellowed   **D.** glowing

____ 3. profusely
    A. angrily   **B.** deeply   **C.** plentifully   **D.** professionally

____ 4. hindered
    A. slowed   **B.** shortened   **C.** hastened   **D.** encouraged

***from* "In Search of Our Mothers' Gardens"** by Alice Walker
Support for Writing an Outline

To prepare to write an **outline** of the excerpt from "In Search of Our Mothers' Gardens," create a word web. Write the main idea in the center circle. In each circle around it, write a key point. In the circles around each key point, write details that support the key point.

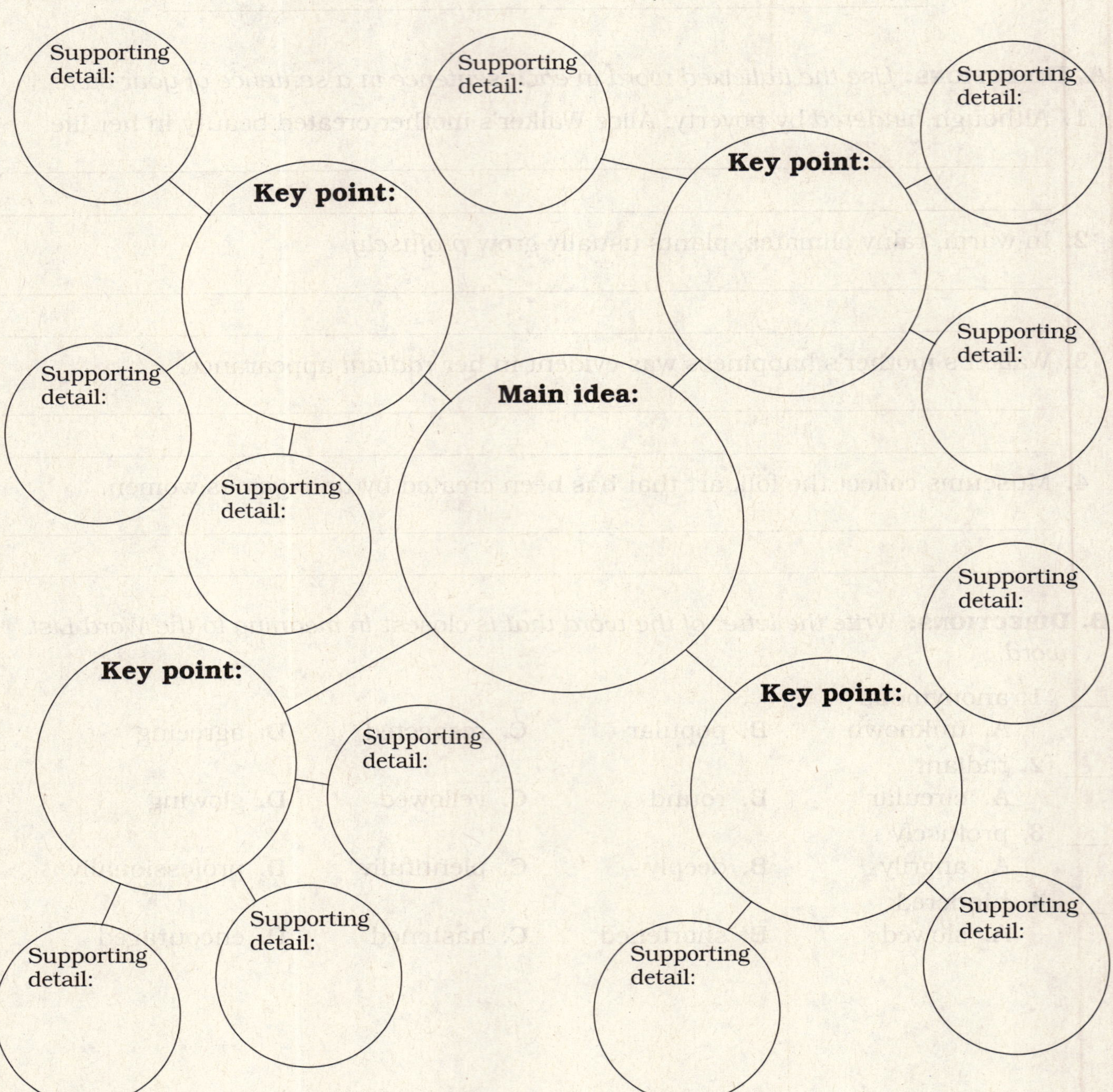

Now, use your word web to make an outline of the essay.

"I Am a Native of North America" by Chief Dan George
from **"In Search of Our Mothers' Gardens"** by Alice Walker
Build Language Skills: Vocabulary Skill

The Prefix *in-*

The word *insignificant* combines the prefix *in-*, which means "without" or "not," and the word *significant*. The word *significant* means "having an important meaning." Adding the prefix creates an antonym, a word with the opposite meaning.

> *in-* + *adequate* = *inadequate*

A. DIRECTIONS: *Revise each sentence so that the italicized vocabulary word is used logically. Be sure to use the vocabulary word in your sentence.*

1. Amanda showed how *insensitive* she was by comforting the crying child.

   ____

2. Brandon's excellent table manners are *inexcusable.*

   ____

3. The report was *incomplete,* so Ashley got an A.

   ____

Academic Vocabulary Practice

B. DIRECTIONS: *Answer each question.*

1. If detectives find stolen property in someone's house, is that *significant* evidence? Why or why not?

   ____

2. If the special effects in a movie have nothing to do with the plot, would they be *irrelevant*? Why or why not?

   ____

3. If you can *identify* all the ingredients in a dish, what do you know?

   ____

4. If a movie director thinks that a scene is *insignificant,* should he or she leave it out? Why or why not?

   ____

5. If information is *relevant* to a report you are writing, should you include it? Why or why not?

   ____

"**I Am a Native of North America**" by Chief Dan George
from "**In Search of Our Mothers' Gardens**" by Alice Walker

Build Language Skills: Grammar

Prepositions and Prepositional Phrases

A **preposition** relates a noun or pronoun that follows the preposition to another word in the sentence. In *The key is in the lock,* the preposition *in* relates *lock* to *key.* These are some common prepositions:

above	beyond	near	outside	to
behind	for	of	over	under
below	into	on	through	with

A **prepositional phrase** begins with a preposition and ends with the noun or pronoun that follows it. In *The key is in the lock,* the prepositional phrase is *in the lock.*

A. DIRECTIONS: *The following sentences are from "I Am a Native of North America" and the excerpt from "In Search of Our Mothers' Gardens." In each sentence, underline each preposition, and circle the prepositional phrase.*

1. In the course of my lifetime, I have lived in two distinct cultures.
2. Their sleeping apartments were separated by blankets made of bull rush reeds.
3. My father was born in such a house and learned from infancy how to love people and be at home with them.
4. I see him strip the hills bare, leaving ugly wounds on the face of mountains.
5. Her day began before sunup, and did not end until late at night.
6. She planted ambitious gardens—and still does—with more than fifty different varieties of plants that bloom profusely from early March until late November.
7. This ability to hold on, even in very simple ways, is work black women have done for a very long time.
8. And perhaps in Africa over two hundred years ago, there was just such a mother.

B. Writing Application: *Write a paragraph about an artistic talent that you or someone you know possesses. Use at least three prepositional phrases. Underline each preposition, and circle the prepositional phrases.*

____

____

____

____

____

"Bernie Williams: Yankee Doodle Dandy" by Joel Poiley
"No Gumption" by Russell Baker

Literary Analysis: Comparing Biography and Autobiography

In an **autobiography,** a person tells his or her own life story. Writers may write about their own experiences to explain their actions, to provide insight into their choices, or to show the personal side of an event. In contrast, in a **biography,** a writer tells the life story of another person. Writers of biographies often write to analyze a person's experiences and actions. Biographies often present their subject as a model, or at least as an example from which readers can learn a lesson.

Some biographies and autobiographies are short essays that focus on a particular episode in the subject's life. Both biography and autobiography focus on actual events and offer insight to explain a person's actions or ideas. The forms have these important differences, however:

Biography	Autobiography
More objective	More personal
Based on research	Based on memory and emotion

DIRECTIONS: *Answer these questions about "Yankee Doodle Dandy" and "No Gumption."*

1. What details in "Yankee Doodle Dandy" show that a biography is more objective than an autobiography?

____

____

2. What details in "No Gumption" show that an autobiography is more personal than a biography?

____

____

3. What details in "Yankee Doodle Dandy" show that a biography is based on research?

____

____

4. What details in "No Gumption" show that an autobiography is based on memory and emotion?

____

____

"Bernie Williams: Yankee Doodle Dandy" by Joel Poiley
"No Gumption" by Russell Baker
Vocabulary Builder

Word List

envisioned   thrive   gumption   paupers   crucial   aptitude

DIRECTIONS: *Identify each statement as* true *or* false. *Then, explain your answer.*

1. A person who has *envisioned* something has drawn a picture of what is on his or her mind.

   True/false: ___________________ **Explanation:** _________________________________

   ____

2. Russell Baker demonstrated that he had *gumption* by reading stories and listening to the radio rather than selling copies of the *Saturday Evening Post*.

   True/false: ___________________ **Explanation:** _________________________________

   ____

3. People who are *paupers* have few possessions and little money.

   True/false: ___________________ **Explanation:** _________________________________

   ____

4. Bernie Williams continues to *thrive* as an athlete and a musician because he is good at sports and music.

   True/false: ___________________ **Explanation:** _________________________________

   ____

5. A person who shows an *aptitude* for something does poorly at it.

   True/false: ___________________ **Explanation:** _________________________________

   ____

6. Choosing what to eat for dinner is a *crucial* decision.

   True/false: ___________________ **Explanation:** _________________________________

   ____

"Bernie Williams: Yankee Doodle Dandy" by Joel Poiley
"No Gumption" by Russell Baker

Support for Writing to Compare Literary Works

On this graphic organizer, record your impressions of Bernie Williams and Russell Baker based on the portraits presented by "Yankee Doodle Dandy" and "No Gumption." Write your impressions of Williams on the left side of each diagram and your impressions of Baker on the right side of each diagram. Write impressions that pertain to both men in the overlapping portions.

My Overall Impression

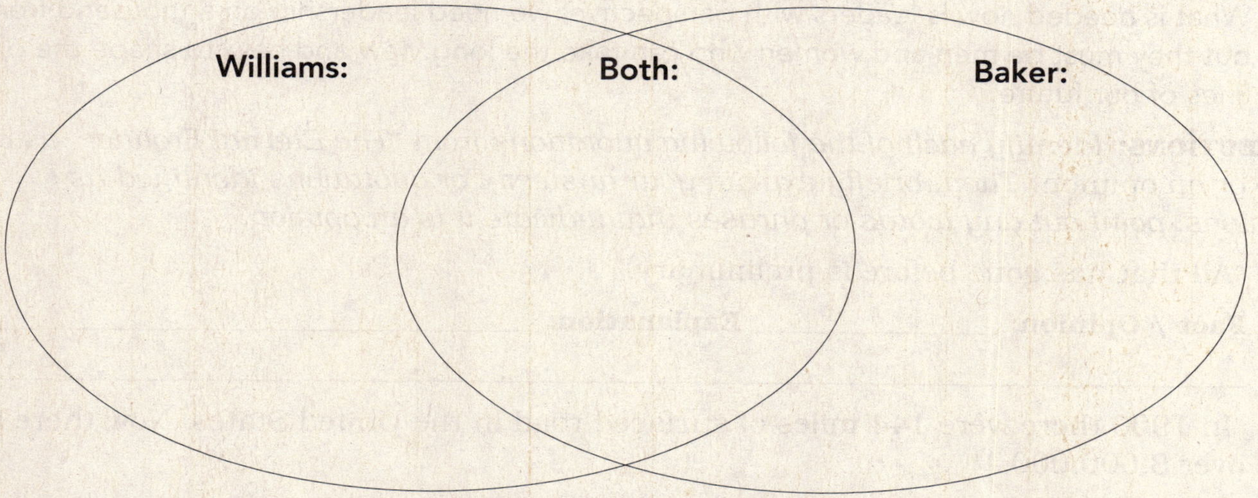

Williams: Both: Baker:

Information That Helped Me Form My Overall Impression

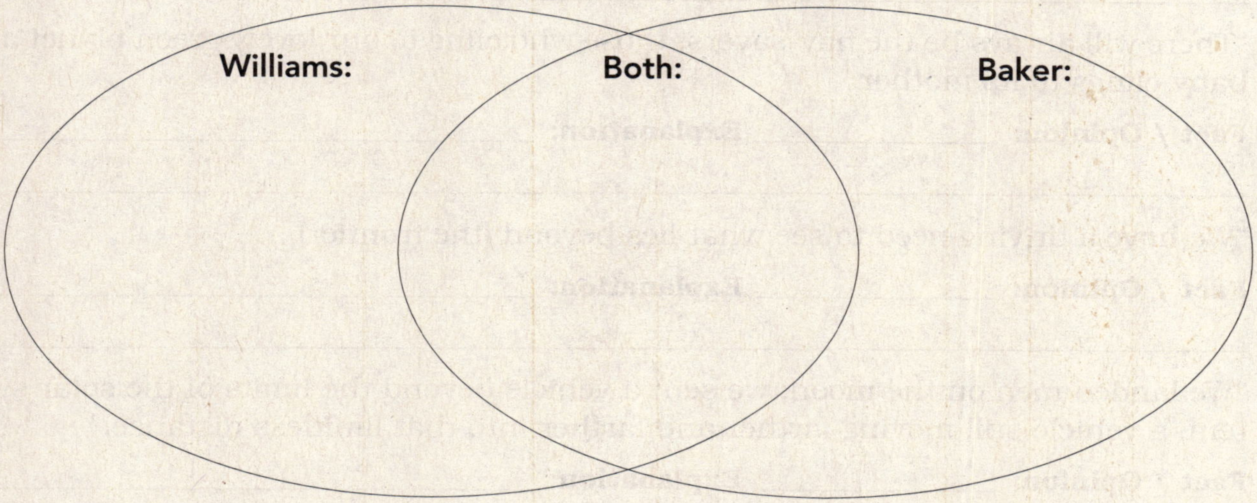

Williams: Both: Baker:

Now, use your notes to write an essay in which you **compare and contrast** what you learned about Bernie Williams and Russell Baker. State your overall impression of each man and the kind of information that helped you form your impression. Then, state which man you understand better.

"The Eternal Frontier" by Louis L'Amour
Reading: Recognize Clue Words That Indicate an Opinion

When you read nonfiction, it is important to be able to distinguish between fact and opinion. A **fact** is something that can be proved true. An **opinion** is a person's judgment or belief. It may be supported by factual evidence, but it cannot be proven.

As you read, **recognize clue words that indicate an opinion,** as in the phrases "I believe" and "in my opinion." Also look for words such as *always, never, must, cannot, best, worst,* and *all,* which may indicate a broad statement that reveals a personal judgment.

You can tell that the statement below from "The Eternal Frontier" is an opinion because it cannot be proven. Another hint is that it contains the word *must.*

> What is needed now is leaders with perspective; we need leadership on a thousand fronts, but they must be men and women who can take the long view and help to shape the outlines of our future.

DIRECTIONS: *Identify each of the following quotations from "The Eternal Frontier" as a fact or an opinion. Then, briefly explain your answer. For quotations identified as opinions, point out any words or phrases that indicate it is an opinion.*

1. "All that has gone before is preliminary."

   Fact / Opinion: ______________ **Explanation:** ______________________________

   ____

2. "In 1900 there were 144 miles of surfaced road in the United States. Now there are over 3,000,000."

   Fact / Opinion: ______________ **Explanation:** ______________________________

   ____

3. "There will always be the nay-sayers, those who cling to our lovely green planet as a baby clings to its mother."

   Fact / Opinion: ______________ **Explanation:** ______________________________

   ____

4. "We have a driving need to see what lies beyond [the frontier] . . ."

   Fact / Opinion: ______________ **Explanation:** ______________________________

   ____

5. "We landed men on the moon; we sent a vehicle beyond the limits of the solar system, a vehicle still moving farther and farther into that limitless distance."

   Fact / Opinion: ______________ **Explanation:** ______________________________

   ____

6. "Nor is the mind of man bound by any limits at all."

   Fact / Opinion: ______________ **Explanation:** ______________________________

   ____

"The Eternal Frontier" by Louis L'Amour
Literary Analysis: Persuasive Essay

A **persuasive essay** is a piece of nonfiction that presents a series of arguments to convince readers that they should believe or act in a certain way. Below are some techniques that are often used in persuasive essays. When you read a persuasive essay, be aware of these techniques; you will need to decide whether they are powerful enough to persuade you to accept the author's ideas.

- **Appeals to authority:** using the opinions of experts and well-known people
- **Appeals to emotion:** using words that convey strong feeling
- **Appeals to reason:** using logical arguments backed by statistics and facts

DIRECTIONS: *In the left-hand column of the following chart, copy down statements from "The Eternal Frontier" that include appeals to emotion. In the right-hand column, copy down statements that include appeals to reason. Find at least two examples of each kind of appeal. (The essay does not make any appeals to authority.)*

Appeals to Emotion	Appeals to Reason

"The Eternal Frontier" by Louis L'Amour
Vocabulary Builder

Word List

frontier   preliminary   antidote   impetus

A. DIRECTIONS: *Answer each question in a complete sentence. In your answer, use one of the Word List words in place of the italicized word or phrase.*

1. What *unexplored region* might you want to learn more about?

   ____

   ____

2. Can you recommend a *cure* for an hour spent working in the hot sun?

   ____

   ____

3. What is the *driving force* behind studying for a test?

   ____

   ____

4. What kind of examination might be given *before* a major examination?

   ____

   ____

B. DIRECTIONS: *Write the letter of the word or phrase whose meaning is most nearly opposite that of the word from the Word List.*

____ 1. antidote
   - A. cure
   - B. reason
   - C. poison
   - D. essay

____ 2. preliminary
   - A. elementary
   - B. fundamental
   - C. secondary
   - D. follow-up

____ 3. frontier
   - A. settled region
   - B. unsettled region
   - C. rural area
   - D. outer space

Name _______________________________________ Date _______________________

Support for Writing a Persuasive Letter

To prepare to write a brief **persuasive letter** advising the government about space travel, complete the chart below. In the left-hand column, write down the priorities you would set and the compromises those priorities might force you to make. In the right-hand column, describe the persuasive technique you will use to make each point.

Points	Persuasive Techniques

Now, use the ideas you have gathered to write your persuasive letter.

"All Together Now" by Barbara Jordan
Reading: Recognize Clue Words That Indicate an Opinion

When you read nonfiction, it is important to be able to distinguish between fact and opinion. A **fact** is something that can be proven true. An **opinion** is a person's judgment or belief. It may be supported by factual evidence, but it cannot be proven.

As you read, **recognize clue words that indicate an opinion,** as in the phrases "I believe" and "In my opinion." Also look for words such as *always, never, must, cannot, best, worst,* and *all,* which may indicate a broad statement that reveals a personal judgment.

You can tell that this statement from "All Together Now" is an opinion because it cannot be proven. Another hint is that it contains the phrase "I don't believe":

> Frankly, I don't believe that the task of bringing us all together can be accomplished by government.

DIRECTIONS: *Identify each of the following quotations from "All Together Now" as a* fact *or an* opinion. *Then, briefly explain your answer. For quotations identified as opinions, point out any words or phrases that indicate it is an opinion.*

1. President Lyndon B. Johnson pushed through the Civil Rights Act of 1964, which remains the fundamental piece of civil rights legislation in this century.

   Fact / Opinion: ____________________ **Explanation:** ______________________

   ____

2. One thing is clear to me: We, as human beings, must be willing to accept people who are different from ourselves.

   Fact / Opinion: ____________________ **Explanation:** ______________________

   ____

3. Children learn ideas and attitudes from the adults who nurture them.

   Fact / Opinion: ____________________ **Explanation:** ______________________

   ____

4. I absolutely believe that children do not adopt prejudices unless they absorb them from their parents or teachers.

   Fact / Opinion: ____________________ **Explanation:** ______________________

   ____

5. It is possible for all of us to work on this at home, in our schools, at our jobs.

   Fact / Opinion: ____________________ **Explanation:** ______________________

   ____

Unit 3 Resources: Types of Nonfiction

"All Together Now" by Barbara Jordan
Literary Analysis: Persuasive Essay

A **persuasive essay** is a piece of nonfiction that presents a series of arguments to convince readers that they should believe or act in a certain way. Below are some techniques that are often used in persuasive essays. When you read a persuasive essay, be aware of these techniques; you will need to decide whether they are powerful enough to persuade you to accept the author's ideas.

- **Appeals to authority:** using the opinions of experts and well-known people
- **Appeals to emotion:** using words that convey strong feeling
- **Appeals to reason:** using logical arguments backed by statistics and facts

DIRECTIONS: *In the first column of the following chart, copy statements from "All Together Now" that include appeals to authority. In the second column, copy statements that include appeals to emotion. In the third column, copy statements that include appeals to reason. Find at least one example of each kind of appeal.*

Appeals to Authority	Appeals to Emotion	Appeals to Reason

"All Together Now" by Barbara Jordan
Vocabulary Builder

Word List

legislation	tolerant	fundamental	optimist

A. DIRECTIONS: *Answer each question in a complete sentence. In your answer, use one of the Word List words in place of the italicized word or phrase.*

1. In what way have civil rights *laws* changed this country?

   ____

   ____

2. What is the *basic* rule for getting along with others?

   ____

   ____

3. What happens when people are not *accepting* of others' differences?

   ____

   ____

4. Are you *someone who takes the most hopeful view of matters?*

   ____

   ____

B. DIRECTIONS: *Write the letter of the word whose meaning is most nearly* opposite *that of the word from the Word List.*

____ 1. tolerant
   A. prejudiced   B. conflicted   C. accepting   D. kind

____ 2. optimist
   A. physicist   B. optician   C. pessimist   D. racist

____ 3. fundamental
   A. necessary   B. unimportant   C. basic   D. able

"All Together Now" by Barbara Jordan

Support for Writing a Persuasive Letter

To prepare to write a brief **persuasive letter** advising a community leader on ways in which residents of the community can promote tolerance, complete the chart below. In the left-hand column, write down the steps people can take in their own homes and explain challenges they might face in trying to achieve their goal. In the right-hand column, describe the persuasive technique you will use to make each point.

Points (Including Challenges)	Persuasive Techniques

Now, use the ideas you have gathered to write your persuasive letter.

"The Eternal Frontier" by Louis L'Amour
"All Together Now" by Barbara Jordan
Build Language Skills: Vocabulary Skill

Borrowed and Foreign Words

Many words in the English language have been borrowed from other languages. Here are just a few of them: *kindergarten* is from German; *magazine* and *almanac* are from Arabic; *trek* is from Afrikaans; and *tycoon* is from Japanese.

A. DIRECTIONS: *Follow the instructions to write sentences using the borrowed words featured in this lesson. If you need to, look up the definition of the word in a dictionary before you write.*

1. In a sentence about someone's first experience at school, use the word *kindergarten.*

   ____

2. In a sentence about something you enjoyed reading about, use the word *magazine.*

   ____

3. In a sentence about a long, difficult journey, use the word *trek.*

   ____

4. In a sentence about an exceptionally wealthy and powerful person, use the word *tycoon.*

   ____

Academic Vocabulary Practice

check   almanac   evaluate   investigate   valid

B. DIRECTIONS: *Answer each question in a complete sentence. Use one of the following Academic Vocabulary words in each answer.*

1. Where might you look to find out the population of your state?

   ____

2. If a detective were attempting to solve a crime, what would he do?

   ____

3. If you are not sure whether a phone number is correct, what might you do?

   ____

4. If you were choosing between several similar products, what would you do?

   ____

5. When a judge is not sure whether an argument is justifiable, with what is she concerned?

   ____

"The Eternal Frontier" by Louis L'Amour
"All Together Now" by Barbara Jordan
Build Language Skills: Grammar

Subjects and Predicates

Every sentence has two parts: the **subject** and the **predicate.** The **subject** describes whom or what the sentence is about. The **simple subject** is the noun or pronoun that states exactly whom or what the sentence is about. The **complete subject** includes the simple subject and all of its modifiers.

The **predicate** is a verb that tells what the subject does, what is done to the subject, or what the condition of the subject is. The **simple predicate** is the verb or verb phrase that tells what the subject of the sentence does or is. It includes the simple predicate and any modifiers or complements.

In the following example, the simple subject and the simple predicate are in bold type. The complete subject is underlined once, and the complete predicate is underlined twice.

Louis L'Amour, a writer of novels about the American West, **has written** a persuasive essay about the importance of space exploration.

A. PRACTICE: *In each sentence, underline the simple subject once and the simple predicate twice.*

1. Louis L'Amour writes about the importance of space travel.

2. In L'Amour's view, outer space is the next frontier.

3. All of humankind longs for exploration and discovery.

4. According to Barbara Jordan, we can win the fight against prejudice.

5. Little children do not hate other people.

6. People learn to hate from parents and teachers.

B. Writing Application: *In a paragraph of at least four sentences, describe a place you would like to explore. Underline each simple subject once and each simple predicate twice.*

____

____

____

____

____

____

____

____

"The Real Story of a Cowboy's Life" by Geoffrey C. Ward
Reading: Use Resources to Check Facts

A **fact** is information you can prove. An **opinion** is a judgment.

Fact: The big herds . . . carried with them a disease . . . that devastated domestic livestock.

Opinion: The settlers' hostility was entirely understandable.

Be aware that some writers present opinions or beliefs as facts. To get to the truth, **use resources to check facts.**

Resource	Characteristics
almanac	a collection of facts and statistics on the climate, planets, stars, people, places, events, and so on, updated yearly
atlas	a collection of maps
biographical dictionary	an alphabetical listing of famous or historically significant persons with identifying information and dates of birth and death
dictionary	an alphabetical listing of words with their pronunciation and definition
encyclopedia	an alphabetically organized collection of articles on a broad range of subjects
reliable Web sites	Internet pages and articles on an extremely wide variety of topics, sponsored by individuals, companies, governments, and organizations

DIRECTIONS: *Read these passages from "The Real Story of a Cowboy's Life." Then, identify each one as a* fact *or an* opinion. *If the statement is a fact, indicate the best resource for checking it.*

1. Most Texas herds numbered about 2,000 head with a trail boss and about a dozen men in charge though herds as large as 15,000 were also driven north with far larger escorts.

   Fact/opinion: _________________ **Resource:** _________________________

2. Regardless of its ultimate destination, every herd had to ford a series of rivers—the Nueces, the Guadalupe, the Brazos, the Wichita, the Red.

   Fact/opinion: _________________ **Resource:** _________________________

3. After you crossed the Red River and got out on the open plains . . . it was sure a pretty sight to see them strung out for almost a mile, the sun shining on their horns.

   Fact/opinion: _________________ **Resource:** _________________________

4. Initially, the land immediately north of the Red River was Indian territory, and some tribes charged tolls for herds crossing their land payable in money or beef.

   Fact/opinion: _________________ **Resource:** _________________________

"The Real Story of a Cowboy's Life" by Geoffrey C. Ward
Literary Analysis: Word Choice and Diction

A writer's **word choice** and **diction** are important elements of his or her writing. The specific words a writer uses can make writing difficult or easy to read, formal or informal. Diction includes not only the vocabulary the writer uses but also the way in which the sentences are put together. Here are some questions writers consider when deciding which words to use:

- What does the audience already know about the topic? If an audience is unfamiliar with a topic, the writer will have to define technical vocabulary or use simpler language.
- What feeling will this work convey? Word choice can make a work serious or funny, academic or personal. The length and style of the sentences can make a work simple or complex.

In this passage from "The Real Story of a Cowboy's Life," notice that the author uses both technical vocabulary (*point, swing, drag*) and informal language ("eating dust"):

> The most experienced men rode "point" and "swing," at the head and sides of the long herd; the least experienced brought up the rear, riding "drag" and eating dust.

DIRECTIONS: *Read each passage. Then, on the lines that follow, write down examples of technical vocabulary, formal language, and informal language. If there are no examples of a particular kind of language, write* none.

1. If . . . the cattle started running you'd hear that low rumbling noise along the ground and the men on herd wouldn't need to come in and tell you, you'd know— then you'd jump for your horse and get out there in the lead, trying to head them and get them into a mill before they scattered. It was riding at a dead run in the dark, with duct banks and prairie dog holes all around you, not knowing if the next jump would land you in a shallow grave.

   Technical vocabulary: ____

   Informal language: ____

   Formal language: ____

2. The big herds ruined their crops, and they carried with them a disease, spread by ticks and called "Texas fever," that devastated domestic livestock. Kansas and other territories along the route soon established quarantine lines, called "deadlines," at the western fringe of settlement, and insisted that trail drives not cross them.

   Technical vocabulary: ____

   Informal language: ____

   Formal language: ____

"The Real Story of a Cowboy's Life" by Geoffrey C. Ward
Vocabulary Builder

Word List

| gauge | ultimate | diversions |

A. DIRECTIONS: *Write the correct word from the Word List on each line.*

1. The teammates want to win the next match, but their ___________________ goal is to win the championship.
2. The fair offered games, rides, and a few other ___________________.
3. The cowboys tried to ___________________ the mood of the cattle by the way the animals moved and the cries they uttered.

B. DIRECTIONS: *Write* true *if a statement is true and* false *if it is false. Then, explain your answer.*

1. If you describe volleyball and tennis as *diversions*, those sports did not amuse you.

   True/false: ___________________ **Explanation:** ___________________

   ____

2. If your *ultimate* goal is to run five miles a week, you should probably run one mile five times a week.

   True/false: ___________________ **Explanation:** ___________________

   ____

3. If you can *gauge* distances, you cannot tell how far a mile is.

   True/false: ___________________ **Explanation:** ___________________

   ____

C. DIRECTIONS: *Write the letter of the word whose meaning is closest to the meaning of the word from the Word List.*

___ 1. ultimate
     A. real   **B.** final   **C.** first   **D.** timely

___ 2. gauge
     A. find   **B.** join   **C.** estimate   **D.** know

___ 3. diversions
     A. amusements   **B.** erasures   **C.** friends   **D.** payments

"The Real Story of a Cowboy's Life" by Geoffrey C. Ward
Support for Writing an Adaptation

In preparation for an **adaptation** of one of the incidents described in "The Real Story of a Cowboy's Life," complete the following graphic organizer. First, note the incident you plan to adapt and the audience you plan to present your adaptation to. Then, in the first column of the chart, copy down the incident. In the second column, write your adaptation, keeping your audience in mind. Finally, look carefully at your adaptation. See if you can simplify it even further. In the last column, note your revisions.

Incident: ____

Audience: ____

Passage	Adaptation	Revision of Adaptation

Now, use your notes to write a final draft of your adaptation.

"**Rattlesnake Hunt**" by Marjorie Kinnan Rawlings
Reading: Use Resources to Check Facts

A **fact** is information you can prove. An **opinion** is a judgment.

Fact: Ross Allen is a young herpetologist from Florida.

Opinion: "The scientific and dispassionate detachment of the material and the man made a desirable approach to rattlesnake territory."

Be aware that some writers present opinions or beliefs as facts. To get to the truth, **use resources to check facts.** You can confirm whether a statement is accurate by using one of these resources:

Resource	Characteristics
almanac	a collection of facts and statistics on the climate, planets, stars, people, places, events and so on, updated yearly
atlas	a collection of maps
geographical dictionary	an alphabetical listing of places with statistical and factual information about them and perhaps some maps
dictionary	an alphabetical listing of words with their pronunciation and definition
encyclopedia	an alphabetically organized collection of articles on a broad range of subjects
reliable Web sites	Internet pages and articles on an extremely wide variety of topics, sponsored by individuals, companies, governments, and organizations

DIRECTIONS: *Read these passages from and about "Rattlesnake Hunt." Then, identify each one as a fact or an opinion. If the statement is a fact, indicate the best resource for checking it.*

1. Big Prairie, Florida, is south of Arcadia and west of the northern tip of Lake Okeechobee.

    Fact/opinion: ___________________   **Resource:** _______________________________

2. A snake takes on the temperature of its surroundings. They can't stand too much heat for that reason, and when the weather is cool, as now, they're sluggish.

    Fact/opinion: ___________________   **Resource:** _______________________________

3. Snakes are not cold and clammy.

    Fact/opinion: ___________________   **Resource:** _______________________________

4. The next day was magnificent. The air was crystal, the sky was aquamarine.

    Fact/opinion: ___________________   **Resource:** _______________________________

5. A rattler will lie quietly without revealing itself if a man passes by and it thinks it is not seen.

    Fact/opinion: ___________________   **Resource:** _______________________________

"**Rattlesnake Hunt**" by Marjorie Kinnan Rawlings
Literary Analysis: Word Choice and Diction

A writer's **word choice** and **diction** are important elements of his or her writing. The specific words a writer uses can make writing difficult or easy to read, formal or informal. Diction includes not only the vocabulary the writer uses but also the way in which the sentences are put together. Here are some questions writers consider when deciding which kinds of words to use:

- What does the audience already know about the topic? If an audience is unfamiliar with a topic, the writer will have to define technical vocabulary or use simpler language.
- What feeling will this work convey? Word choice can make a work serious or funny, academic or personal. The length or style of the sentences can make a work simple or complex.

In this passage from "Rattlesnake Hunt," note that the author uses formal language and difficult vocabulary, but she also uses the informal word *varmints*:

> The scientific and dispassionate detachment of the material and the man made a desirable approach to rattlesnake territory. As I had discovered with the insects and varmints, it is difficult to be afraid of anything about which enough is known.

DIRECTIONS: *Read each passage. Then, on the lines that follow, write down examples of technical vocabulary, formal language, and informal language. If there are no examples of a particular kind of language, write* none.

1. They lived in winter, he said, in gopher holes, coming out in the midday warmth to forage, and would move ahead of the flames and be easily taken.

   Technical vocabulary: ____

   Informal language: ____

   Formal language: ____

2. After the rattlers, water snakes seemed innocuous enough. We worked along the edge of the stream and here Ross did not use his L-shaped steel.

   Technical vocabulary: ____

   Informal language: ____

   Formal language: ____

3. Yet having learned that it was we who were the aggressors; that immobility meant complete safety; that the snakes, for all their lightning flash in striking, were inaccurate in their aim, . . . suddenly I understood that I was drinking in freely the magnificent sweep of the horizon, with no fear of what might be at the moment under my feet.

   Technical vocabulary: ____

   Informal language: ____

   Formal language: ____

"**Rattlesnake Hunt**" by Marjorie Kinnan Rawlings
Vocabulary Builder

Word List

desolate   arid   mortality

A. DIRECTIONS: *Write the correct word from the Word List in each blank. Use each word only once.*

1. The creek bed was _____________________, as there had been no rain in months.

2. Being close to a dangerous reptile can make you aware of your

   _____________________.

3. The rocky, dry landscape was _____________________ and depressing.

B. DIRECTIONS: *Write* true *if a statement is true and* false *if it is false. Then, explain your answer.*

1. If a region is *arid*, crops will grow there easily.

   True/false: _____________________ **Explanation:** _____________________

   ____

2. If a character in a book faces his *mortality*, he believes he will live forever.

   True/false: _____________________ **Explanation:** _____________________

   ____

3. If a scene in a movie is set in a *desolate* location, the mood will likely be lonely.

   True/false: _____________________ **Explanation:** _____________________

   ____

C. DIRECTIONS: *Write the letter of the word whose meaning is* closest *to the meaning of the word from the Word List.*

___ 1. mortality
    A. life   B. eternity   C. death   D. fear

___ 2. desolate
    A. huge   B. lonely   C. scary   D. crowded

___ 3. arid
    A. mistaken   B. cold   C. airy   D. dry

"Rattlesnake Hunt" by Marjorie Kinnan Rawlings
Support for Writing an Adaptation

In preparation for an **adaptation** of one of the incidents described in "Rattlesnake Hunt," complete the following graphic organizer. First note the incident you plan to adapt and the audience you plan to present your adaptation to. Then, in the first column of the chart, copy down the incident. In the second column, write your adaptation, keeping your audience in mind. Finally, look carefully at your adaptation. See if you can simplify it even further. In the last column, note your revisions.

Incident: ____

Audience: ____

Passage	Adaptation	Revision of Adaptation

Now, use your notes to write a final draft of your adaptation.

143

"The Real Story of a Cowboy's Life" by Geoffrey C. Ward
"Rattlesnake Hunt" by Marjorie Kinnan Rawlings
Build Language Skills: Vocabulary Skill

Borrowed and Foreign Words

Here are some commonly used English words that have been borrowed from foreign languages: *ballet* and *bizarre* come from French; *bungalow* is from Hindi and Urdu; *mammoth* is from Russian; *safari* is from Swahili.

A. DIRECTIONS: *Explain your answer to each question. If you are unsure of the meaning of the word, look it up in a dictionary before answering the question.*

1. Is someone likely to live on the third floor of a *bungalow*?

    ____

2. Was Marjorie Kinnan Rawlings's hunt for rattlesnakes a *safari*?

    ____

3. Are you likely to see hip-hop dancing at a *ballet*?

    ____

4. Is a *bizarre* scene one that you are likely to see every day?

    ____

Academic Vocabulary Practice

B. DIRECTIONS: *Revise each sentence so that the underlined Academic Vocabulary word is used logically.*

1. Reporters <u>investigate</u> stories after they have been published.

    ____

2. We used an <u>almanac</u> to look up the spelling of *prairie*.

    ____

3. If I am sure of the spelling of a word, I look it up in a <u>dictionary</u>.

    ____

4. It is best to <u>evaluate</u> a movie before you watch it.

    ____

5. A <u>valid</u> excuse is one that no one is likely to believe.

    ____

"The Real Story of a Cowboy's Life" by Geoffrey C. Ward
"Rattlesnake Hunt" by Marjorie Kinnan Rawlings

Build Language Skills: Grammar

Compound Subjects and Predicates

A **compound subject** contains two or more subjects that share the same verb. A **compound predicate** contains two or more verbs that share the same subject. Both compound subjects and compound predicates are joined by conjunctions such as *and, or, but,* and *nor.*

Compound subject:	<u>Discipline</u> *and* <u>planning</u> were essential to the success of a cattle drive.
Compound predicate:	"The snake <u>did</u> not <u>coil</u>, *but* <u>lifted</u> its head *and* <u>whirred</u> its rattles lightly."

A. PRACTICE: *In these sentences, underline the compound subjects once and the compound predicates twice.*

1. On trail rides, cowboys keep the herd together and guide them along the trail.
2. Trail bosses and cowboys work together to keep the cattle safe.
3. Sometimes bosses pay homesteaders or face their anger.
4. Most trail bosses forbid gambling and punish cowboys for drinking.
5. Rattlesnakes warn intruders but strike quickly.
6. Snakes and other reptiles are cold-blooded.
7. Sun and warm temperatures bring snakes out of hiding.
8. Snake catchers must move carefully or suffer the consequences.

B. Writing Application: *Imagine that you are describing an attempt at catching a rattlesnake. Follow these instructions.*

1. Write a sentence with a compound predicate; use *walked* and *searched*.

____

____

2. Write a sentence with a compound subject; use *insects* and *snakes*.

____

____

3. Write a sentence with a compound predicate; use *hissed* and *rattled*.

____

____

4. Write a sentence with a compound predicate; use *found* and *caught*.

____

____

"Alligator" by Bailey White
"The Night the Bed Fell" by James Thurber
Literary Analysis: Comparing Humorous Essays

Humorous essays are works of nonfiction meant to amuse readers. To entertain, authors may use one or more of these comic techniques:

- presenting an illogical, inappropriate, improper, or unusual situation
- contrasting reality with characters' mistaken views
- exaggerating the truth or exaggerating the feelings, ideas, and actions of characters

While most humorists want to entertain the reader, many also want to convey a serious message.

Writers of humorous essays often develop the humor through the characters they present. For example, humorous characters are central to "Alligator" and "The Night the Bed Fell."

DIRECTIONS: *Explain your answers to the following questions, using examples from the selections.*

Question	"Alligator"	"The Night the Bed Fell"
1. Does the essay describe illogical, inappropriate, improper, or unusual situations?		
2. Does the writer contrast reality with characters' mistaken views?		
3. Does the writer exaggerate the truth or the feelings, ideas, and actions of characters?		
4. Which character did you find the most humorous? How is that character's appearance described? How are his or her actions described? What does the character say, or what do other characters say about him or her, to add to the humor?		

"Alligator" by Bailey White
"The Night the Bed Fell" by James Thurber
Vocabulary Builder

Word List

cattails	bellow	ominous	deluge

A. DIRECTIONS: *Read each sentence, paying attention to the italicized word from the Word List. Then, explain whether the sentence makes sense. If it does not make sense, rewrite the sentence using the Word List word correctly, or write a new sentence using the word.*

1. On our trip to the desert, we found *cattails* growing everywhere.

   Explanation: ____

   New sentence: ____

2. The crowds in the arena *bellow* when the referee makes an unfair call.

   Explanation: ____

   New sentence: ____

3. The girl's smile was *ominous* as she happily and gently hugged her new puppy.

   Explanation: ____

   New sentence: ____

4. The *deluge* of rain has caused the river to overflow.

   Explanation: ____

   New sentence: ____

B. DIRECTIONS: *Write the letter of the word that is most similar in meaning to the word from the Word List.*

____ 1. perilous
   A. happy   B. tired   C. safe   D. dangerous

____ 2. exultant
   A. depressed   B. overjoyed   C. weeping   D. slow

____ 3. pungent
   A. sharp   B. silly   C. serious   D. light

____ 4. culprit
   A. judge   B. criminal   C. jury   D. lawyer

Name ____ Date _______________________

"Alligator" by Bailey White
"The Night the Bed Fell" by James Thurber
Support for Writing to Compare Literary Works

To prepare to write an essay **comparing humorous essays,** complete this graphic organizer.

Which events made you laugh?

Which characters made you laugh?

Which character was the funniest?

"Alligator" and "The Night the Bed Fell"

Which character did you like the most?

What purpose might the authors have had beyond amusing you?

Would you read another work by either author? Why or why not?

Now, use your notes to write an essay explaining why you found "Alligator" funnier than "The Night the Bed Fell" or why you found "The Night the Bed Fell" funnier than "Alligator."

Pat Mora
Listening and Viewing

Segment 1: Meet Pat Mora
- Why does Pat Mora use both English and Spanish when she writes?
- What are some reasons that it is important to read literature by or about people of many different cultures?

____

____

____

Segment 2: Poetry
- Why does Pat Mora write the last line of "The Desert Is My Mother" in Spanish?
- What effect do the Spanish lines in this poem have on you as a reader?

____

____

____

Segment 3: The Writing Process
- How does Pat Mora prepare to begin writing?
- Which one of her writing strategies would you use, and why?

____

____

____

Segment 4: The Rewards of Writing
- How are poetry readings particularly rewarding to Pat Mora?
- Has a certain piece of literature had a strong impact on you as a reader? Explain.

____

____

____

Learning About Poetry

Poetry is the most musical, and often the most imaginative, of all literary forms. A common characteristic of poetry is **figurative language,** which is writing or speech that is not meant to be taken literally, or as though it is realistic.

FIGURATIVE LANGUAGE	• **metaphor:** describes one thing as if it were something else (*You are the sunshine of my life.*)
	• **simile:** uses *like* or *as* to compare two unlike things (*Your smile is as bright as the sun.*)
	• **personification:** gives human qualities to a nonhuman thing (*The sun smiled on our picnic.*)
	• **symbol:** something that represents something else (*The flag is a symbol of our country; a dove is a symbol of peace.*)

A. DIRECTIONS: *On the lines, write the letter of the type of figurative language used in each line of poetry.*

   ___ 1. bubbly and bright like a mountain stream   **A.** simile

   ___ 2. a bright lantern that welcomed me home   **B.** metaphor

   ___ 3. your eyes are moonlight to my earth   **C.** symbol

   ___ 4. the apple pie that means "home"   **D.** personification

B. DIRECTIONS: *Follow each direction by writing an original phrase or sentence.*

1. Use a metaphor to write about the moon.

____

2. Use a simile to write about a dog.

____

3. Use personification to write about a clock.

____

4. Write a sentence containing a symbol.

____

The Poetry of Pat Mora
Model Selection: Poetry

In addition to figurative language, Pat Mora's three poems contain examples of **sound devices,** or writing or speech that adds a musical quality.

SOUND DEVICES	• **alliteration:** repetition of consonant sounds at the beginning of words (*a busy bee*)
	• **repetition:** use of a sound, word, or group of words more than once (*the beat of the drum and the beat of my heart*)
	• **onomatopoeia:** use of words that imitate sounds (*quack, bang*)
	• **rhyme:** repetition of sounds at the ends of words (*sit, lit, hit*)
	• **meter:** arrangement of stressed and unstressed syllables (*The day began at eight o'clock.*)

A. DIRECTIONS: *Answer these questions about the characteristics in Pat Mora's poems.*

1. In the first stanza of "Maestro," what verb is an example of onomatopoeia?
   ____

2. What example of repetition appears in the first five lines of "Bailando"?
   ____

3. What type of sound device is represented by the word *whispers*?
   ____

4. What type of sound device is represented by the phrase *the snow's silence*?
   ____

B. DIRECTIONS: *In these poems, Pat Mora speaks of family members. On the lines below, write your own short poem about a family member or friend. Include at least two examples of figurative language and sound devices.*

____

____

____

____

____

____

Poetry Collection: Naomi Shihab Nye, William Jay Smith, Buson
Reading: Ask Questions to Draw a Conclusion

Drawing conclusions means arriving at an overall judgment or idea by pulling together several details. By drawing conclusions, you recognize meanings that are not directly stated. **Asking questions** can help you identify details and make connections that lead to a conclusion. You might ask yourself questions such as these:

- What details does the writer include and emphasize?
- How are the details related?
- What do the details mean all together?

Consider, for example, this haiku by Buson:

After the moon sets,

slow through the forest, shadows

drift and disappear

What do the details suggest? The moon has set, so it must be morning. Why, though, do "shadows / drift and disappear"? Is it because it has grown darker or because it has grown lighter, because the sun is rising? The reader might conclude that Buson's haiku vividly evokes the darkness that precedes dawn.

DIRECTIONS: *Complete the following chart. First, ask a question about the poem. Then, record the details that prompted the question. Finally, write a conclusion that you can draw based on the question and the related details.*

Poem	Question	Details Relating to Question	Conclusion
"The Rider"			
"Seal"			
"O foolish ducklings"			
"Deep in a windless wood"			

Poetry Collection: Naomi Shihab Nye, William Jay Smith, Buson
Literary Analysis: Forms of Poetry

There are many different **forms of poetry.** A poet will follow different rules depending on the structure of a poem. These are the three forms represented by the poems in this collection:

- A **lyric poem** expresses the poet's thoughts and feelings about a single image or idea in vivid, musical language.
- In a **concrete poem,** the poet arranges the letters and lines to create a visual image that suggests the poem's subject.
- **Haiku** is a traditional form of Japanese poetry that is often about nature. In a traditional haiku, the first line always has five syllables, the second line always has seven syllables, and the third line always has five syllables.

DIRECTIONS: *Write your responses to the following questions.*

1. If you were to rewrite "The Rider" as a concrete poem, what shape would you use to express the main idea of the poem? Why?

   ____

   ____

2. If you were to rewrite "Seal" as a haiku, what seven-syllable line might you write that contained the phrase "Quicksilver-quick"?

   ____

3. If you were to rewrite one of Buson's haiku as a lyric poem, on what single image would you focus? Why?

   ____

   ____

4. If you were to rewrite "The Rider" as a haiku, what would one of your lines be?

   ____

5. If you were to rewrite "Seal" as a lyric poem, how would you change it? Why?

   ____

   ____

Unit 4 Resources: Poetry

153

Poetry Collection: Naomi Shihab Nye, William Jay Smith, Buson
Vocabulary Builder

Word List

luminous	swerve	utter	weasel

A. DIRECTIONS: *Provide an explanation for your answer to each question.*

1. Would you be able to see *luminous* stars in a clear night sky?

   ____

   ____

2. If someone did not *utter* a word, would she be likely to win a debate?

   ____

   ____

3. Would you be likely to see a *weasel* in the Large Mammals section of a zoo?

   ____

   ____

4. Would a driver likely go into a *swerve* to avoid hitting something in the road?

   ____

   ____

B. DIRECTIONS: *Write the letter of the pair of words that best expresses a relationship* similar *to that expressed by the pair in capital letters.*

____ 1. WEASEL : MAMMAL
  A. animal : giraffe
  B. mongoose : snake
  C. owl : bird
  D. frog : toad

____ 2. LUMINOUS : BRIGHT
  A. funny : humorous
  B. lamp : bulb
  C. happy : sad
  D. shiny : metal

____ 3. UTTER : SPEAK
  A. smile : frown
  B. talk : shout
  C. speech : debate
  D. cry : weep

____ 4. SWERVE : CURVE
  A. stop : halt
  B. straight : line
  C. walk : run
  D. open : close

Name ____ Date _______________________

Support for Writing a Lyric Poem, Concrete Poem, or Haiku

In the chart below, write details that you might use in your poem.

Subject: ____

Vivid Descriptions	Action Words	Thoughts	Feelings

Now, use the details you have collected to draft a **lyric poem, concrete poem,** or **haiku.**

Poetry Collection: Nikki Giovanni, Mary Ellen Solt, Bashō
Reading: Ask Questions to Draw a Conclusion

Drawing conclusions means arriving at an overall judgment or idea by pulling together several details. By drawing conclusions, you recognize meanings that are not directly stated. **Asking questions** can help you identify details and make connections that lead to a conclusion. You might ask yourself questions such as these:

- What details does the writer include and emphasize?
- How are the details related?
- Taken together, what do all the details mean?

Consider, for example, this haiku by Bashō:

On sweet plum blossoms

The sun rises suddenly.

Look, a mountain path!

What do those details mean? As the sun rises, it shines on a blossoming plum tree. You can conclude that it is a spring morning.

DIRECTIONS: *Complete the following chart. First, ask a question about the poem. Then, record the details that prompted the question. Finally, write a conclusion that you can draw based on the question and the related details.*

Poem	Question	Details Relating to Question	Conclusion
"Winter"			
"Forsythia"			
"Has spring come indeed?"			
"Temple bells die out"			

Poetry Collection: Nikki Giovanni, Mary Ellen Solt, Bashō
Literary Analysis: Forms of Poetry

There are many different **forms of poetry.** A poet will follow different rules, depending on the structure of a poem. These are the three forms represented by poems in this collection:

- A **lyric poem** expresses the poet's thoughts and feelings about a single image or idea in vivid, musical language.
- In a **concrete poem,** the poet arranges the letters and lines to create a visual image that suggests the poem's subject.
- **Haiku** is a traditional form of Japanese poetry that is often about nature. In a traditional haiku, the first line always has five syllables, the second line always has seven syllables, and the third line always has five syllables.

DIRECTIONS: *Write your answers to the following questions.*

1. If you were to rewrite one of Bashō's haiku as a concrete poem, what shape would you use to express the main idea? Why?

   ____

   ____

2. If you were to rewrite "Winter" as a haiku, what seven-syllable line might you write that contained the phrase "Bears store fat"?

   ____

3. If you were to rewrite "Forsythia" as a lyric poem, on what single idea would you focus? Why?

   ____

   ____

4. If you were to rewrite "Forsythia" as a haiku, what would one of your lines be?

   ____

5. If you were to rewrite one of Bashō's haiku as a lyric poem, how would you change it? Why?

   ____

   ____

Poetry Collection: Nikki Giovanni, Mary Ellen Solt, Bashō
Vocabulary Builder

Word List

burrow

A. DIRECTIONS: *Complete this word web with details about* burrow.

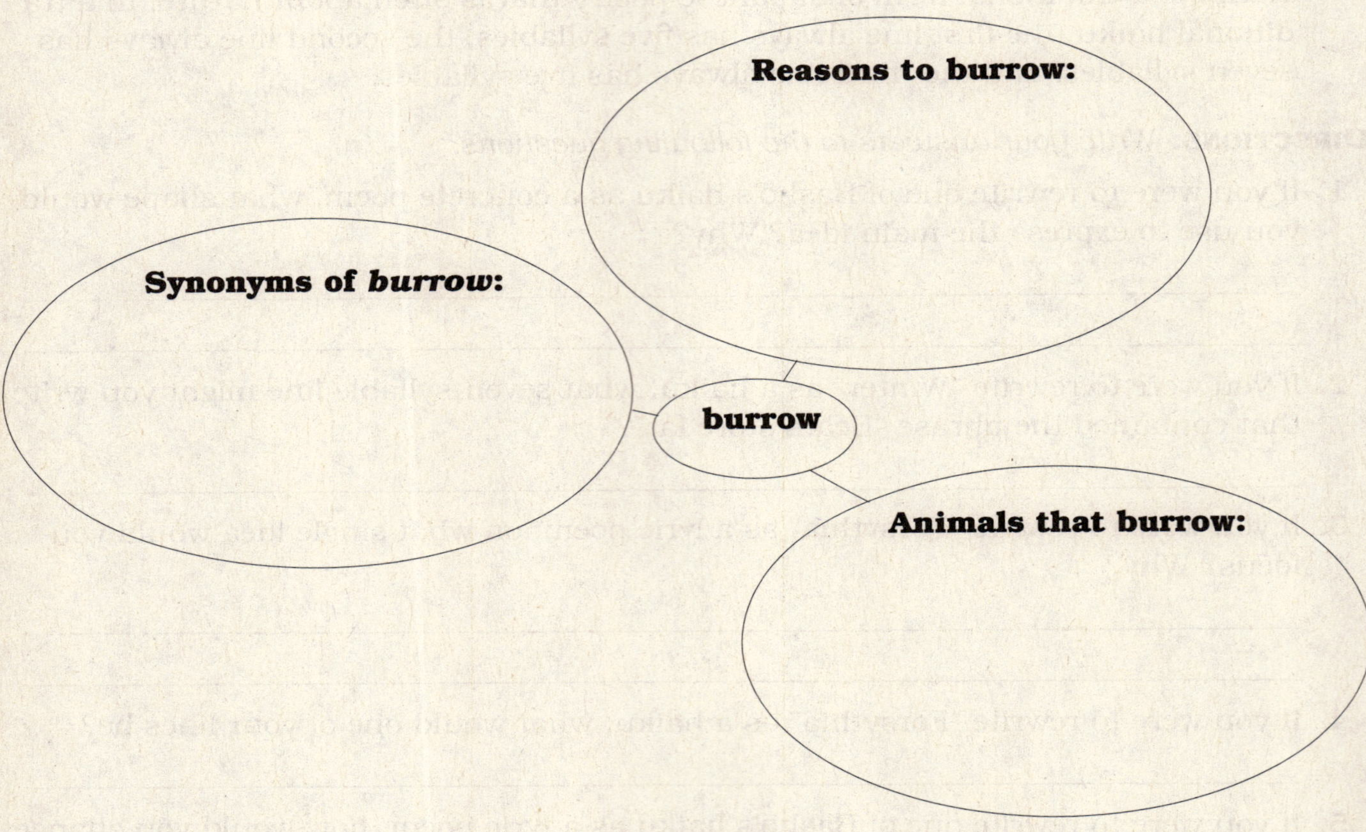

B. DIRECTIONS: *Write a description of an animal that is burrowing. Explain what it is doing and why it is doing it.*

____

____

____

____

Poetry Collection: Nikki Giovanni, Mary Ellen Solt, Bashō
Support for Writing a Lyric Poem, Concrete Poem, or Haiku

In the chart below, write details that you might use in your poem.

Subject: ____

Vivid Descriptions	Action Words	Thoughts	Feelings

Now, use the details you have collected to draft a **lyric poem, concrete poem,** or **haiku.**

Poetry Collections: Naomi Shihab Nye, William Jay Smith, Buson;
Nikki Giovanni, Mary Ellen Solt, Bashō
Build Language Skills: Vocabulary

Roots

The word *transform* contains the root *-trans-*, which means "across" or "through." *Transform* means "change the nature or form of." Words that contain the root *-trans-* will have something to do with the idea of *across* or *through.*

> The first snowfall <u>transforms</u> the autumn landscape into a winter wonderland.

A. DIRECTIONS: *Indicate whether each statement is* true *or* false. *Then, explain your answer.*

1. If a man *transforms* his appearance, he looks the same as before.

   True/false: _________________ **Explanation:** _______________________

   ____

2. If you *transfer* to another school, you attend a school somewhere else.

   True/false: _________________ **Explanation:** _______________________

   ____

Academic Vocabulary

infer	refer	transform	detect	conclude

B. DIRECTIONS: *Answer each question with a complete sentence using the Academic Vocabulary word that means the same as the underlined word or words.*

1. You could <u>make a logical assumption</u> about a dog that is begging. What would it be?

   ____

2. What kind of smell might you <u>notice</u> in a bakery?

   ____

3. What is an easy way to <u>change</u> the way you look?

   ____

4. You could <u>consult a source</u> to find out about animals that burrow. What source would you consult?

   ____

5. If a classmate does well on a difficult test, you can <u>form a judgment based on the evidence</u>. What judgment would you form?

   ____

Unit 4 Resources: Poetry

Poetry Collections: Naomi Shihab Nye, William Jay Smith, Buson;
Nikki Giovanni, Mary Ellen Solt, Bashō

Build Language Skills: Grammar

Infinitives and Infinitive Phrases

An **infinitive** is a verb that acts as a noun, an adjective, or an adverb. An infinitive usually begins with the word *to.*

Some dogs like *to swim.* (infinitive as a noun serving as the object of the verb *like*)

To travel is my objective. (infinitive as a noun serving as the subject of the sentence)

Paris is the city *to visit.* (infinitive as an adjective modifying the noun *city*)

Everyone waited *to hear.* (infinitive as an adverb modifying the verb *waited*)

An **infinitive phrase** is an infinitive plus its own modifiers or complements.

Some dogs like *to swim all year round.* (phrase serving as object of the verb *like*)

To travel in Europe is my objective. (phrase serving as subject of the sentence)

Paris is the city *to visit in the spring.* (phrase modifying the noun *city*)

Everyone waited *to hear the news.* (phrase modifying the verb *waited*)

A. PRACTICE: *Underline the infinitive in each sentence, and circle any infinitive phrases.*

1. In "Winter," the speaker goes outside to air her quilts.
2. To create a poem that looks like a forsythia bush was the aim of Mary Ellen Solt.
3. In "The Rider," the roller skater wants to escape his loneliness.
4. In one of Buson's haiku, "not one leaf dares to move."
5. In "Seal," the seal loves to swim fast.

B. Writing Application: *Review the poems in these collections. Then, write a sentence that captures your reaction to each poem and includes an infinitive or an infinitive phrase.*

1. **"The Rider":** ____

   ____

2. **"Seal":** ____

   ____

3. **One of Buson's haiku:** ____

   ____

4. **"Winter":** ____

   ____

5. **"Forsythia":** ____

   ____

Poetry Collection: Naomi Long Madgett, Wendy Rose, Edna St. Vincent Millay
Reading: Connect the Details to Draw a Conclusion

A **conclusion** is a decision or opinion that you reach after considering the details in a literary work. **Connecting the details** can help you draw conclusions as you read. For example, if the speaker in a poem uses the words *spits, growls, snarls, trembling, shudder, unravel,* and *dislodge,* you might conclude that he or she is expressing dissatisfaction, anger, or some aspect of violence. As you read, identify important details. Then, look at the details together and draw a conclusion about the poem or the speaker.

DIRECTIONS: *In the first column of the chart below are details from the poems in this collection. Consider each set of details, and use them to draw a conclusion about the poem. Write your conclusion in the second column.*

Details	Conclusion
"Life": • The speaker says that life is a toy. • The toy ticks for a while, amusing an infant. • The toy, a watch, stops running.	
"Loo-Wit": • The old woman is "bound" by cedar. • Huckleberry "ropes" lie around her neck. • Machinery operates on her skin.	
"The Courage That My Mother Had": • The speaker's mother had courage. • The speaker has a brooch her mother wore. • The speaker wants her mother's courage.	

Poetry Collection: Naomi Long Madgett, Wendy Rose, Edna St. Vincent Millay
Literary Analysis: Figurative Language

Figurative language is language that is not meant to be taken literally. Writers use figures of speech to express ideas in vivid and imaginative ways. Common figures of speech include the following:

- A **simile** compares two unlike things using a word such as *like* or *as.*
- A **metaphor** compares two unlike things by stating that one thing is another thing. In an **extended metaphor,** several related comparisons extend over a number of lines.
- **Personification** gives human characteristics to a nonhuman subject.
- A **symbol** is an object, person, animal, place, or image that represents something else.

Look at this line from "Life." What figure of speech does the speaker use?

Life is but a toy that swings on a bright gold chain.

The speaker uses a metaphor to compare life to a toy, one "that swings on a bright gold chain."

DIRECTIONS: *As you read the poems in this collection, record the similes, metaphors, extended metaphors, personification, and symbols.*

Poem	Passage	Figurative Language
"Life"		
"Loo-Wit"		
"The Courage That My Mother Had"		

Name _______________________________________ Date _______________________

Poetry Collection: Naomi Long Madgett, Wendy Rose, Edna St. Vincent Millay
Vocabulary Builder

Word List

crouches   unravel   dislodge

A. DIRECTIONS: *Read each sentence, paying attention to the italicized word. Then, explain whether the sentence makes sense. If it does not make sense, rewrite the sentence or write a new sentence, using the italicized word correctly.*

1. The angry woman *crouches* as she stretches herself on her bumpy bed.

   Explanation: ____

   ____

   New sentence: ____

2. If you *dislodge* the stones, they may start an avalanche.

   Explanation: ____

   ____

   New sentence: ____

3. The sweater was so well made that it began to *unravel.*

   Explanation: ____

   ____

   New sentence: ____

B. DIRECTIONS: *Write the letter of the word whose meaning is most nearly* opposite *that of the word from the Word List.*

____ 1. dislodge
    A. throw   B. bind   C. uproot   D. move

____ 2. crouches
    A. stands   B. walks   C. stoops   D. falls

____ 3. unravel
    A. untangle   B. toss   C. separate   D. tangle

Poetry Collection: Naomi Long Madgett, Wendy Rose, Edna St. Vincent Millay
Support for Writing an Extended Metaphor

Use the word web below to collect ideas for an **extended metaphor** about life. First, decide what you will compare life to, and write that idea at the center of the web. Then, complete the web by writing down ideas that relate to your central idea. Use vivid images and descriptive language. Your extended metaphor may include similes, metaphors, personification, and symbols.

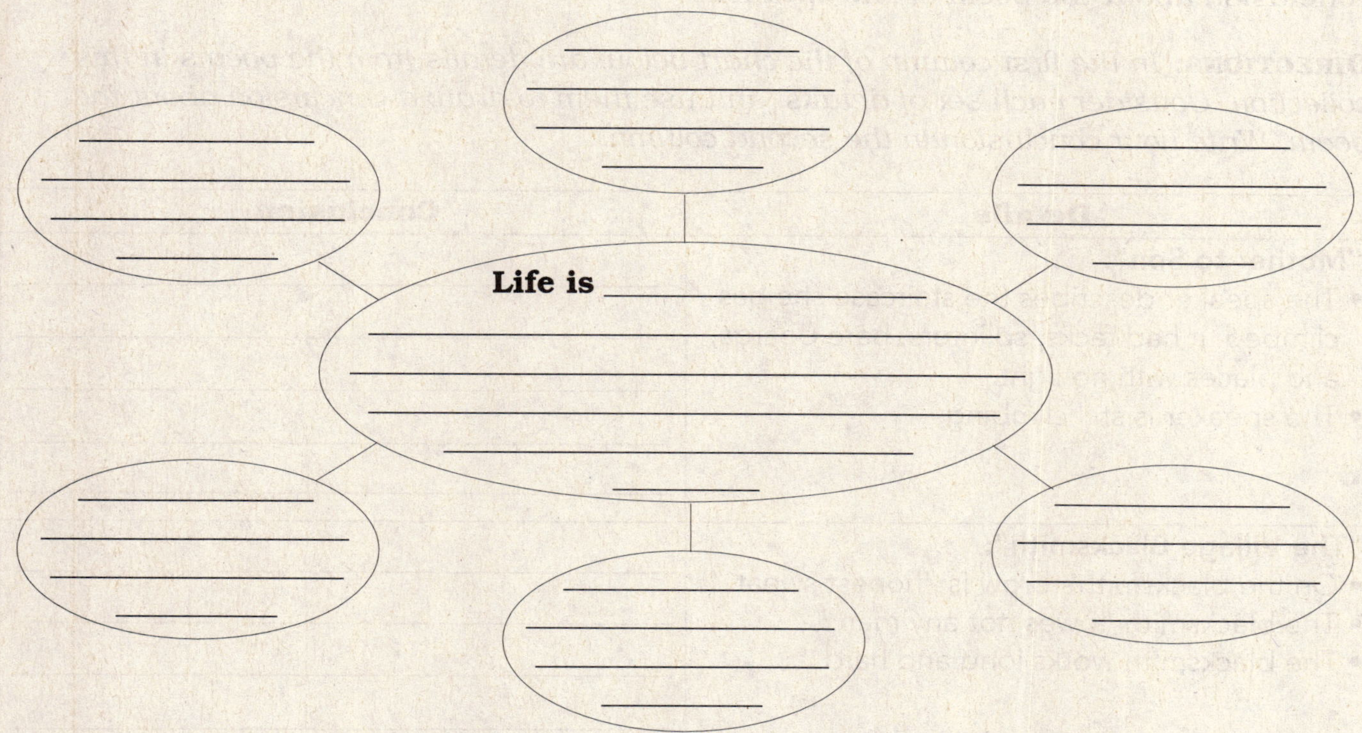

Now, use your notes to write an extended metaphor about life. Be sure to use vivid images and descriptive language.

Poetry Collection: Langston Hughes, Henry Wadsworth Longfellow, Carl Sandburg
Reading: Connect the Details to Draw a Conclusion

A **conclusion** is a decision or opinion that you reach after considering the details in a literary work. **Connecting the details** can help you draw conclusions as you read. For example, if the speaker in a poem uses the words *tacks*, *splinters*, *boards*, *bare*, and *dark*, you might conclude that he or she wishes to create an image of hardship. As you read, identify important details. Then, look at the details together and draw a conclusion about the poem or the speaker.

DIRECTIONS: *In the first column of the chart below are details from the poems in this collection. Consider each set of details, and use them to draw a conclusion about the poem. Write your conclusion in the second column.*

Details	Conclusion
"Mother to Son": • The speaker describes the staircase she has climbed: it had tacks, splinters, bare boards, and places with no light. • The speaker is still climbing.	
"The Village Blacksmith": • On the blacksmith's brow is "honest sweat." • The blacksmith "owes not any man." • The blacksmith works long and hard.	
"Fog": • The fog arrives "on little cat feet." • The fog sits "on silent haunches." • The fog looks "over harbor and city / . . . and then moves on."	

Poetry Collection: Langston Hughes, Henry Wadsworth Longfellow, Carl Sandburg
Literary Analysis: Figurative Language

Figurative language is language that is not meant to be taken literally. Writers use figures of speech to express ideas in vivid and imaginative ways. Common figures of speech include the following:

- A **simile** compares two unlike things using a word such as *like* or *as*.
- A **metaphor** compares two unlike things by stating that one thing is another thing. In an **extended metaphor,** several related comparisons extend over a number of lines.
- **Personification** gives human characteristics to a nonhuman subject.
- A **symbol** is an object, person, animal, place, or image that represents something else.

Look at this line from "The Village Blacksmith." What figure of speech does the speaker use?

> And the muscles of his brawny arms
>
> Are strong as iron bands.

The speaker uses a simile to compare the blacksmith's muscles to iron bands.

DIRECTIONS: *As you read the poems in this collection, record the similes, metaphors, extended metaphors, personification, and symbols you find in the poems.*

Poem	Passage	Figurative Language
"Mother to Son"		
"The Village Blacksmith"		
"Fog"		

Name ____   Date _______________________

Vocabulary Builder

Word List

haunches	sinewy	brawny

A. DIRECTIONS: *Read each sentence, paying attention to the italicized word. Then, explain whether the sentence makes sense. If it does not make sense, rewrite the sentence or write a new sentence, using the italicized word correctly.*

1. The cheetah sprang from its *haunches* to bring down the fleeing antelope.

   Explanation: ____

   ____

   New sentence: ____

2. Because the blacksmith was *brawny*, he easily lifted the heavy sledgehammer.

   Explanation: ____

   ____

   New sentence: ____

3. The *sinewy* construction worker could carry only the lightest loads.

   Explanation: ____

   ____

   New sentence: ____

B. DIRECTIONS: *Provide an explanation for your answer to each question.*

1. Would a person who is balancing on his or her *haunches* be lying down?

   ____

   ____

2. Would a person who got no exercise be *brawny*?

   ____

   ____

3. Would a person with *sinewy* hands be able to carve granite?

   ____

   ____

Poetry Collection: Langston Hughes, Henry Wadsworth Longfellow, Carl Sandburg
Support for Writing an Extended Metaphor

Use the word web below to collect ideas for an **extended metaphor** about a quality or an idea, such as love, loyalty, or death. Decide on the quality or idea, and then decide what you will compare it to. It may be an object, an animal, or an idea. Write your ideas in the center of the web. Then, complete the web by writing down ideas that relate to your central idea. Use vivid images and descriptive language. Your extended metaphor may include similes, metaphors, personification, and symbols.

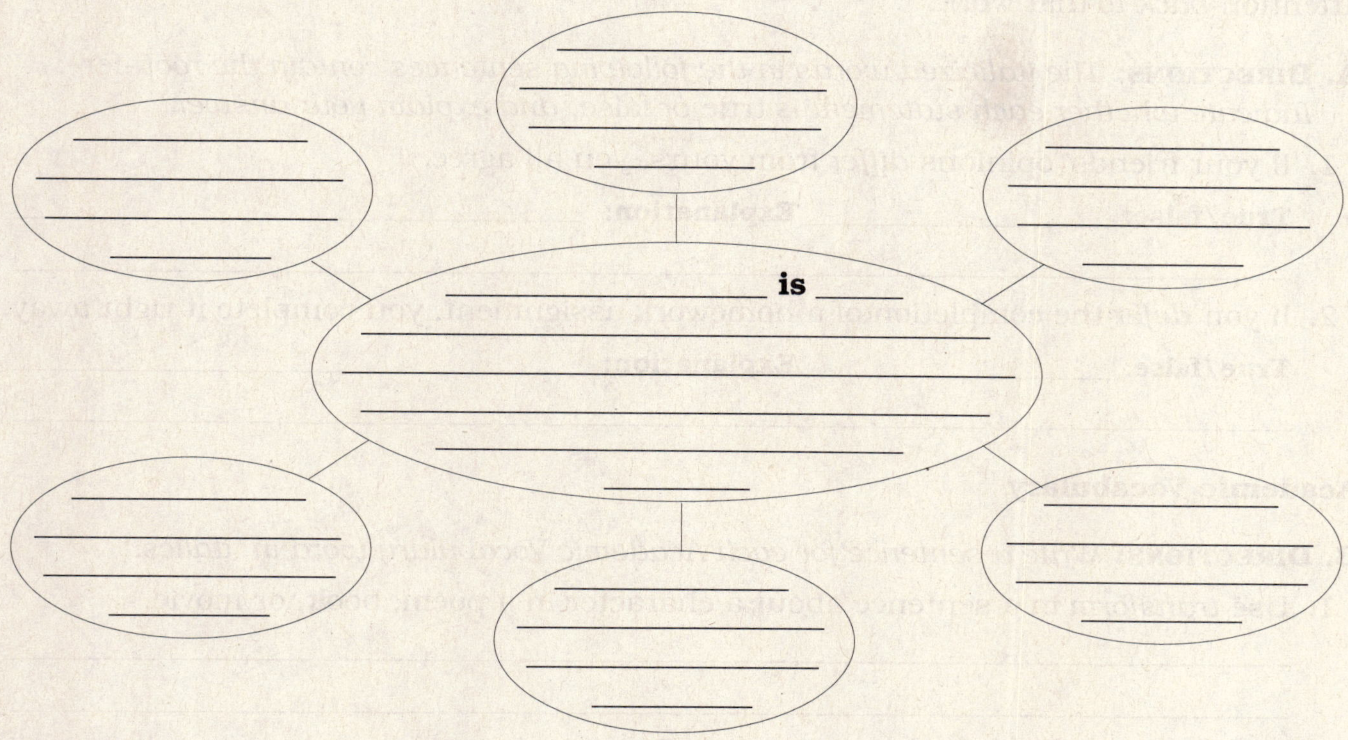

Now, use your notes to write an extended metaphor about a quality or an idea. Be sure to use vivid images and descriptive language.

Poetry Collections: Naomi Long Madgett, Wendy Rose, Edna St. Vincent Millay;
Langston Hughes, Henry Wadsworth Longfellow, Carl Sandburg

Build Language Skills: Vocabulary

Roots

The root *-fer-* means "bring" or "carry." When you **infer** something, you read between the lines and, in effect, *bring to* a piece of literature a meaning that is not directly stated in it.

Refer comes from the root *-fer-* and the prefix *re-*, which means "back." When you **refer** to information you have read in a work of literature, you *bring* the reader's attention *back to* that work.

A. DIRECTIONS: *The italicized words in the following sentences contain the root -fer-. Indicate whether each statement is* true *or* false, *and explain your answer.*

1. If your friends' opinions *differ* from yours, you all agree.

   True/false: ________________ **Explanation:** ________________________

   ____

2. If you *defer* the completion of a homework assignment, you complete it right away.

   True/false: ________________ **Explanation:** ________________________

   ____

Academic Vocabulary

B. DIRECTIONS: *Write a sentence for each Academic Vocabulary word in italics.*

1. Use *transform* in a sentence about a character in a poem, book, or movie.

   ____

   ____

2. Use *conclude* in a sentence about the village blacksmith.

   ____

   ____

3. Use *refer* in a sentence about advice that a mother might give her son or daughter.

   ____

   ____

4. Use *detect* in a sentence about volcanoes.

   ____

   ____

5. Use *infer* in a sentence about fog.

   ____

   ____

Poetry Collections: Naomi Long Madgett, Wendy Rose, Edna St. Vincent Millay; Langston Hughes, Henry Wadsworth Longfellow, Carl Sandburg

Build Language Skills: Grammar

Appositives and Appositive Phrases

An **appositive** is a noun or pronoun that is placed after another noun or pronoun to identify, rename, or explain it. In the following sentence, the appositive is underlined:

> In "Fog," the poet compares an animal, a <u>cat</u>, to fog.

An **appositive phrase** is a noun or pronoun, along with any modifiers, that is placed after another noun or pronoun to identify, rename, or explain it. In the following sentence, the appositive is underlined; the words that make up the appositive phrase are in italics:

> Longfellow made the village blacksmith, *an honest and reliable <u>man</u>*, into a hero.

A. PRACTICE: *In each sentence, underline the appositive phrase. Then, circle the noun that the appositive phrase identifies or explains.*

1. Loo-Wit, a volcano, is about to erupt.
2. Death, an old man, lets the watch run down.
3. The speaker in "The Courage That My Mother Had" mentions New England, a region in the northeast.
4. The speaker in "The Courage That My Mother Had" compares her mother's courage to granite, a hard rock.
5. The village blacksmith weeps when he hears the voice of his daughter, a singer in the choir.
6. In "Mother to Son," a poem by Langston Hughes, a mother gives advice to her son.

B. Writing Application: *Use each phrase in brackets as an appositive phrase in the sentence that follows it. Set off each phrase with commas or dashes.*

1. [a beautiful golden pin] In "The Courage That My Mother Had," the speaker's mother has given the speaker a brooch.

____

____

2. [a blanket of white mist] In "Fog," fog covers a harbor.

____

3. [a symbol of an easy life] The mother in "Mother to Son" speaks of the crystal stair.

____

____

Poetry by Alfred Noyes, Robert Service, and Gregory Djanikian
Literary Analysis: Comparing Narrative Poems

Narrative poetry combines elements of fiction and poetry to tell a story. Like short stories, narrative poetry usually includes characters, setting, plot, conflict, and point of view. Like other poems, narrative poetry uses sound devices, such as rhythm and rhyme, to bring out the musical qualities of the language. It also uses figurative language to create memorable images, or word pictures.

Narrative poetry is well suited to a wide range of stories. For example, narrative poems may tell romantic tales about knights and ladies, heroic deeds, amazing events, or larger-than-life characters. In contrast, the form may be used to relate everyday stories about ordinary people.

The poems presented in this collection blend elements of fiction and poetry in a memorable way. As you read these poems, look for ways in which each one blends the elements of narration and poetry.

DIRECTIONS: *Complete this chart about the narrative poems in this collection. In the second column, briefly describe the poem's plot and conflict. In the third column, describe the sound devices and/or figurative language in the poem.*

Poem	Plot and Conflict	Poetic Devices
"The Highwayman"		
"The Cremation of Sam McGee"		
"How I Learned English"		

Poetry by Alfred Noyes, Robert Service, and Gregory Djanikian
Vocabulary Builder

Word List

torrent	bound	strive	whimper	loathed	transfixed	writhing

A. DIRECTIONS: *Pay attention to the way the italicized vocabulary word is used in each sentence. Then, indicate whether the statement is* true *or* false, *and explain your answer.*

1. If a dog were *bound* to a tree, it would be free to roam.

   T / F: ______ **Explanation:** ____________________________________

2. Someone who *loathed* cold weather would want to visit Alaska in the winter.

   T / F: ______ **Explanation:** ____________________________________

3. Someone *writhing* in pain is lying still.

   T / F: ______ **Explanation:** ____________________________________

4. A *torrent* of rain is likely to cause a river to overflow its banks.

   T / F: ______ **Explanation:** ____________________________________

5. If children *whimper,* they are probably content.

   T / F: ______ **Explanation:** ____________________________________

6. Someone *transfixed* by fear is running to escape danger.

   T / F: ______ **Explanation:** ____________________________________

7. People who *strive* are usually very lazy.

   T / F: ______ **Explanation:** ____________________________________

B. DIRECTIONS: *Write the letter of the word or words whose meaning is most* opposite *that of the word from the Word List.*

____ 1. whimper
   A. laugh   B. complain   C. whine   D. cry

____ 2. bound
   A. tied   B. released   C. confined   D. restrained

____ 3. loathed
   A. detested   B. loved   C. hated   D. despised

____ 4. strive
   A. attempt   B. try   C. give up   D. fight for

Poetry by Alfred Noyes, Robert Service, and Gregory Djanikian
Support for Writing to Compare Literary Works

Use this chart to take notes for an essay comparing and contrasting the stories that are told in the three narrative poems in this collection.

Point of Comparison	"The Highwayman"	"The Cremation of Sam McGee"	"How I Learned English"
Who narrates the poem? Is it a character in the poem or someone outside the poem?			
Is there any suspense? If so, when does it occur and why?			
How do the poetic elements increase my interest in or my appreciation of the story?			

Now, use your notes to write an essay comparing and contrasting the poems' stories.

Poetry Collection: Shel Silverstein, Eve Merriam, James Berry

Reading: Read Aloud According to Punctuation
in Order to Paraphrase

When you **paraphrase,** you restate something in your own words. To paraphrase a poem, you must first understand it. **Reading aloud according to punctuation** can help you identify complete thoughts in a poem and therefore grasp its meaning. Because poets do not always complete a sentence at the end of a line, pausing simply because a line ends can interfere with your understanding of the meaning. Follow these rules when you read aloud:

- Keep reading when a line has no end punctuation.
- Pause at commas, dashes, and semicolons.
- Stop at end marks, such as periods, question marks, or exclamation points.

As you read poetry, allow the punctuation to help you paraphrase the poet's ideas.

DIRECTIONS: *The following items are from "Sarah Cynthia Sylvia Stout Would Not Take the Garbage Out," "Weather," or "One." Read each item aloud, following the rules above. Then, paraphrase the lines. That is, restate them in your own words.*

1. Dot a dot dot dot a dot dot
   Spotting the windowpane.

   ____

   ____

2. Nobody can get into my clothes for me
   or feel my fall for me, or do my running.
   Nobody hears my music for me, either.

   ____

   ____

3. Poor Sarah met an awful fate,
   That I cannot right now relate
   Because the hour is much too late.
   But children, remember Sarah Stout
   And always take the garbage out!

   ____

   ____

   ____

   ____

   ____

Name ____ Date _________________________

Literary Analysis: Sound Devices

Sound devices create musical effects that appeal to the ear. Here are some common sound devices used in poetry:

- **Onomatopoeia** is the use of words whose sounds suggest their meaning:

  The explosion made a thunderous <u>boom</u>. The snake uttered a <u>hiss</u>.

- **Alliteration** is the repetition of sounds at the beginnings of words:

  <u>Sh</u>e <u>s</u>ells <u>s</u>ea <u>sh</u>ells by the <u>s</u>ea <u>sh</u>ore.

- **Repetition** is the repeated use of words, phrases, and/or rhythms:

  I said, "Come," / I said, "Sit," / My dog would have none of it.

In the last example, there is repetition of both the words (*I said*) and the rhythm. In poetry, a line may contain more than one sound device.

DIRECTIONS: *The following items are from "Sarah Cynthia Sylvia Stout Would Not Take the Garbage Out," "Weather," or "One." Read each item, and decide which sound devices the lines contain. Then, identify the sound devices in each line by writing* Onomatopoeia, Alliteration, *and/or* Repetition. *An item may contain more than one sound device.*

1. Prune pits, peach pits, orange peel

   ____

2. Crusts of black burned buttered toast

   ____

3. A spatter a scatter a wet cat a clatter
   A splatter a rumble outside.

   ____

4. And mirrors can show me multiplied
   Many times

   ____

5. Umbrella umbrella umbrella umbrella
   Bumbershoot barrel of rain.

   ____

6. Sarah Cynthia Sylvia Stout
   Would not take the garbage out!

   ____

7. Slosh a galosh slosh a galosh
   Slither and slather a glide

   ____

Poetry Collection: Shel Silverstein, Eve Merriam, James Berry
Vocabulary Builder

Word List

withered   rancid   stutter

A. DIRECTIONS: *Read each item, and think about the meaning of the italicized word from the Word List. Then, answer the question, and explain your answer.*

1. The *withered* flowers had been in the vase for a week. Were the flowers brightly colored?

   ____

2. The hungry twins found *rancid* cheese in the refrigerator. Would they have thrown it out or eaten it?

   ____

3. The suspect began to *stutter* when he was questioned. Was he nervous? How can you tell?

   ____

B. DIRECTIONS: *Revise each sentence so that the italicized vocabulary word is used logically. Be sure to keep the vocabulary word in your revision.*

1. The florist made up a bouquet of *withered* roses and daisies.

   ____

2. The fresh salad contained tomatoes, lettuce, and *rancid* dressing.

   ____

3. The announcer did not hesitate or falter, speaking with a *stutter.*

   ____

C. DIRECTIONS: *Write the letter of the word or group of words that mean the same or about the same as the word from the Word List.*

____ 1. withered
   A. freshly cut   B. dried out   C. well watered   D. newly planted

____ 2. rancid
   A. fragrant   B. expensive   C. spoiled   D. burned

____ 3. stutter
   A. falter   B. close   C. quarrel   D. shout

Poetry Collection: Shel Silverstein, Eve Merriam, James Berry
Support for Writing a Poem Called "Alliteration"

Use this chart as you draft a **poem** called "Alliteration."

"Alliteration": A Poem
Alliteration, defined by the textbook: "Alliteration is the repetition of sounds at the beginning of words."
Alliteration, defined in my own words: ________________________________   ____   ____
Example of alliteration: <u>Sh</u>e <u>s</u>ells <u>s</u>ea <u>sh</u>ells by the <u>s</u>ea <u>sh</u>ore.
My own example of alliteration: _______________________________   ____   ____   ____
My poem, combining my definition of alliteration with my examples of alliteration: ____   ____   ____   ____   ____   ____   ____   ____

Look over your poem to be sure your examples work. Do they contain words that begin with the same sound? Then, check your definition. Does it correctly define alliteration? Revise your poem before creating your final draft.

Poetry Collection: William Shakespeare, Eve Merriam, Louise Bogan
Reading: Read Aloud According to Punctuation
in Order to Paraphrase

When you **paraphrase,** you restate something in your own words. To paraphrase a poem, you must first understand it. **Reading aloud according to punctuation** can help you identify complete thoughts in a poem and therefore grasp its meaning. Because poets do not always complete a sentence at the end of a line, pausing simply because a line ends can interfere with your understanding of the meaning. Follow these rules when you read aloud:

- Keep reading when a line has no end punctuation.
- Pause at commas, dashes, and semicolons.
- Stop at end marks, such as periods, question marks, or exclamation points.

As you read poetry, allow the punctuation to help you paraphrase the poet's ideas.

DIRECTIONS: *The following items are from "Full Fathom Five," "Onomatopoeia," or "Train Tune." Read each item aloud, following the rules above. Then, paraphrase the lines. That is, restate them in your own words.*

1. spurts,
   finally stops sputtering
   and plash!
   gushes rushes splashes
   clear water dashes.

   ____

   ____

2. Back through lightning
   Back through cities
   Back through stars
   Back through hours

   ____

   ____

3. Sea nymphs hourly ring his knell;
   Ding-dong.
   Hark! Now I hear them ding-dong bell.

   ____

   ____

Poetry Collection: William Shakespeare, Eve Merriam, Louise Bogan

Literary Analysis: Sound Devices

Sound devices create musical effects that appeal to the ear. Here are some common sound devices used in poetry:

- **Onomatopoeia** is the use of words whose sounds suggest their meaning:

  The saw cut through the tree with a <u>buzz</u>. The librarian <u>murmured</u> her answer.

- **Alliteration** is the repetition of sounds at the beginnings of words:

  <u>P</u>eter <u>P</u>iper <u>p</u>icked a <u>p</u>eck of <u>p</u>ickled <u>p</u>eppers.

- **Repetition** is the repeated use of words, phrases, and/or rhythms:

  <u>The leaves blew</u> up, / <u>The leaves blew</u> down, / <u>The leaves blew</u> all around the town.

In the last example, there is repetition of both the words (*The leaves blew*) and the rhythm. In poetry, a line may contain more than one sound device.

DIRECTIONS: *The following items are from "Full Fathom Five," "Onomatopoeia," or "Train Tune." Read each item, and decide which sound devices the lines contain. Then, identify the sound devices in each line by writing* Onomatopoeia, Alliteration, *and/or* Repetition. *An item may contain more than one sound device.*

1. Full fathom five thy father lies

   ____

2. The rusty spigot
   sputters,
   utters
   a splutter

   ____

3. Back through clouds
   Back through clearing
   Back through distance
   Back through silence

   ____

4. finally stops sputtering
   and plash!
   gushes rushes splashes
   clear water dashes

   ____

5. Nothing of him that doth fade
   But doth suffer a sea change
   Into something rich and strange.

   ____

Poetry Collection: William Shakespeare, Eve Merriam, Louise Bogan
Vocabulary Builder

Word List

spigot   sputters   groves

A. DIRECTIONS: *Read each item, and think about the meaning of the italicized word from the Word List. Then, answer the question, and explain your answer.*

1. If a plumber says you need a new *spigot*, should you purchase a device to keep water from running down the drain?

   ____

2. If a person *sputters* as she speaks, is she likely to be calm?

   ____

3. If there are orange *groves* on your property, are there trees on your property?

   ____

B. DIRECTIONS: *Decide whether each statement is true or false. Write* T *or* F. *Then, explain your answer.*

1. If a spigot has been shut off, water will not flow through it.

   T / F: ______ **Explanation:** ____

2. Most of the time, a newly tuned-up car sputters when you start it.

   T / F: ______ **Explanation:** ____

3. Groves are good places to play soccer.

   T / F: ______ **Explanation:** ____

C. DIRECTIONS: *Write the letter of the word or group of words that* mean the same or *about the same as* the word from the Word List.

____ 1. spigot

    A. bouquet   B. pipe   C. faucet   D. twig

____ 2. sputters

    A. sings   B. spits   C. growls   D. screeches

____ 3. groves

    A. slopes   B. gardens   C. fields   D. woods

Poetry Collection: William Shakespeare, Eve Merriam, Louise Bogan
Support for Writing a Poem Called "Alliteration"

Use this chart as you draft a **poem** called "Alliteration."

"Alliteration": A Poem
Alliteration, defined by the textbook: "Alliteration is the repetition of sounds at the beginning of words."
Alliteration, defined in my own words: ___________________________   ____   ____
Example of alliteration: <u>P</u>eter <u>P</u>iper <u>p</u>icked a <u>p</u>eck of <u>p</u>ickled <u>p</u>eppers.
My own example of alliteration: ______________________________   ____   ____   ____
My poem, combining my definition of alliteration with my examples of alliteration: ____   ____   ____   ____   ____   ____   ____

Look over your poem to be sure your examples work. Do they contain words that begin with the same sound? Then, check your definition. Does it correctly define alliteration? Revise your poem before creating your final draft.

Unit 4 Resources: Poetry

Poetry Collections: Shel Silverstein, Eve Merriam, James Berry;
William Shakespeare, Eve Merriam, Louise Bogan

Build Language Skills: Vocabulary

Synonyms

The words *emphasize* and *highlight* are **synonyms**. That is, their meanings may be similar, depending on the context of the sentence. In many cases, one synonym can replace another in a sentence without changing the basic meaning of the sentence. Almost always, there are slight differences in meaning between synonyms.

Notice that either *highlight* or *emphasize* can be used in either of these sentences:

Use a yellow marker to <u>highlight</u> the important material in your reading.

To be sure your reader can understand your argument, <u>emphasize</u> your main ideas.

A. DIRECTIONS: *Underline the synonyms in each pair of sentences.*

1. Sam says he can imitate the way James dances.
   Have you ever noticed how babies mimic the faces we make?
2. The speaker used presentation software to highlight her important ideas.
   Will the test emphasize the material we studied today?
3. "Sarah Cynthia Sylvia Stout would not take the garbage out."
   Remember to take out the trash before you go to bed.
4. The garden hose is attached to the spigot on the side of the house.
   The faucet in our kitchen sink needs a new washer.
5. It was too rough to go swimming in the sea.
   The ship crossed the ocean in just three days.

Academic Vocabulary Practice

B. DIRECTIONS: *Decide whether each statement is true or false. Write T or F. Then, explain your answer.*

1. A *paraphrase* of a sentence should be longer than the original sentence.

   T / F: ______ **Explanation:** ____

2. If you read a *passage* in a book, you have read the whole book.

   T / F: ______ **Explanation:** ____

3. A good way to study for a test is to *highlight* the main ideas.

   T / F: ______ **Explanation:** ____

4. When you *restate* what a speaker has said, you add your interpretation of what the speaker has said.

   T / F: ______ **Explanation:** ____

5. If you want to *emphasize* something, do not draw attention to it.

   T / F: ______ **Explanation:** ____

Poetry Collections: Shel Silverstein, Eve Merriam, James Berry;
William Shakespeare, Eve Merriam, Louise Bogan

Build Language Skills: Grammar

Independent and Subordinate Clauses

A **clause** is a group of words with its own subject and verb. There are two types of clauses: independent clauses and subordinate clauses. An **independent clause** expresses a complete thought and can stand alone as a sentence.

A **subordinate clause** (also called a **dependent clause**) has a subject and a verb, but it does not express a complete thought. Therefore, it cannot stand alone as a sentence. The following sentence contains both an independent clause and a subordinate clause. The subject in each clause is underlined once, and the verb is underlined twice. The subordinate clause appears in italics:

Shel Silverstein was a cartoonist and a writer, *though he also composed songs.*

A subordinate clause may appear either before or after the independent clause:

Though he also composed songs, Shel Silverstein was a cartoonist and a writer.

A. DIRECTIONS: *In each sentence, underline the independent clause once and the subordinate clause twice.*

1. Eve Merriam's lifelong love was poetry even though she wrote fiction, nonfiction, and drama.
2. Because language and its sound gave Eve Merriam great joy, she tried to communicate her enjoyment by writing poetry for children.
3. Berry moved to the United States when he was seventeen.
4. If Berry had not lost his job as a telegraph operator, he might not have become a writer.
5. Because he did not play ball or dance when he was young, Shel Silverstein began to draw and write.
6. Silverstein began to draw cartoons after he served in the military.

B. Writing Application: *Rewrite each sentence by adding a subordinate clause.*

1. Sarah Stout was a stubborn young woman.

   ____

2. The rain spotted the windowpane.

   ____

3. Anyone can dance like me.

   ____

4. The drowned man's bones had turned to coral.

   ____

Poetry Collection: Edgar Allan Poe, Raymond Richard Patterson, Emily Dickinson
Reading: Reread in Order to Paraphrase

To **paraphrase** means to restate or explain something in your own words. When you paraphrase lines of poetry, you make the meaning clear to yourself. If you are unsure of a poem's meaning, **reread** the parts that are difficult. Follow these steps:

- Look up unfamiliar words, and replace them with words you know.
- Restate the line or passage using your own everyday words.
- Reread the passage to make sure that your version makes sense.

Look at these lines from the poem "Martin Luther King":

He came upon an age / Beset by grief, by rage

The first line tells you that King "came upon an age." If you look up "come upon" in a dictionary, you will learn that it means "meet by chance." In this case, you might use a looser definition: "happen to live in." *Age* can refer to the number of years a person has lived or to a period in history. In this case, it refers to a period of history a time when African Americans did not have the same rights as white Americans.

If you looked up *beset,* you would discover that one of its meanings is "troubled." You probably know that *grief* is a synonym for *sorrow* or *sadness* and that *rage* is a synonym for *anger.* Now you have all the ingredients for a paraphrase of the line. It might look like this:

He happened to live at a time that was troubled by sorrow and anger.

DIRECTIONS: *Read these passages from "Annabel Lee," "Martin Luther King," and "I'm Nobody." Following the process described above, write a paraphrase of each passage.*

1. "A wind blew out of a cloud by night / Chilling my Annabel Lee; /
   So that her highborn kinsmen came / And bore her away from me, /
   To shut her up in a sepulcher / In this kingdom by the sea."

   ____

   ____

   ____

2. "He came upon an age / Beset by grief and rage—
   His love so deep, so wide / He could not turn aside."

   ____

   ____

   ____

3. "How dreary to be Somebody! / How public like a Frog /
   To tell your name the livelong June / To an admiring Bog!"

   ____

   ____

   ____

Poetry Collection: Edgar Allan Poe, Raymond Richard Patterson, Emily Dickinson

Literary Analysis: Rhythm, Meter, and Rhyme

Rhythm and rhyme make poetry musical. **Rhythm** is a poem's pattern of stressed (´) and unstressed (˘) syllables.

Meter is a poem's rhythmical pattern. It is measured in *feet,* or single units of stressed and unstressed syllables. In the examples below, stressed and unstressed syllables are marked, and the feet are separated by vertical lines (|). The first line of "Annabel Lee" contains four feet, and the second line contains three feet. The two lines of "Martin Luther King" contain three feet each.

Rhyme is the repetition of sounds at the ends of lines. The two words that rhyme in the lines from "Martin Luther King" are underlined.

It was MÁN | -y and MÁN | -y a YEÁR | a-GÓ. | / In a KÍNG | -dom BÝ | the SÉA.

He CÁME | up-ÓN | an <u>AGE</u> | be-SÉT | by GRIEF, | by <u>RAGE</u>.

A. DIRECTIONS: *Mark the stressed (´) and unstressed (˘) syllables in these lines. Then, show the meter by drawing a vertical rule after each foot.*

1. But our love it was stronger by far than the love / Of those who were older than we

2. His passion, so profound, / He would not turn around.

B. DIRECTIONS: *The words that end each line of "Annabel Lee" and "Martin Luther King" are listed in the following items. In each item, circle each word that rhymes with another word. Then draw lines to connect all the words that rhyme with each other in that item.*

1. ago sea know Lee thought me

2. child sea love Lee Heaven me

3. ago sea night Lee came me sepulcher sea

4. Heaven me know sea chilling Lee

5. love we we above sea soul Lee

6. dreams Lee Lee side bride sea sea

7. age rage / wide aside / profound around / Earth worth / be free

Poetry Collection: Edgar Allan Poe, Raymond Richard Patterson, Emily Dickinson

Vocabulary Builder

Word List

coveted   profound   banish

A. DIRECTIONS: *Read each sentence, and think about the meaning of the italicized word from the Word List. Then, answer the question, and explain your answer.*

1. The speaker in "Annabel Lee" says that the angels *coveted* the love between him and Annabel Lee. Did the angels criticize their love?

   ____

2. The speaker in "Martin Luther King" says that King's passion was *profound*. Was King very passionate?

   ____

3. The speaker in "I'm Nobody" says that "they" will *banish* her if they find out that she is a Nobody. Will "they" accept her in their social circle?

   ____

B. DIRECTIONS: *Answer each question in a complete sentence. In your answer, use a word from the Word List in place of the italicized word or words.*

1. On what subject do you have *weighty* feelings?

   ____

2. What is something you have recently *wished for seriously*?

   ____

3. For what reason might a club *permanently send away* one of its members?

   ____

C. DIRECTIONS: *Write the letter of the word that means* about the same as *the word from the Word List.*

_____ 1. coveted
    A. covered   B. questioned   C. desired   D. hid

_____ 2. profound
    A. deep   B. supportive   C. sideways   D. interested

_____ 3. banish
    A. clean   B. exile   C. imprison   D. relax

Poetry Collection: Edgar Allan Poe, Raymond Richard Patterson, Emily Dickinson
Support for Writing a Paraphrase

Use these charts to draft a **paraphrase** of "Annabel Lee," "Martin Luther King," or "I'm Nobody." In the first chart, write down unfamiliar words from the poem, their dictionary definition, and the restated definition in your own words. In the second chart, write each line of the poem in the first column. In the second column, restate the meaning of the line in your own words.

Title of poem: _______________________________

Word to Look Up	Dictionary Definition	Definition in My Own Words

Poem, Line by Line	Paraphrase, Line by Line

Now, read over your paraphrase to make sure it has the same meaning as the original. Make your revisions as you prepare your final draft.

Poetry Collection: Gwendolyn Brooks, Lewis Carroll, Robert Frost
Reading: Reread in Order to Paraphrase

To **paraphrase** means to restate or explain something in your own words. When you paraphrase lines of poetry, you make the meaning clear to yourself. If you are unsure of a poem's meaning, **reread** the parts that are difficult. Follow these steps:

- Look up unfamiliar words, and replace them with words you know.
- Restate the line or passage using your own everyday words.
- Reread the passage to make sure that your version makes sense.

Look at these lines from "Father William":

"In my youth," said his father, "I took to the law
   And argued each case with my wife;
And the muscular strength which it gave to my jaw
   Has lasted the rest of my life."

The first line tells you that Father William "took to the law." If you look up *law* in a dictionary, you will learn that one of its meanings is "the legal profession." Father William is saying that he was a lawyer. That knowledge will help you understand the second line: Father William prepared for his legal cases by arguing them with his wife. You probably know or can guess that *muscular* has to do with muscles. Now you have all the ingredients to write a paraphrase of the verse. It might look like this:

"When I was young," Father William said, "I was a lawyer
   And I talked over every case with my wife;
And as a result, I developed strong jaw muscles
   That I still have today."

DIRECTIONS: *Read these passages from "Jim," "Father William," and "Stopping by Woods on a Snowy Evening." Following the process described above, write a paraphrase of each passage.*

1. "The sun should drop its greatest gold / On him."

   ____

2. "'In my youth,' said the sage, as he shook his gray locks, / 'I kept all my limbs very supple / By the use of this ointment one shilling the box / Allow me to sell you a couple?'"

   ____

   ____

   ____

3. "He gives his harness bells a shake / To ask if there is some mistake. / The only other sound's the sweep / Of easy wind and downy flake."

   ____

   ____

   ____

Poetry Collection: Gwendolyn Brooks, Lewis Carroll, Robert Frost
Literary Analysis: Rhythm, Meter, and Rhyme

Rhythm and rhyme make poetry musical. **Rhythm** is a poem's pattern of stressed (´) and unstressed (˘) syllables.

Meter is a poem's rhythmical pattern. It is measured in *feet,* or single units of stressed and unstressed syllables. In the examples below, stressed and unstressed syllables are marked, and the feet are separated by vertical lines (|). The first line of "Father William" contains four feet, and the second line contains three feet. The two lines of "Stopping by Woods on a Snowy Evening" contain four feet each.

"You are OLD, | Fa-ther WILL- | iam," the YOUNG | man SAID, |

And your HAIR | has be-COME | ver-y WHITE" |

Rhyme is the repetition of a sounds at the ends of lines. The two words that rhyme in the lines from "Stopping by Woods on a Snowy Evening" are underlined.

My LIT- | tle HORSE | must THINK | it QUEER |

to STOP | with-OUT | a FARM- | house NEAR |

A. DIRECTIONS: *Mark the stressed (´) and unstressed (˘) syllables in these lines. Then, show the meter by drawing a vertical rule after each foot.*

1. "'You are old,' said the youth, 'as I mentioned before. / And have grown most

   uncommonly fat.'"

2. "He gives his harness bells a shake / To ask if there is some mistake. / The only

   other sound's the sweep / Of easy wind and downy flake."

B. DIRECTIONS: *The words that end each verse of "Jim," "Father William," and "Stopping by Woods on a Snowy Evening" are listed in the following items. In each item, circle each word that rhymes with another word. Then draw lines to connect all the words that rhyme with each other in that item.*

1. boy Jim gold him / sick in bread medicine / room see baseball Terribly

2. said white head right / son brain none again before fat door that

3. locks supple box couple / weak suet beak do it law wife jaw life

4. suppose ever nose clever / enough airs stuff downstairs

5. know though here snow / queer near lake year

6. shake mistake sweep flake / deep keep sleep sleep

Poetry Collection: Gwendolyn Brooks, Lewis Carroll, Robert Frost
Vocabulary Builder

Word List

incessantly   sage   supple

A. DIRECTIONS: *Read each item, and think about the meaning of the italicized word from the Word List. Then, answer the question, and explain your answer.*

1. Father William stands on his head *incessantly*. Does he stand on his head for an hour at a time, taking breaks when he gets tired?

   ____

2. Father William is a *sage*. Would he be likely to do well on a quiz show?

   ____

3. Father William used an ointment to keep his joints *supple*. Was he likely to have had trouble bending down to tie his shoes?

   ____

B. DIRECTIONS: *Answer each question in a complete sentence. In your answer, use a word from the Word List in place of the italicized word or words.*

1. What would you do if the person sitting next to you on an airplane talked *continually*?

   ____

2. Is a dancer likely to be *flexible*?

   ____

3. Where are you likely to meet a *very wise person*?

   ____

C. DIRECTIONS: *Write the letter of the word that means about the same as the word from the Word List.*

_____ 1. incessantly
    A. innocently   B. constantly   C. haltingly   D. uncomfortably

_____ 2. sage
    A. salary   B. green   C. seasoning   D. scholar

_____ 3. supple
    A. elastic   B. strong   C. stiff   D. understated

Poetry Collection: Gwendolyn Brooks, Lewis Carroll, Robert Frost

Support for Writing a Paraphrase

Use these charts to draft a **paraphrase** of "Jim," "Father William," or "Stopping by Woods on a Snowy Evening." In the first chart, write down unfamiliar words from the poem, their dictionary definition, and the definition restated in your own words. In the second chart, write each line of the poem in the first column. In the second column, restate the meaning of the line in your own words. If you are paraphrasing "Father William," finish your paraphrase on a separate sheet of paper.

Title of poem: ____

Word to Look Up	Dictionary Definition	Definition in My Own Words

Poem, Line by Line	Paraphrase, Line by Line

Now, read over your paraphrase to make sure it has the same meaning as the original. Make your revisions as you prepare your final draft.

Unit 4 Resources: Poetry

Poetry Collections: Edgar Allan Poe, Raymond Richard Patterson, Emily Dickinson; Gwendolyn Brooks, Lewis Carroll, Robert Frost

Build Language Skills: Vocabulary

Synonyms

The words *paraphrase* and *restate* are **synonyms.** That is, their meanings may be similar, depending on how they are used in a sentence. In many cases, one synonym can replace another in a sentence without changing the basic meaning of the sentence. Almost always, there are slight differences in meaning between synonyms.

Notice that either *paraphrase* or *restate* can be used in either of these sentences:

When you do research, <u>paraphrase</u> information that is not important enough to put in quotation marks.

To show you understand it, please <u>restate</u> the first paragraph of this news article.

A. DIRECTIONS: *Underline the synonyms in each pair of sentences.*

1. I highlight some words when I read a poem silently.
   Doing that reminds me to emphasize those words when I read the poem aloud.

2. If I restate my argument, perhaps you will understand what I am saying.
   If you can paraphrase that difficult poem, it will be clear that you understand it.

3. Jim's mother was sick, and he brought her cocoa, broth, and medicine.
   If you are feeling ill, you should stay in bed.

4. Father William worried that standing on his head would injure the brain.
   If you exercise without stretching first, you may hurt yourself.

5. Father William's son calls his father "uncommonly fat."
   Father William's son is remarkably disrespectful.

Academic Vocabulary Practice

B. DIRECTIONS: *Revise each sentence so that the italicized vocabulary word is used logically. Be sure to keep the vocabulary word in your revision.*

1. *Paraphrase* the last paragraph of the editorial by revising it.

   ____

2. *Emphasize* important points when you read aloud by speaking without expression.

   ____

3. The actors took three hours to perform a *passage* in the play.

   ____

4. You can *restate* what you have read by rereading the entire selection.

   ____

5. In order to *highlight* a section of your reading, cross it out completely.

   ____

Poetry Collections: Edgar Allan Poe, Raymond Richard Patterson, Emily Dickinson;
Gwendolyn Brooks, Lewis Carroll, Robert Frost

Build Language Skills: Grammar

Sentence Structure

A **simple sentence** is an independent clause. That is, it is a group of words that has a
subject and a verb and can stand by itself as a complete thought.

A **compound sentence** consists of two or more independent clauses that are joined
by a conjunction such as *and, but, or,* or *for.*

Lewis Carroll was a mathematician, <u>but</u> he also wrote stories and poetry.

A **complex sentence** contains one independent clause and one or more subordinate
clauses. In this sentence, the subordinate clause is underlined:

<u>Although he was a mathematician</u>, Lewis Carroll also wrote novels.

A. DIRECTIONS: *Identify each sentence below by writing* Simple, Compound, *or*
Complex.

1. Gwendolyn Brooks lived in an area of Chicago known as Bronzeville, and one of her
   volumes of poetry is called *A Street in Bronzeville.*

   ____

2. Although she was primarily a poet, Brooks published a novel, *Maud Martha.*

   ____

3. Gwendolyn Brooks served as the poet laureate of Illinois.

   ____

4. Lewis Carroll's *Alice's Adventures in Wonderland* has been translated into more
   than thirty languages.

   ____

5. Carroll liked to write nonsense verse, and he invented nonsense characters, such
   as the Snark, the Jabberwock, and the twins Tweedledee and Tweedledum.

   ____

B. Writing Application: *Write a short paragraph in which you describe your reaction to
one of the poems in these collections. Tell what you liked most about the poem and
why it appeals to you. Use at least one simple sentence, one compound sentence, and
one complex sentence. Label your sentences by writing* Simple, Compound, *or*
Complex *in parentheses after each one.*

____

____

____

____

Poetry by Walt Whitman and E. E. Cummings
Literary Analysis: Comparing Imagery

In poetry, an **image** is a word or phrase that appeals to one or more of the five senses. Writers use **imagery** to bring poetry to life with descriptions of how their subjects look, sound, feel, taste, and smell.

Both "Miracles" and "in Just-" contain images that appeal to the senses. For example, "wade with naked feet along the beach" appeals to the sense of touch, and "the little lame balloonman" appeals to sight.

DIRECTIONS: *Read each image in the first column, and mark an x in the column or columns to indicate the sense or senses that the image appeals to. The first fifteen images are from "Miracles"; the last nine are from "in Just-."*

Image	Sight	Hearing	Touch	Taste	Smell
1. "walk the streets of Manhattan"					
2. "dart my sight over the roofs"					
3. "stand under trees in the woods"					
4. "talk by day with any one I love"					
5. "sit at table at dinner with the rest"					
6. "look at strangers opposite me"					
7. "honeybees busy around the hive"					
8. "animals feeding in the fields"					
9. "birds, or . . . insects in the air"					
10. "the sundown"					
11. "stars shining so quiet and bright"					
12. "thin curve of the new moon"					
13. "fishes that swim the rocks"					
14. "the motion of the waves"					
15. "the ships with men in them"					
16. "the world is mud-luscious"					
17. "little lame balloonman whistles"					
18. "eddieandbill come running"					
19. "from marbles and piracies"					
20. "the world is puddle-wonderful"					
21. "queer old balloonman whistles"					
22. "bettyandisbel come dancing"					
23. "from hop-scotch and jump-rope"					
24. "goat-footed balloonMan whistles"					

Poetry by Walt Whitman and E. E. Cummings
Vocabulary Builder

Word List

exquisite   distinct

A. DIRECTIONS: *Complete these word maps by writing synonyms, antonyms, and an example sentence for each vocabulary word.*

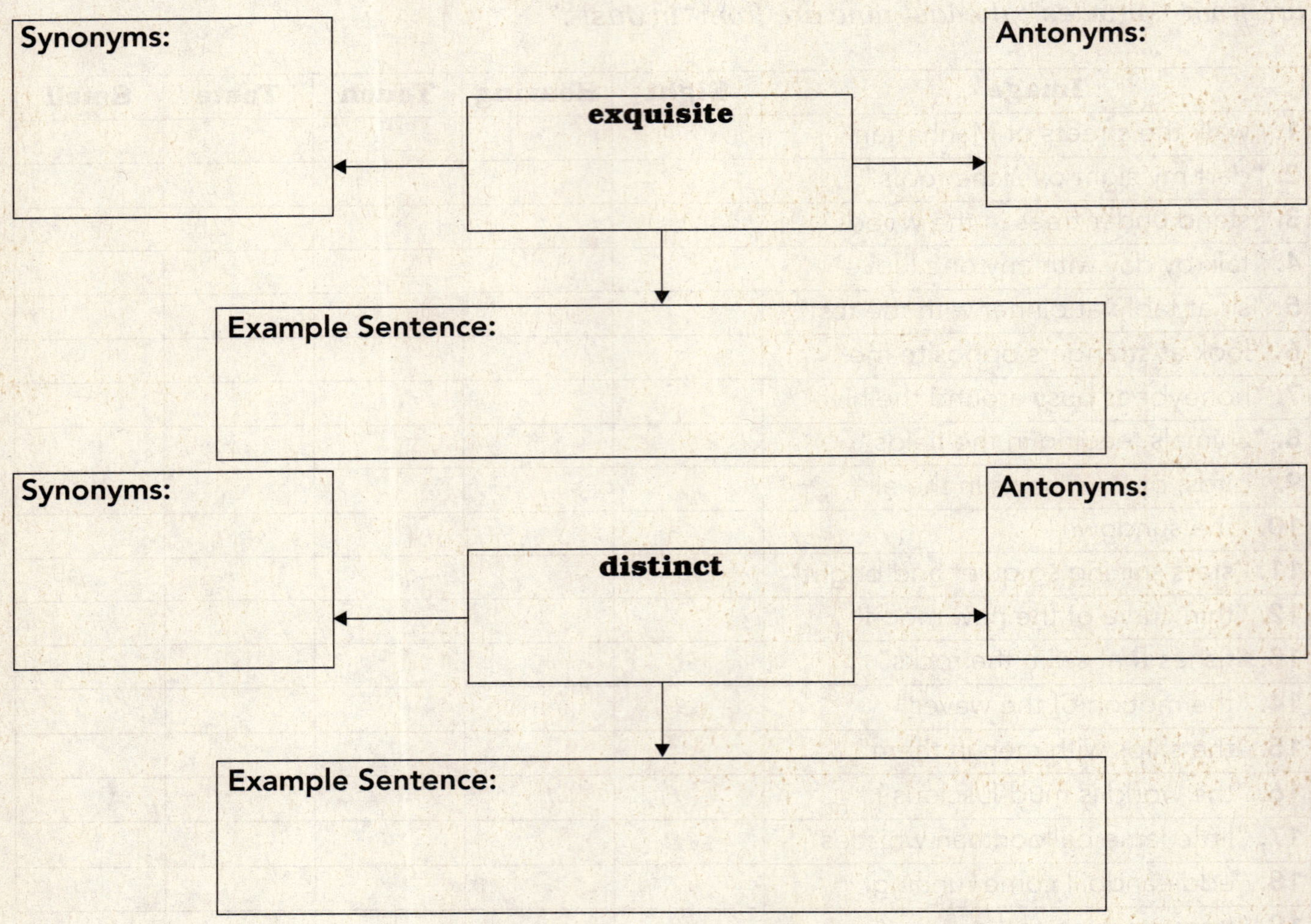

B. DIRECTIONS: *Write the letter of the word or words whose meaning is most nearly the same as the word from the Word List.*

____ 1. exquisite
    A. quaint   B. significant   C. costly   D. beautiful

____ 2. distinct
    A. blurry   B. separate   C. similar   D. pure

Poetry by Walt Whitman and E. E. Cummings
Support for Writing to Compare Literary Works

Use the following graphic organizers as you prepare to write an essay recommending either "Miracles" or "in Just-" to someone your age.

Imagery from "Miracles" that appeals to me:

Sight	Hearing	Touch

Imagery from "in Just-" that appeals to me:

Sight	Hearing	Touch

Which poem's imagery is fascinating or strange? What about it is fascinating or strange?

____

____

Which poem is more musical? Why?

____

____

Which poem's images do I find more meaningful? Why?

____

____

____

Now, use your notes to write an essay about the poem that you would recommend.

Laurence Yep
Listening and Viewing

Segment 1: Meet Laurence Yep
- Why did Laurence Yep identify with the themes he encountered in science fiction?
- Does it surprise you that he chose to write science fiction? Why or why not?

____

____

____

Segment 2: Drama
- According to Yep, what are the differences between a drama and a novel?
- Which form, the drama or the novel, might be more difficult to write? Why?

____

____

____

Segment 3: The Writing Process
- Why does Yep adjust his drafts as he writes?
- What method of Yep's would you be most inclined to try in your own writing? Why?

____

____

____

Segment 4: The Rewards of Writing
- What does Yep think literature can do for young readers?

____

____

____

Unit 5 Resources: Drama

Learning About Drama

Drama is a story told in dialogue by performers in front of an audience. The **playwright** is the author of a drama, which may also be called a *play.* The play itself is written in segments, called **acts.** Acts are often divided into **scenes.**

A playwright uses **characterization** to create believable characters. To advance the action, the playwright creates **dramatic speech.** Two types of dramatic speech are **dialogue,** conversation between two or more characters, and **monologue,** a long speech by a single character. A monologue often reveals a character's thoughts and feelings.

Stage directions describe the scenery and tell how the characters move and speak. The **set** is the construction onstage that suggests the time and place of the action (the setting). **Props** are small movable items that make the set look realistic.

Two types of drama are comedy and tragedy. A **comedy** has a happy ending. It often features ordinary characters in funny situations. In a **tragedy,** the events lead to the downfall of the main character. The main character may be an ordinary person, but the traditional tragic hero is a man of great significance, such as a king.

A. DIRECTIONS: *Read the following excerpt from a drama. Then, answer the questions.*

[*The FISCHERS' kitchen, 7 A.M. MRS. FISCHER sits at kitchen table, reading a newspaper. The door opens. BECKY rushes in. She wears school clothes and carries a book bag.*]

BECKY. Mom! I overslept! I'll miss the tryouts for the play. Why didn't you wake me?

MRS. FISCHER [*getting up from the table*]. Calm down. Let me make you some breakfast.

BECKY [*almost shouting*]. Breakfast? I'm already late!

MRS. FISCHER [*patiently*]. No, dear, you're early. It's Saturday. Tryouts aren't until Monday.

1. Describe the set. ____

2. What props are used? ____

3. Quote a stage direction that tells how a character speaks.

____

4. Quote a stage direction that tells how a character moves.

____

5. Is the passage a dialogue or a monologue? Explain.

____

6. Is this scene more likely from a comedy or a tragedy? Explain. _____________

____

from **Dragonwings** by Laurence Yep
Model Selection: Drama

Dragonwings is a **drama,** or *play*, a story told in dialogue and meant to be performed by actors before an audience. Laurence Yep is the **playwright,** the author of the play. A play is written in segments. You have read just one segment, a **scene.** In a full-length work, several scenes usually make up an **act,** and several acts make up the play.

To advance the action, Yep wrote **dramatic speech.** Most of the excerpt from *Dragonwings* contains **dialogue,** conversation between several characters. One section might be considered a **monologue,** a long speech by a single character. A monologue often reveals a character's thoughts and feelings.

Stage directions describe the scenery and sound effects and tell how the characters move and speak. The **set** is the construction onstage that suggests the time and place of the action (the setting). **Props** are small movable items that make the set look realistic.

In a drama, as the **main character** develops, the audience should identify with his or her emotions. The **climax** of a drama, the moment of greatest tension, concerns the main character in some way. With the climax comes some insight or revelation.

A. DIRECTIONS: *Answer these questions about Scene 9 of* Dragonwings.

1. What is the setting? ____

2. What props is Moon Shadow most likely using during his opening speech?

   ____

3. Describe one sound effect that is used. ______________________________________

4. After Windrider takes off in the airplane, Moon Shadow speaks these lines:

   I thought he'd fly forever and ever. Up, up to heaven and never come down. But then . . . Dragonwings came crashing to earth. Father had a few broken bones, but it was nothing serious. Only the aeroplane was wrecked. . . . Father didn't say much, just thought a lot I figured he was busy designing the next aeroplane. . . .

   What type of dramatic speech would you call this passage? Explain your answer.

   ____

5. Who is the main character? How can you tell?

   ____

B. DIRECTIONS: *What is the climax of events in Scene 9 of* Dragonwings? *What insight does Windrider gain in response to the climax? What insight does Moon Shadow gain?*

____

____

____

A Christmas Carol: Scrooge and Marley, **Act I,** by Israel Horovitz
Reading: Preview a Text to Set a Purpose for Reading

When you **set a purpose for reading,** you decide what you want to get from a text. Setting a purpose gives you a focus as you read. These are some of the reasons you might have for reading something:

- to learn about a subject
- to be entertained
- to gain understanding
- to prepare to take action or make a decision
- to find inspiration
- to complete a task

In order to set a purpose, **preview a text** before you read it. Look at the title, the pictures, the captions, the organization, and the beginnings of passages. If you already have a purpose in mind, previewing will help you decide whether the text will fit that purpose. If you do not have a purpose in mind, previewing the text will help you determine one.

DIRECTIONS: *Read the passages from Act I of* A Christmas Carol: Scrooge and Marley *indicated below, and then complete each item.*

1. Following the list of "The People of the Play," read the information labeled "The Place of the Play." Where is the play set?

   ____

2. Read the information labeled "The Time of the Play." When does the play take place?

   ____

3. What purpose or purposes might you set based on that information?

   ____

   ____

4. The illustrations that accompany the text of Act I of the play are photographs from a production of the play. Look at those photographs now, but ignore the one of the ghostly character in chains. How are the characters dressed?

   ____

5. Based on that information, what purpose might you set for reading Act I of the play?

   ____

6. Read the opening lines of Act I, Scene 1, spoken by a character called Marley. Then, look at the photograph of the ghostly character in chains. What purpose might you set based on that information?

   ____

A Christmas Carol: Scrooge and Marley, Act I, by Israel Horovitz
Literary Analysis: Dialogue

Dialogue is a conversation between characters. In a play, the characters are developed almost entirely through dialogue. Dialogue also advances the action of the plot and develops the conflict.

In the script of a dramatic work, you can tell which character is speaking by the name that appears before the character's lines. In this example of dialogue, you are introduced to two of the characters in *A Christmas Carol: Scrooge and Marley:*

> **NEPHEW.** [*Cheerfully; surprising* SCROOGE] A merry Christmas to you, Uncle! God save you!
>
> **SCROOGE.** Bah! Humbug!
>
> **NEPHEW.** Christmas a "humbug," Uncle? I'm sure you don't mean that.
>
> **SCROOGE.** I do! Merry Christmas? What right do you have to be merry? What reason have you to be merry? You're poor enough!

In just a few words apiece, the characters establish a conflict between them. The nephew thinks Christmas is a joyful holiday, and Scrooge thinks it is nonsense. This conflict will reappear throughout the play until it is resolved. Those lines of dialogue also give you a look at the character traits of Scrooge and his nephew. Scrooge is quarrelsome and unpleasant; the nephew is upbeat and friendly.

DIRECTIONS: *Answer the following questions about this passage from* A Christmas Carol: Scrooge and Marley, *Act I, Scene 2.*

> **PORTLY MAN.** . . . [*Pen in hand; as well as notepad*] What shall I put you down for, sir?
>
> **SCROOGE.** Nothing!
>
> **PORTLY MAN.** You wish to be left anonymous?
>
> **SCROOGE.** I wish to be left alone! [*Pauses; turns away; turns back to them*] Since you ask me what I wish, gentlemen, that is my answer. I help to support the establishments that I have mentioned; they cost enough: and those who are badly off must go there.
>
> **THIN MAN.** Many can't go there; and many would rather die.
>
> **SCROOGE.** If they would rather die, they had better do it, and decrease the surplus population. . . .

1. How many characters are speaking? Who are they?

   ____

2. What is Scrooge like in this scene?

   ____

3. How is he different from the men he is talking to?

   ____

   ____

4. Based on the identification of the characters, whom would you expect to speak next?

   ____

A Christmas Carol: Scrooge and Marley, **Act I,** by Israel Horovitz
Vocabulary Builder

Word List

implored   morose   destitute   void   conveyed   benevolence

A. DIRECTIONS: *Think about the meaning of the italicized word from the Word List in each sentence. Then, answer the question, and explain your answer.*

1. Marley *implored* Scrooge to pay attention to him. Did Marley ask casually?
   ____

2. Scrooge was *morose*. Did he enjoy celebrating Christmas?
   ____

3. Are the *destitute* able to save money?
   ____

4. Scrooge looked into the *void*. Did he see anything?
   ____

5. In Act I, Scene 3, of *A Christmas Carol: Scrooge and Marley,* has Scrooge *conveyed* his fear?
   ____

6. Was Marley known for his *benevolence*?
   ____

B. DIRECTIONS: *For each item, write the letter of the word that means* the same or about the same as *the word from the Word List.*

____ 1. implored
    A. shouted   B. refused   C. begged   D. rejected

____ 2. morose
    A. cheerful   B. quarrelsome   C. sleepy   D. gloomy

____ 3. destitute
    A. poor   B. ill   C. rich   D. well

____ 4. void
    A. completion   B. remains   C. fullness   D. emptiness

____ 5. conveyed
    A. expressed   B. responded   C. activated   D. overcame

____ 6. benevolence
    A. indifference   B. remorse   C. kindness   D. happiness

A Christmas Carol: Scrooge and Marley, **Act I,** by Israel Horovitz
Support for Writing a Letter

Use this form to prepare to **write a letter** to Scrooge.

Salutation
State your main point: Scrooge is missing out in life by being cranky and negative with the people around him.

State a specific thing that Scrooge is missing out on. Include a detail from the play or from your experience to support your point.

State another specific thing that Scrooge is missing out on. Include a detail from the play or from your experience to support your point.

Conclude with a summary or a request that Scrooge change his behavior.

Closing, Signature

Dear ____________________,

Now, prepare a final draft of your letter.

A Christmas Carol: Scrooge and Marley, Act I, by Israel Horovitz
Build Language Skills: Vocabulary

Suffixes: *-ment*

The suffix *-ment* means "the act or quality of." Adding *-ment* to a verb creates a noun. *Pave* becomes *pavement,* "the quality of being paved; a paved surface." *Employ* becomes *employment,* "the act of being employed."

A. DIRECTIONS: *Add the suffix* -ment *to the italicized verb in each sentence. Then, write a new sentence using the noun you have created.*

1. The columns of text in the school newsletter did not *align.*

   ____

2. How would you *assess* the swimmer's chance of victory?

   ____

3. The witness will *state* her version of what occurred on the night of the crime.

   ____

4. Our principal will *announce* the winners of the spelling bee at tomorrow's assembly.

   ____

Academic Vocabulary Practice

B. DIRECTIONS: *Read each sentence, paying attention to the italicized Academic Vocabulary word. Indicate whether each statement is* true *or* false. *Then, explain your answer.*

1. A rousing cheer is a natural *reaction* to the loss of a championship game.

   T / F: _______ **Explanation:** _____________________________________

2. A teacher would be pleased to see her students' *involvement* with their schoolwork.

   T / F: _______ **Explanation:** _____________________________________

3. *Conflict* is the opposite of peacefulness.

   T / F: _______ **Explanation:** _____________________________________

4. You can get a good idea of a play by reading a *critique* of the production.

   T / F: _______ **Explanation:** _____________________________________

5. An *assumption* is the same as a certainty.

   T / F: _______ **Explanation:** _____________________________________

A Christmas Carol: Scrooge and Marley, **Act I,** by Israel Horovitz
Build Language Skills: Grammar

Interjections

An **interjection** is a part of speech that exclaims and expresses a feeling, such as pain or excitement. It may stand on its own, or it may appear within a sentence, but it functions independently of the sentence—it is not related to it grammatically. If an interjection stands on its own, it is set off with a period or an exclamation point. If it appears in a sentence, it is set off with commas.

> <u>Wow</u>, look at that sunset!

> My pants are covered with mud. <u>Yuck</u>!

> <u>Boy</u>, do my legs ache after climbing all those stairs.

Here are some common interjections:

Boy	Hmmm	Oh	Ugh	Whew	Yikes
Hey	Huh	Oops	Well	Wow	Yuck

A. DIRECTIONS: *Rewrite each item. Punctuate the sentence or pair of sentences to set off the interjections. Some sentences or pairs of sentences may be written in more than one way.*

1. Oops the cat spilled his food all over the floor

   ____

2. Ouch I dropped the hammer on my foot

   ____

3. I worked for two hours in the hot sun Whew

   ____

4. Hmmm I think this CD costs way too much

   ____

5. Hey do not go near that downed electric wire

   ____

B. Writing Application: *Write three sentences using interjections. Be sure to punctuate the sentences correctly.*

1. ____

2. ____

3. ____

A Christmas Carol: Scrooge and Marley, *Act II,* by Israel Horovitz

Reading: Adjust Your Reading Rate to Suit Your Purpose

Setting a purpose for reading is deciding before you read what you want to get out of a text. The purpose you set will affect the way you read.

Adjust your reading rate to suit your purpose. When you read a play, follow these guidelines:

- Read stage directions slowly and carefully. They describe action that may not be revealed by the dialogue.
- Read short lines of dialogue quickly in order to create the feeling of conversation.
- Read longer speeches by a single character slowly in order to reflect on the character's words and look for clues to the message.

DIRECTIONS: *Read the following passages, and answer the questions that follow each one.*

MAN # 1. Hey, you, watch where you're going.

MAN # 2. Watch it yourself, mate!

[PRESENT *sprinkles them directly, they change.*]

MAN # 1. I pray go in ahead of me. It's Christmas. You be first!

MAN # 2. No, no. I must insist that YOU be first!

1. How would you read the preceding dialogue? Why?

   ____

2. How would you read the stage directions? Why?

   ____

3. What important information do the stage directions contain? How does it affect your understanding of the lines that follow it?

   ____

   ____

   ____

PRESENT. Mark my words, Ebenezer Scrooge. I do not present the Cratchits to you because they are a handsome, or brilliant family. They are not handsome. They are not brilliant. They are not well-dressed, or tasteful to the times. Their shoes are not even waterproofed by virtue of money or cleverness spent. So when the pavement is wet, so are the insides of their shoes and the tops of their toes. They are the Cratchits, Mr. Scrooge. They are not highly special. They are happy, grateful, pleased with one another, contented with the time and how it passes. They don't sing very well, do they? But, nonetheless, they do sing . . . [*Pauses*] think of that, Scrooge. Fifteen shillings a week and they do sing . . . hear their song until its end.

4. How would you read the preceding passage? Why?

   ____

   ____

A Christmas Carol: Scrooge and Marley, *Act II,* by Israel Horovitz
Literary Analysis: Stage Directions

Stage directions are the words in the script of a drama that are not spoken by characters. When a play is performed, you can see the set, the characters, and the movements, and you can hear the sound effects. When you read a play, you get this information from the stage directions. Stage directions are usually printed in italic type and set off by brackets or parentheses.

DIRECTIONS: *Read the following passages, and answer the questions that follow each one.*

[BOB CRATCHIT *enters, carrying* TINY TIM *atop his shoulder. He wears a threadbare and fringe-less comforter hanging down in front of him.* TINY TIM *carries small crutches and his small legs are bound in an iron frame brace.*]

1. Who appears in this scene?

   ____

2. What does the description of Bob Cratchit reveal about the Cratchit family?

   ____

3. What does the description of Tiny Tim reveal about him?

   ____

   ____

SCROOGE. Specter, something informs me that our parting moment is at hand. I know it, but I know not how I know it.

[FUTURE *points to the other side of the stage. Lights out on* CRATCHITS. FUTURE *moves slowing, gliding . . .* FUTURE *points opposite.* FUTURE *leads* SCROOGE *to a wall and a tombstone. He points to the stone.*]

Am I that man those ghoulish parasites so gloated over?

4. Who appears in this scene? How do you know?

   ____

   ____

5. What do the stage directions reveal that the dialogue does not reveal?

   ____

   ____

   ____

A Christmas Carol: Scrooge and Marley, *Act II*, by Israel Horovitz
Vocabulary Builder

Word List

astonish   compulsion   severe   meager   audible

A. DIRECTIONS: *Think about the meaning of the italicized word from the Word List in each sentence. Then, answer the question, and explain your answer.*

1. Scrooge's new attitude will *astonish* his family. Will they be surprised by it?

   ____

2. Scrooge has a *compulsion* to go with each of the ghosts. Can he easily resist going?

   ____

3. Mrs. Cratchit's judgment of Scrooge is *severe*. Does she think highly of him?

   ____

4. Scrooge paid Cratchit a *meager* salary. Was the salary generous?

   ____

5. The actor's voice is *audible* when he whispers. Can the audience hear him?

   ____

B. DIRECTIONS: *Write the letter of the word whose meaning is* the same or about the same as *the meaning of the word from the Word List.*

____ 1. astonish
   A. frighten   B. puzzle   C. amaze   D. question

____ 2. compulsion
   A. rejection   B. desire   C. expectation   D. need

____ 3. severe
   A. mild   B. tall   C. fast   D. harsh

____ 4. meager
   A. insufficient   B. nonsensical   C. mistaken   D. required

____ 5. audible
   A. loud   B. visible   C. hidden   D. silent

A Christmas Carol: Scrooge and Marley, *Act II,* **by Israel Horovitz**
Support for Writing a Tribute

To prepare to write a **tribute,** or expression of admiration, to the changed Ebenezer Scrooge, answer the following questions.

What is Scrooge like before the change?

____

____

What anecdotes—brief stories that make a point—illustrate Scrooge's character before the change?

____

____

____

____

What causes Scrooge to change?

____

____

What is Scrooge like after the change?

____

____

What anecdotes illustrate Scrooge's character after the change?

____

____

____

____

Now, write a draft of your tribute to Scrooge. Be sure to explain how Scrooge has changed and why his new behavior deserves to be honored. Use this space to write your first draft.

____

____

____

____

A Christmas Carol: Scrooge and Marley, *Act II*, by Israel Horovitz
Build Language Skills: Vocabulary

Suffixes: *-tion*

The suffix *-tion* creates a noun that names the quality, act, or result of the word to which it is added. When you add *-tion* to the verb *react*, for example, you create the noun *reaction*, which means "the act of reacting." When you add *-tion* to the verb *assume*, you create the noun *assumption*, which means "the act of assuming or taking for granted."

A. DIRECTIONS: *Add the suffix* -tion *to the italicized verb in each sentence. Then, write a new sentence using the noun you have created.*

1. When I was younger, I had difficulty with problems that ask you to *subtract.*

   ____

2. Will the stores *reduce* their prices after the holidays?

   ____

3. Do not *assume* that the weather will remain sunny all day.

   ____

4. Do you have a device that can *detect* carbon monoxide in your home?

   ____

5. Can the team afford to *add* new uniforms to its budget?

   ____

Academic Vocabulary Practice

B. DIRECTIONS: *Read each sentence, paying attention to the italicized Academic Vocabulary word. Then, revise the sentence so that the vocabulary word is used logically. Be sure to use the vocabulary word in your revised sentence.*

1. I knew I had no *reaction* to the scary movie because after I saw it, I had nightmares.

   ____

2. The philanthropist's lack of interest in the project was evidence of his *involvement* in it.

   ____

3. The two characters' friendliness to each other was proof of their *conflict.*

   ____

4. Before the critic saw the play, she wrote a *critique* predicting that it would succeed.

   ____

5. Because we were sure of all the facts about Dickens's life, we made an *assumption* about the writer's character.

   ____

A Christmas Carol: Scrooge and Marley, *Act II*, by Israel Horovitz
Build Language Skills: Grammar

Double Negatives

Double negatives occur when two negative words appear in a sentence but only one is needed. Examples of negative words are *nothing, not, never,* and *no.* You can correct a double negative by revising the sentence.

Incorrect	**Correct**
I do <u>not</u> have <u>no</u> homework tonight.	I do <u>not</u> have <u>any</u> homework tonight.
You <u>never</u> said <u>nothing</u> about that movie.	You <u>never</u> said <u>anything</u> about that movie.

A. DIRECTIONS: *Put a checkmark (✓) next to each sentence that uses a negative word correctly. Put an ✗ next to each sentence that contains a double negative.*

____ 1. Do not ever say nothing to Mom about the surprise party.

____ 2. You never told me anything about your new coach.

____ 3. The team never had time to make a comeback.

____ 4. We do not have no reason to get up early tomorrow.

____ 5. They did not have no money for the movie.

B. Writing Application: *Rewrite each sentence to eliminate the double negative.*

1. We do not have no bread for sandwiches.

   ____

2. The spy never had no intention of giving himself up.

   ____

3. This article does not have nothing to do with our assignment.

   ____

4. They are not going to no championship game tonight.

   ____

5. Our dog will not ever eat no food she does not like.

   ____

from **A Christmas Carol: Scrooge and Marley,** *Act I, Scenes 2 & 5* by Israel Horovitz
Literary Analysis: Comparing Characters

A **character** is a person who takes part in a literary work. Like main characters in stories and novels, main characters in drama have traits that make them unique. These may include qualities such as dependability, intelligence, selfishness, and stubbornness. The characters in dramas have motives, or reasons, for behaving the way they do. For example, one character may be motivated by compassion, while another may be motivated by guilt.

When you read a drama, pay attention to what each character says and does, and note the reactions those words and actions spark in others. Notice what those words and actions reveal about the character's traits and motives.

In drama, one way to develop a character is through a **foil,** a character whose behavior and attitude contrast with those of the main character. With a foil, audiences can see good in contrast with bad or generousness in contrast with selfishness.

DIRECTIONS: *Answer the following questions to compare the older Scrooge with Fezziwig.*

Question	Scrooge	Fezziwig
1. What does the character say?		
2. What does the character do?		
3. How does the character react to Christmas?		
4. What do other characters say to or about him?		
5. What adjectives describe the character?		

from **A Christmas Carol: Scrooge and Marley,** *Act I, Scenes 2 & 5* by Israel Horovitz
Vocabulary Builder

Word List

fiddler   suitors   snuffs

A. DIRECTIONS: *Complete the word maps by writing a definition, synonyms, and an example sentence for each word from the Word List.*

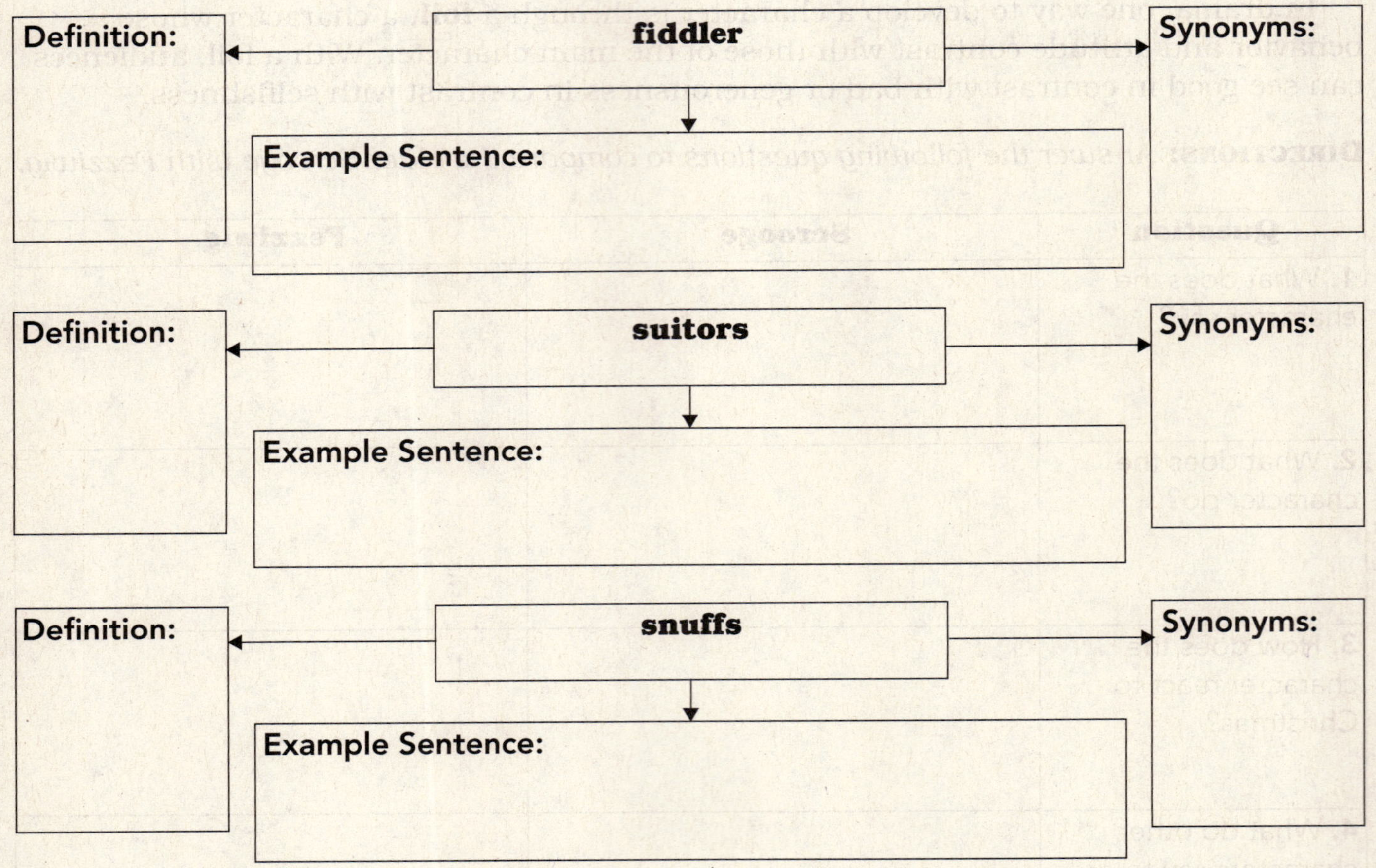

B. DIRECTIONS: *Write the letter of the word whose meaning is* most like *that of the word from the Word List.*

____ 1. fiddler
    A. crab   B. musician   C. violinist   D. tinkerer

____ 2. suitors
    A. boyfriends   B. tailors   C. lawyers   D. apprentices

____ 3. snuffs
    A. sniffs   B. erases   C. blots   D. extinguishes

Unit 5 Resources: Drama

***from* A Christmas Carol: Scrooge and Marley, *Act I, Scenes 2 & 5* by Israel Horovitz**

Support for Writing to Compare Literary Works

Use this graphic organizer to gather notes for an essay in which you compare and contrast Fezziwig and Scrooge.

Scrooge   **Fezziwig**

	How does each character behave? Think about what each one says and does.	
	Why does each character act as he does? What might motivate each one?	
	Which character do you prefer? Why? Why do you not prefer the other character?	
	What does the audience learn about Scrooge in the scene with Fezziwig?	
	How does Fezziwig help Scrooge change?	

Now, use your notes to write an essay comparing and contrasting Fezziwig and Scrooge. Be sure to discuss how each character's actions and words help the playwright make a point about Scrooge and his behavior.

"The Monsters Are Due on Maple Street" by Rod Serling

Reading: Distinguish Between Important and Unimportant Details to Write a Summary

A **summary** is a brief statement that presents only the main ideas and most important details. Summarizing helps you review and understand what you are reading. To summarize, you must first **distinguish between important and unimportant details.** Ask yourself questions like these:

- Is the detail necessary to an understanding of the literary work?
- Would the work hold together without the inclusion of this information?

As you read, pause periodically to recall and restate only the key events and important details.

DIRECTIONS: *Read these summaries of portions of "The Monsters Are Due on Maple Street." Then, answer the questions that follow each summary.*

It is an ordinary September evening on Maple Street when a roar is heard and a flash is seen. The power goes off, and telephones and portable radios stop working. One neighbor leaves to see what is happening on another street. Another neighbor says that he will go downtown to find out what is going on. For no explainable reason, his car will not start. He and a third neighbor decide to walk downtown. Tommy, a fourteen-year-old boy who wears eyeglasses, tells the men not to go. Tommy tells the crowd that what is happening is like every story about aliens he has read. He says that before they land, aliens send a family that looks human to live in a community and prepare for the aliens' arrival.

1. What is the main idea of the preceding summary?

   ____

2. Which detail in the preceding summary is unnecessary?

   ____

After Les Goodman's car starts on its own, the neighbors become suspicious of Goodman. A neighbor says that she has seen him standing on his porch in the middle of the night, looking at the sky. Goodman explains that he often has insomnia. He compares his neighbors to frightened rabbits. He says that they are letting a nightmare begin.

3. What is the main idea of the preceding summary?

   ____

   ____

4. Which detail in the preceding summary is unimportant? How do you know it is unimportant?

   ____

"The Monsters Are Due on Maple Street" by Rod Serling
Literary Analysis: A Character's Motives

A character's motives are the reasons for his or her actions. Motives are usually related to what a character wants, needs, or feels. Powerful motives include love, anger, fear, and greed. As you read, think about what motivates each character.

DIRECTIONS: *Read the following passages from "The Monsters Are Due on Maple Street." Then, answer the questions that follow, about the characters' motives.*

STEVE. It isn't just the power failure, Charlie. If it was, we'd still be able to get a broadcast on the portable.

[*There's a murmur of reaction to this.* STEVE *looks from face to face and then over to his car.*]

STEVE. I'll run downtown. We'll get this all straightened out.

1. What are Steve's motives for volunteering to go downtown?

   ____

   ____

GOODMAN. I just don't understand it. I tried to start it and it wouldn't start. You saw me. All of you saw me.

[*And now, just as suddenly as the engine started, it stops and there's a long silence that is gradually intruded upon by the frightened murmuring of the people.*]

GOODMAN. I don't understand. I swear . . . I don't understand. What's happening?

DON. Maybe you better tell us. Nothing's working on this street. Nothing. No lights, no power, no radio. . . . Nothing except one car—yours!

[*The people pick this up and now their murmuring becomes a loud chant filling the air with accusations and demands for action. Two of the men . . . head toward* GOODMAN, *who backs away, backing into his car and now at bay.*]

GOODMAN. Wait a minute now. You keep your distance—all of you. So I've got a car that starts by itself—well, that's a freak thing. I admit it. But does that make me some kind of a criminal or something? I don't know why the car works—it just does!

2. Which speaker appears to be motivated by confusion? ___________________________

3. Which speaker appears to be motivated by suspicion? ___________________________

4. What emotion or emotions appear to be motivating Goodman after the crowd has accused him? ____

5. Why might Goodman be feeling this emotion? ___________________________________

   ____

"The Monsters Are Due on Maple Street" by Rod Serling
Vocabulary Builder

Word List

flustered	sluggishly	persistently	defiant	metamorphosis

A. DIRECTIONS: *Read each sentence, and think about the meaning of the italicized word from the Word List. Then, answer the question, and explain your answer.*

1. Would you expect a *flustered* person to speak clearly?

   ____

2. If a heavy rain fills a riverbed, will the river move *sluggishly*?

   ____

3. If someone *persistently* asks a question, would you assume that she is eager to know the answer?

   ____

4. Would a *defiant* child be likely to refuse to do his chores?

   ____

5. If a rude person undergoes a *metamorphosis*, is she likely to continue to be rude?

   ____

B. DIRECTIONS: *Write the letter of the word or group of words whose meaning is* most nearly the opposite *of the word from the Word List.*

____ 1. flustered
  A. nervous   B. calm   C. neat   D. suspicious

____ 2. sluggishly
  A. speedily   B. hopefully   C. listlessly   D. carelessly

____ 3. persistently
  A. confidently   B. appreciatively C. halfheartedly D. importantly

____ 4. defiant
  A. responsive   B. weak   C. worthless   D. combative

____ 5. metamorphosis
  A. long speech   B. resistance   C. dejection   D. lack of change

"The Monsters Are Due on Maple Street" by Rod Serling
Support for Writing a Report

Use this chart to take notes for your **report** from the point of view of Figure One or Figure Two. In your report, you will inform your leader of the events on Maple Street.

Report to Leader on Visit to Maple Street, Earth

Human Beings

Steve: ____
____

Tommy: ____
____

Charlie: ____
____

Pete Van Horn: ____
____

Les Goodman: ____
____

Other residents of Maple Street: _____________________________________
____

Events

Act I: ____
____
____

Act II: ____
____
____

Recommendations
____
____
____

Now, write a draft of your report. Be sure to focus on the important details.

"The Monsters Are Due on Maple Street" by Rod Serling
Build Language Skills: Vocabulary

Suffixes: *-ize*

The suffix *-ize* (or *-yze*) means "to make." This suffix forms verbs. When you add *-ize* to the noun *summary*, for example, you create the verb *summarize*, meaning "to make a summary." When you add *-yze* to the noun *analysis*, you create the verb *analyze*, meaning "to make an analysis."

A. DIRECTIONS: *Add the suffix -ize or -yze to the italicized noun in each sentence. Then, write a sentence using the new verb.*

1. Put these names in order according to the letters of the *alphabet*.

   ____

2. Jason worked hard to make his dreams become *real*.

   ____

3. The scientists will work on an *analysis* of the evidence.

   ____

4. Can you commit this poem to *memory*?

   ____

5. The prairie dogs will form a *colony* on the plains.

   ____

Academic Vocabulary Practice

B. DIRECTIONS: *Revise each sentence so that the italicized Academic Vocabulary word is defined correctly or used logically. Be sure to use the vocabulary word in your revision.*

1. If you are arranging events in *chronological* order, you may arrange them in any order.

   ____

2. When asked to describe the *sequence* of events, the witness began with the end of the story, skipped to the middle, and ended with the beginning.

   ____

3. When you *summarize* a work, you tell everything that happened in the order in which it happened.

   ____

4. A *characteristic* is a quality that makes one thing just like another thing.

   ____

5. To *focus* on a scene is to look at it as if from a distance, so that it is blurry and indistinct.

   ____

Name ____ Date _____________________________

"The Monsters Are Due on Maple Street" by Rod Serling
Build Language Skills: Grammar

Sentence Functions and Endmarks

Sentences are classified into four categories, according to their function.

Category, Function, and Endmark	Example
A **declarative sentence** makes a statement. It ends with a period. (.)	Monsters are due on Maple Street.
An **interrogative sentence** asks a question. It ends with a question mark. (?)	What is going on?
An **imperative sentence** gives a command. It ends with a period or an exclamation point. (. or !)	Do not leave town. Watch out!
An **exclamatory sentence** calls out or exclaims. It ends with an exclamation point. (!)	Hey! How frightened we were!

Note that the subject of an imperative sentence is always the word *you*, and it is never stated: *(You) do not leave town. (You) watch out!*

Also note that in your writing, you should use exclamatory sentences as if they were a powerful spice. For the greatest effect, use them sparingly.

A. DIRECTIONS: *Add the correct endmark to each sentence. Then, identify the sentence as* declarative, interrogative, imperative, *or* exclamatory.

1. Where did you go on your field trip on Saturday ______ ____________________
2. We drove to a quarry and looked for fossils ______ ____________________
3. What cool fossils ______ ____________________
4. This one is a trilobite ______ ____________________
5. Don't drop it ______ ____________________
6. Next time we go, you should come with us ______ ____________________
7. Will you tell me when you plan to go again ______ ____________________

B. Writing Application: *Write a short dialogue between two characters. Use at least one of each kind of sentence. Label your sentences* dec *for declarative,* int *for interrogative,* imp *for imperative, and* exclam *for exclamatory.*

____

____

____

____

Unit 5 Resources: Drama

221

from **Grandpa and the Statue** by Arthur Miller
"My Head Is Full of Starshine" by Peg Kehret
Literary Analysis: Comparing Dramatic Speeches

Dramatic speeches are performed by actors in a drama or play. Whether spoken by a character who is onstage alone or given by a character who is part of a larger scene, these speeches move the action of the story forward and help define the conflict in a play. There are two main types of dramatic speeches:

- **Monologues** are long, uninterrupted speeches that are spoken by a single character. They reveal the private thoughts and feelings of the character.
- **Dialogues** are conversations between characters. They reveal characters' traits, develop conflict, and move the plot forward.

Grandpa and the Statue is a dialogue, and "My Head Is Full of Starshine" is a monologue. As you read these selections, consider what you learn about the characters. Also, think about how other key information is revealed.

DIRECTIONS: *Answer the following questions about the excerpts from* Grandpa and the Statue *and "My Head Is Full of Starshine."*

1. In the excerpt from *Grandpa and the Statue*, what does the audience learn about Monaghan's character?

____

____

2. What conflict is revealed in Monaghan and Sheean's dialogue in the excerpt from *Grandpa and the Statue*?

____

____

3. In the excerpt from *Grandpa and the Statue*, what does Monaghan reveal about himself in the speech about his experiences when he first came to America?

____

____

4. How does the reader learn about the writer's tendency to daydream in "My Head Is Full of Starshine"?

____

____

5. What does the writer reveal about her feelings toward having library fines in "My Head Is Full of Starshine"?

____

____

from **Grandpa and the Statue** by Arthur Miller
"My Head Is Full of Starshine" by Peg Kehret
Vocabulary Builder

Word List

peeved	practical	rummaging	potential

A. DIRECTIONS: *Read each sentence, paying attention to the italicized word from the Word List. Then, answer each question, and explain your answer.*

1. If you accidentally threw away a diamond ring, might you be *rummaging* through the trash?

   ____

2. Is a *practical* person one who daydreams and puts things off until the last minute?

   ____

3. Is a relaxed, easygoing person likely to be easily *peeved*?

   ____

4. Is someone with great *potential* as an athlete likely to compete in the Olympics someday?

   ____

B. DIRECTIONS: *Write the letter of the word whose meaning is* most like *that of the word from the Word List.*

____ 1. peeved
   A. outgoing   B. happy   C. realistic   D. annoyed

____ 2. practical
   A. happy   B. realistic   C. strong   D. imaginative

____ 3. rummaging
   A. reselling   B. organizing   C. searching   D. destroying

____ 4. potential
   A. capability   B. intelligence   C. sharpness   D. volume

Name _______________________________________ Date _______________________

from **Grandpa and the Statue** by Arthur Miller
"My Head Is Full of Starshine" by Peg Kehret

Support for Writing to Compare Dramatic Speeches

Use this graphic organizer to take notes for your essay comparing and contrasting the dramatic speech by Monaghan in the excerpt from *Grandpa and the Statue* with the one by the speaker in "My Head Is Full of Starshine."

Which ideas in the speech are familiar to you? _______________________________________

With which ideas in the speech do you agree or disagree? _______________________________________

Which character do you relate to more? Why? _______________________________________

The speaker in "My Head Is Full of Starshine"

Monaghan in *Grandpa and the Statue*

From which character do you think you learn more? Why? _______________________________________

Which ideas in the speech are familiar to you? _______________________________________

With which ideas in the speech do you agree or disagree? _______________________________________

Now, use your notes to write a draft of an essay comparing and contrasting the two speeches.

Unit 5 Resources: Drama

Jon Scieszka
Listening and Viewing

Segment 1: Meet Jon Scieszka
- How did Jon Scieszka choose his audience? Scieszka reads all different types of literature.
- How do you think this helps him come up with writing ideas?

____

____

____

____

Segment 2: Themes in the Oral Tradition
- Why is Jon Scieszka "amazed" by fairy tales, myths, and legends?
- Why do you think that the retelling of these stories over time is important?

____

____

____

____

Segment 3: The Writing Process
- Who is Lane Smith, and how is he involved in Jon Scieszka's writing process?
- Why are illustrations important in fairy tales, myths, and fables like the stories that Jon Scieszka writes?

____

____

____

____

Segment 4: The Rewards of Writing
- Why is being a writer rewarding to Jon Scieszka?
- Why do you think that reading is a valuable activity for young people in today's age of technology?

____

____

____

____

Learning About the Oral Tradition

The sharing of stories, cultures, and ideas by word of mouth is called the **oral tradition.** Here are common elements of the oral tradition.

- The **theme** is a central idea, message, or insight that a story reveals.
- A **moral** is a lesson about life that is taught by a story.
- **Heroes** and **heroines** are larger-than-life figures whose virtues and deeds are often celebrated in stories from the oral tradition.
- **Storytelling** calls on the talents and personality of the teller to bring the narrative to life. Storytelling techniques include **hyperbole,** or the use of exaggeration or overstatement, and **personification,** the giving of human characteristics to a non-human subject.

Many stories have been written down for readers. Categories of stories in the oral tradition that have been committed to paper include the following.

- **Myths** are ancient tales that describe the actions of gods, goddesses, and the heroes who interact with them.
- **Legends** are traditional stories about the past. They are based on real-life events or people, but they are more fiction than fact.
- **Folk tales** tell about ordinary people. These stories reveal the traditions and values of a culture and teach a lesson about life.
- **Tall tales** are folk tales that contain hyperbole.
- **Fables** are brief animal stories that contain personification. Fables often end with a moral or lesson.
- **Epics** are long narrative poems about a hero who engages in a dangerous journey.

A. DIRECTIONS: *The following items are elements of stories in the oral tradition. Decide which of the two terms matches the preceding description. Underline your choice.*

1. A woman spins cloth out of gold.   hyperbole   personification
2. The god Apollo drives his chariot across the sky.   myth   legend
3. Baseball great Babe Ruth hits the ball into another state.   fable   legend
4. The sun refuses to shine on an evil character's birthday.   personification   theme
5. It is best to be prepared.   moral   hero

B. DIRECTIONS: *On the lines below, write a plot summary for an original fable. Include one or more animal characters, and include an example of personification. End your fable with a moral. Use a separate sheet of paper if more space is needed.*

____

____

____

"Grasshopper Logic," "The Other Frog Prince," and "duckbilled platypus vs. beefsnakstik®" by Jon Scieszka and Lane Smith
Model Selection: The Oral Tradition

Jon Scieszka entertains readers with his comical versions of traditional **fairy tales** and **fables. Fables** are brief animal stories that contain personification. Fables often end with a moral or lesson. These three short selections are humorous examples of stories in the **oral tradition**—the sharing of stories, cultures, and ideas by word of mouth. Elements of the oral tradition include the following.

- The **theme** is a central idea, message, or insight that a story reveals.
- A **moral** is a lesson about life that is taught by a story. An example of a moral is "Hard work leads to success."
- **Hyperbole** is a deliberate exaggeration or overstatement. It is often used to create humor. For example, a man might be as strong as an ox.
- **Personification** is the granting of human characteristics to a nonhuman subject. This would include a talking fox or an angry tree.

A. DIRECTIONS: *Answer the following questions.*

1. Give an example of hyperbole from "Grasshopper Logic." Tell why it is a hyperbole.

   ____

   ____

2. How does the ending of "The Other Frog Prince" differ from the ending of the traditional "Frog Prince" fairy tale?

   ____

   ____

3. What types of characters are in "duckbilled platypus vs. beefsnakstik®," and in what specific ways are they examples of personification?

   ____

   ____

B. DIRECTIONS: *On the lines below, describe the specific ways in which the grasshopper and his mother talk and act like humans.*

   ____

   ____

   ____

   ____

   ____

"Icarus and Daedalus" by Josephine Preston Peabody

Reading: Ask Questions to Analyze Cause-and-Effect Relationships

A **cause** is an event, action, or feeling that produces a result. An **effect** is the result. In some literary works, multiple causes result in one single effect. In other works, a single cause results in multiple effects. Effects can also become causes for events that follow. The linking of causes and effects propels the action forward.

As you read, **ask questions** such as "What happened?" and "What will happen as a result of this?" **to analyze cause-and-effect relationships.**

DIRECTIONS: *Use the following graphic organizer to analyze some of the cause-and-effect relationships in "Icarus and Daedalus." The first response has been filled in as an example. Where there is no box in which to write the question you would ask yourself, ask the question mentally, and then write the effect in the next box.*

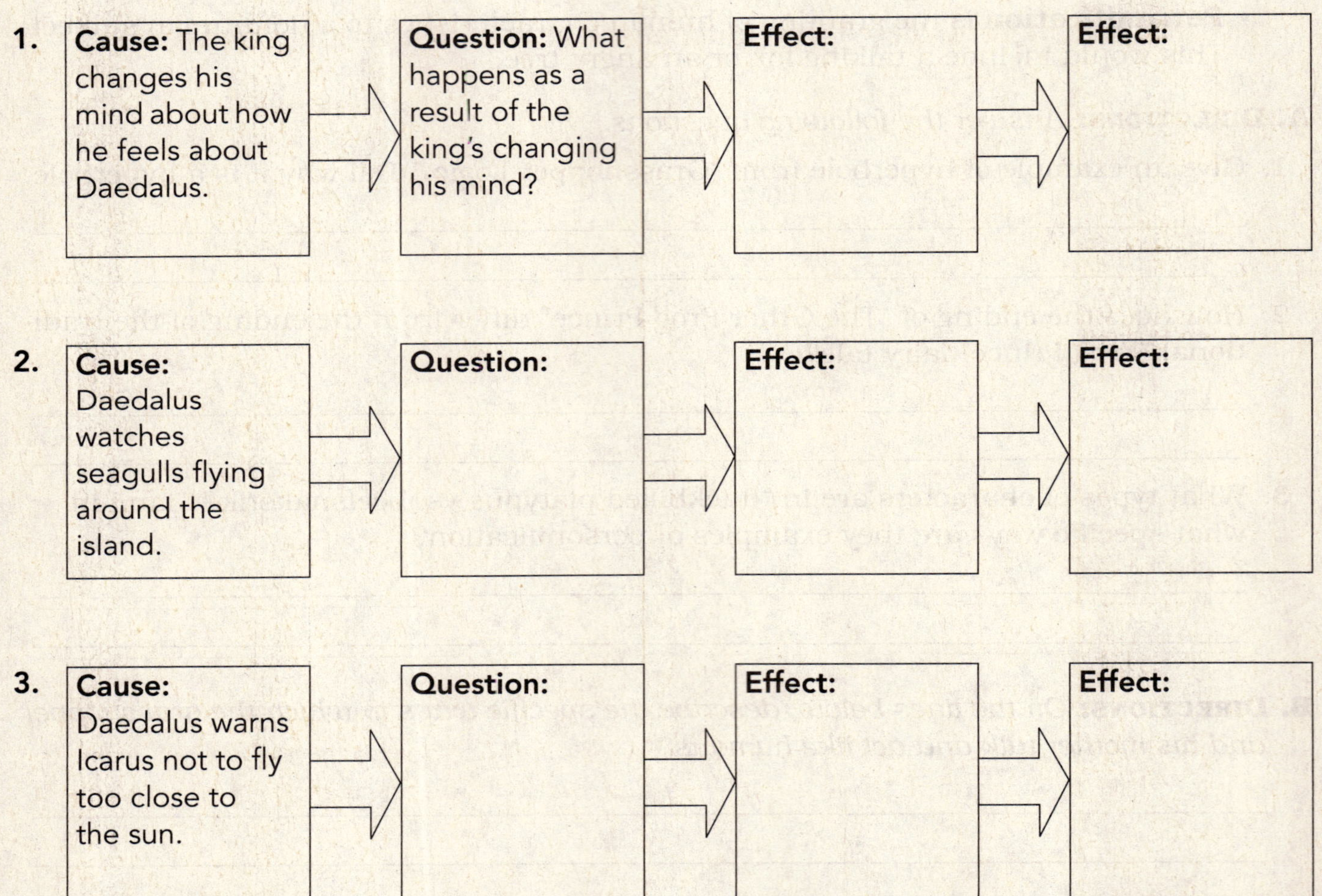

"**Icarus and Daedalus**" by Josephine Preston Peabody
Literary Analysis: Myth

Since time began, people have tried to understand the world around them. Ancient peoples created **myths**—stories that explain natural occurrences and express beliefs about right and wrong. Every culture has its own collection of myths, or *mythology*. In many myths, gods and goddesses have human traits, and human heroes have superhuman traits. Myths explore universal themes and explain the world in human terms.

Most myths perform some of the following functions:

- explain natural occurrences
- express beliefs about right and wrong
- show gods or goddesses with human traits
- show human heroes with superhuman traits
- explore universal themes

Not all myths perform all of those functions, however. "Icarus and Daedalus" illustrates only a few of them.

DIRECTIONS: *Read each excerpt from "Icarus and Daedalus" that follows, and answer the question about the functions of a myth that the excerpt illustrates.*

Among all those mortals who grew so wise that they learned the secrets of the gods, none was more cunning than Daedalus.

1. Which function of a myth does the excerpt illustrate? How can you tell?

____

____

____

"Remember," said the father, "never to fly very low or very high."

2. Which function of a myth does the excerpt illustrate? How can you tell?

____

____

____

The nearest island he named Icaria, in memory of the child; but he, in heavy grief, went to the temple of Apollo in Sicily, and there hung up his wings as an offering. Never again did he attempt to fly.

3. Which function of a myth does the excerpt illustrate? How can you tell?

____

____

____

"Icarus and Daedalus" by Josephine Preston Peabody
Vocabulary Builder

Word List

vacancy   sustained

A. DIRECTIONS: *Read each item, and think about the meaning of the underlined word from the Word List. Then, answer the question, and explain your answer.*

1. There is no <u>vacancy</u> at a motel. Can someone get a room there?

   ____

   ____

2. The villagers felt themselves <u>sustained</u> by the politicians' promises. Did the villagers trust that the promises would be fulfilled?

   ____

   ____

B. DIRECTIONS: *Revise each sentence so that the underlined vocabulary word is used logically.*

1. The <u>vacancy</u> in the look on the man's face made me think that he had a lot on his mind.

   ____

   ____

2. <u>Sustained</u> by the food, the villagers were starving.

   ____

   ____

C. DIRECTIONS: *Write the letter of the word that means* the same or about the same as *the word from the Word List.*

____ 1. vacancy
     A. property   C. emptiness
     B. appointment   D. discount

____ 2. sustained
     A. supported   C. deprived
     B. starved   D. competed

"Icarus and Daedalus" by Josephine Preston Peabody

Support for Writing a Myth

Use the following graphic organizer to take notes for a **myth** you will write to explain a natural phenomenon. You do not have to respond to each prompt in the chart in the order in which it appears, but you should probably decide on the phenomenon you want to explain before you decide on anything else. You might describe the problem and the resolution next and then work on the characters. Coming up with the title may be the last thing you do.

Natural phenomenon that myth will explain:

Title of myth:

Names and traits of characters—how they look, what they do, what they say to one another:
____
____
____
____
____
____
____
____

Problem to be solved and creative way in which it will be solved:
____
____
____
____
____
____
____
____

Now, write the first draft of your myth.

Unit 6 Resources: Themes in the Oral Tradition

"Demeter and Persephone" by Anne Terry White

Reading: Ask Questions to Analyze Cause-and-Effect Relationships

A **cause** is an event, action, or feeling that produces a result. An **effect** is the result. In some literary works, multiple causes result in one single effect. In other works, a single cause results in multiple effects. Effects can also become causes for events that follow. The linking of causes and effects propels the action forward.

As you read, **ask questions** such as "What happened?" and "What will happen as a result of this?" **to analyze cause-and-effect relationships.**

DIRECTIONS: *Use the following graphic organizer to analyze some of the cause-and-effect relationships in "Demeter and Persephone." The first response has been filled in as example. Where there is no box in which to write the question you would ask yourself, ask the question mentally, and then write the effect in the next box.*

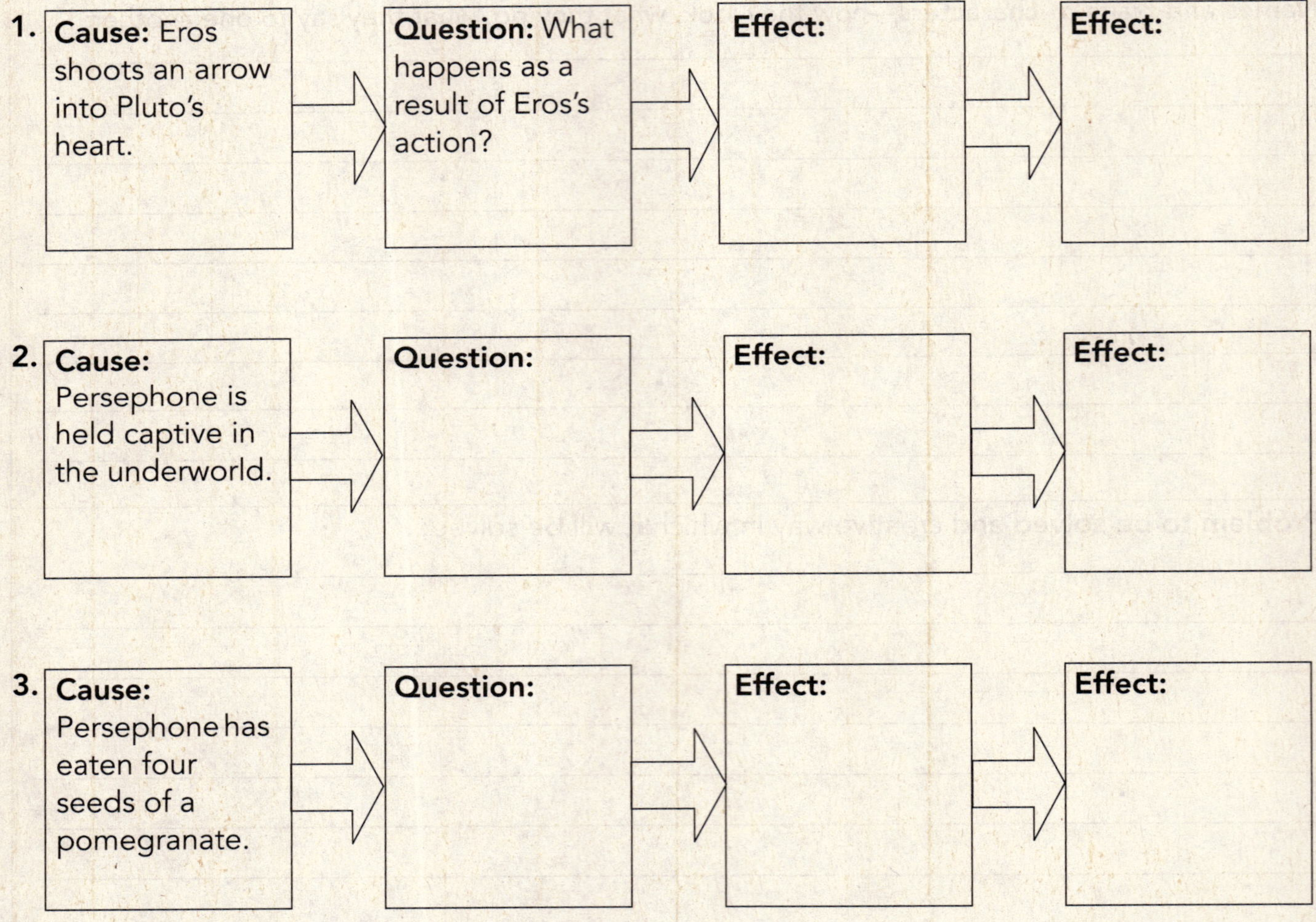

232

"Demeter and Persephone" by Anne Terry White
Literary Analysis: Myth

Since time began, people have tried to understand the world around them. Ancient peoples created **myths**—stories that explain natural occurrences and express beliefs about right and wrong. Every culture has its own collection of myths, or *mythology*. In many myths, gods and goddesses have human traits, and human heroes have superhuman traits. Myths explore universal themes and explain the world in human terms.

Most myths perform some of the following functions:

- explain natural occurrences
- express beliefs about right and wrong
- show gods or goddesses with human traits
- show human heroes with superhuman traits
- explore universal themes

Not all myths perform all of those functions, however. "Demeter and Persephone" illustrates only a few of them.

DIRECTIONS: *Read each excerpt from "Demeter and Persephone" that follows, and answer the question about the function of a myth that the excerpt illustrates.*

Deep under Mt. Aetna, the gods had buried alive a number of fearful, fire-breathing giants. The monsters heaved and struggled to get free. And so mightily did they shake the earth . . .

1. Which function of a myth does the excerpt illustrate? How can you tell?

____

____

____

Now an unaccustomed warmth stole through his veins. His stern eyes softened. . . . The god looked at Persephone and loved her at once.

2. Which function of a myth does the excerpt illustrate? How can you tell?

____

____

____

It seems that all mankind would die of hunger.

"This cannot go on," said mighty Zeus. "I see that I must intervene."

3. Which function of a myth does the excerpt illustrate? How can you tell?

____

____

____

"Demeter and Persephone" by Anne Terry White
Vocabulary Builder

Word List

> defies   intervene

A. DIRECTIONS: *Read each item, and think about the meaning of the underlined word from the Word List. Then, answer the question, and explain your answer.*

1. If a soldier <u>defies</u> orders, is he or she likely to be given a medal?

   ____

   ____

2. If you <u>intervene</u> in a fight, is there a possibility that you will get hurt?

   ____

   ____

B. DIRECTIONS: *Revise each sentence so that the underlined vocabulary word is used logically.*

1. Zeus is pleased when a god or goddess <u>defies</u> his orders.

   ____

2. When the world is calm and at peace, Zeus is likely to <u>intervene</u>.

   ____

C. DIRECTIONS: *Write the letter of the word that means* the same or about the same as *the word from the Word List.*

____ 1. intervene

    A. ignore   C. congregate

    B. interfere   D. lecture

____ 2. defies

    A. competes   C. opposes

    B. compliments   D. reports

"Demeter and Persephone" by Anne Terry White
Support for Writing a Myth

Use the following graphic organizer to take notes for a **myth** you will write to explain a natural phenomenon. You do not have to respond to each prompt in the chart in the order in which it appears, but you should probably decide on the phenomenon you want to explain before you decide on anything else. You might describe the problem and the resolution next and then work on the characters. Coming up with the title may be the last thing you do.

Natural phenomenon that myth will explain:

Title of myth:

Names and traits of characters—how they look, what they do, what they say to one another:

Problem to be solved and creative way in which it will be solved:

Now, write the first draft of your myth.

"Icarus and Daedalus" by Josephine Preston Peabody
"Demeter and Persephone" by Anne Terry White
Build Language Skills: Vocabulary

Denotation and Connotation

A word's **denotation** is its literal meaning, the meaning you find when you look up the word in a dictionary. A word's **connotations** are the associations the word has in our culture. For example, the denotation of *consequence* is "something resulting from a cause." In many cases, the connotations of *consequence* are negative. Consider this sentence:

If you break the law, you will suffer the <u>consequence</u>.

Clearly, you are not likely to want to have anything to do with that consequence.

Yet in certain contexts, words have no connotations. For example, *outcome, result,* and *effect* have meanings similar to that of *consequence,* but those words have no negative connotations.

A. DIRECTIONS: *Use a dictionary to look up the meaning of the following words. Write the definition, and indicate whether the connotation is* positive, negative, *or* neutral. *Then, write a sentence using the word in such a way that its connotation is clear.*

1. hero   **Connotation:** _______________________

   Definition: ____

   Sentence: ____

2. arrogant   **Connotation:** _______________________

   Definition: ____

   Sentence: ____

Academic Vocabulary Practice

B. DIRECTIONS: *Answer each question using the underlined Academic Vocabulary word. Be sure to include the vocabulary word in your answer.*

1. Why might a player's illness have an <u>effect</u> on his or her soccer game?

   ____

2. Why will a slippery sidewalk <u>affect</u> the speed at which people walk?

   ____

3. What might be a <u>consequence</u> of learning to play the trumpet?

   ____

4. What might <u>occur</u> if someone breaks the law?

   ____

5. Why might you <u>alter</u> your routine?

   ____

"Icarus and Daedalus" by Josephine Preston Peabody
"Demeter and Persephone" by Anne Terry White
Build Language Skills: Grammar

Punctuation: Colons

A **colon** looks like two periods, one above the other (:). Colons are used to introduce a list that follows an independent clause.

To make wings, Daedalus gathered the following materials: feathers, wax, and thread.

A. PRACTICE: *Each of the following sentences is missing a colon. Rewrite the sentences, and insert a colon in the correct place.*

1. All of the characters in "Demeter and Persephone" are gods or goddesses Aphrodite, Eros, Pluto, Persephone, Demeter, Zeus, and Hermes.

   ____

   ____

2. Daedalus warns Icarus not to do these things fly too low, fly too high, and fly too far from him.

   ____

   ____

B. Writing Application: *Write two sentences about Greek mythology. In each sentence, use a colon to introduce a list.*

____

____

____

____

____

____

____

____

____

____

____

____

Name ____ Date ____________________

"Tenochtitlan: Inside the Aztec Capital" by Jacqueline Dineen

Reading: Reread to Look for Connections That Indicate Cause-and-Effect Relationships

A **cause** is an event or situation that produces a result. An **effect** is the result produced. In a story or an essay, each effect may eventually become a cause for the next event. This series of events results in a cause-and-effect chain, which propels the action forward.

As you read, think about the causes and effects of events. If you do not see a clear cause-and-effect relationship in a passage, **reread to look for connections** in the text. Look for words and phrases that identify cause-and-effect relationships, for example, *because, due to, for that reason, therefore,* and *as a result.*

DIRECTIONS: *Read the following sequences of events. Underline any words or phrases that help you identify a cause-and-effect relationship. Then, identify each event as a* cause, *an* effect, *or both* cause and effect.

__________________ 1. The Aztecs were excellent engineers.

__________________ 2. Therefore, they were able to build three causeways linking the island city to the mainland.

__________________ 3. Because of their skill as engineers, they were also able to build bridges that could be removed.

__________________ 4. As a result, they could prevent their enemies from reaching the city.

__________________ 5. The land around Lake Texcoco was dry.

__________________ 6. Because the land was dry, the Aztecs built ditches to irrigate the land.

__________________ 7. As they dug, they piled up the earth from the ditches in shallow parts of the lake, thus forming swamp gardens.

__________________ 8. Because they had formed swamp gardens, they had land on which to grow crops.

__________________ 9. Because they had land on which to grow crops, a portion of the population was able to grow its own food.

__________________ 10. Two of the lakes that fed into Lake Texcoco contained salt water.

__________________ 11. For that reason, the Aztecs built an embankment to keep out the salt water.

__________________ 12. The embankment also protected the city from floods.

Unit 6 Resources: Themes in the Oral Tradition

"Tenochtitlan: Inside the Aztec Capital" by Jacqueline Dineen
Literary Analysis: Legends and Facts

A **legend** is a traditional story about the past. Legends are based on facts that have grown into fiction over generations of retelling. Legends usually include these elements: a larger-than-life hero or heroine; fantastic events; roots, or a basis, in historical facts; and actions and events that reflect the culture that created the legend.

A **fact** is something that can be proved true. We uncover facts about ancient cultures by studying a variety of sources: written material, paintings, objects, and excavated ruins. When historians are unable to prove a theory about the past, they may speculate, or make a guess, based on the available evidence.

DIRECTIONS: *Read each excerpt from "Tenochtitlan: Inside the Aztec Capital." Then, tell whether the statement describes a* fact *or a* speculation, *and explain how you know.*

1. The Aztecs . . . built three causeways over the swamp to link the city with the mainland.

   Fact / Speculation: ___________________ **Explanation:** ___________________________

   ____

2. These bridges could be removed to leave gaps and this prevented enemies from getting to the city.

   Fact / Speculation: ___________________ **Explanation:** ___________________________

   ____

3. The Spaniards' first view of Tenochtitlan was described by one of Cortés's soldiers, Bernal Diaz.

   Fact / Speculation: ___________________ **Explanation:** ___________________________

   ____

4. Tenochtitlan was built in a huge valley, the Valley of Mexico.

   Fact / Speculation: ___________________ **Explanation:** ___________________________

   ____

5. Archaeologists think that when Tenochtitlan was at its greatest, about one million people lived in the Valley of Mexico.

   Fact / Speculation: ___________________ **Explanation:** ___________________________

   ____

6. Historians are not sure how many people in Tenochtitlan were farmers, but they think it may have been between one third and one half of the population.

   Fact / Speculation: ___________________ **Explanation:** ___________________________

   ____

"Tenochtitlan: Inside the Aztec Capital" by Jacqueline Dineen
Vocabulary Builder

Word List

outskirts	reeds	goblets

A. DIRECTIONS: *Read each item, and think about the meaning of the underlined word from the Word List. Then, answer each question, and explain your answer.*

1. Poorer people lived on the <u>outskirts</u> of Tenochtitlan. Did they live near the Temple Mayor?

   ____

2. <u>Reeds</u> were cut down in the swamps, dried, and woven into baskets. Are reeds trees?

   ____

3. The host passed <u>goblets</u> to his guests. Was he serving food?

   ____

B. DIRECTIONS: *Revise each sentence so that the underlined vocabulary word is used logically. Be sure to use the vocabulary word in your revised sentence.*

1. Michael liked living on the <u>outskirts</u> of the city so that he could be close to the center of activity.

   ____

   ____

2. The builders used <u>reeds</u> for the foundation, to bear the weight of the three-story house.

   ____

   ____

3. The servants placed slabs of juicy meat on the <u>goblets</u>.

   ____

C. DIRECTIONS: *Write the letter of the word that means the same or about the same as the word from the Word List.*

____ 1. outskirts
      A. dresses   B. suburbs   C. contests   D. cities

____ 2. reeds
      A. books   B. swamps   C. castles   D. grasses

____ 3. goblets
      A. cups   B. plates   C. silverware   D. ghosts

Unit 6 Resources: Themes in the Oral Tradition

Name ____ Date _______________

"Tenochtitlan: Inside the Aztec Capital" by Jacqueline Dineen

Support for Writing a Description

Use this chart to take notes as you prepare to write a **description** of Tenochtitlan. Write down as many details as you can to describe the various aspects of the city. Include verbs and adjectives that appeal to the five senses: sight, touch, taste, smell, and hearing.

Tenochtitlan: The Aztec Capital

When did Tenochtitlan exist?
Where was the city located?
What was the location of the city like?
What was the surrounding area like?
What kinds of infrastructures (roads, bridges, waterways, and so on) did the residents build?
How did the residents feed themselves?
What were the homes of the wealthy residents like?
What were the homes of the poorer residents like?

Now, use your notes to write a draft of a description of Tenochtitlan. Be sure to use vivid verbs and adjectives that will make your description interesting to your readers. Use words that appeal to the senses of sight, touch, taste, smell, and hearing.

241

"Popocatepetl and Ixtlaccihuatl" by Juliet Piggott Wood

Reading: Reread to Look for Connections That Indicate Cause-and-Effect Relationships

A **cause** is an event or situation that produces a result. An **effect** is the result produced. In a story or an essay, each effect may eventually become a cause for the next event. This series of events results in a cause-and-effect chain, which propels the action forward.

As you read, think about the causes and effects of events. If you do not see a clear cause-and-effect relationship in a passage, **reread to look for connections** in the text. Look for words and phrases that identify cause-and-effect relationships, for example, *because, due to, for that reason, therefore,* and *as a result.*

DIRECTIONS: *Read the following sequences of events. Underline any words or phrases that help you identify a cause-and-effect relationship. Then, identify each event as a* cause, *an* effect, *or both* cause and effect.

_____________________ 1. The Emperor wants Ixtla to rule the empire after he dies.

_____________________ 2. Therefore, Ixtla becomes more serious and more studious.

_____________________ 3. Ixtla also studies harder because she has fallen in love.

_____________________ 4. The Emperor becomes ill.

_____________________ 5. As a result, he rules the empire less effectively.

_____________________ 6. Because the empire has grown weaker, enemies are emboldened to surround it.

_____________________ 7. Because enemies surround the empire, the Emperor commands his warriors to defeat them.

_____________________ 8. Jealous warriors tell the Emperor that Popo has been killed in battle.

_____________________ 9. The Emperor tells Ixtla that Popo has died.

_____________________ 10. Because she is heartbroken and does not want to marry anyone but Popo, Ixtla grows sick and dies.

_____________________ 11. When Popo learns the circumstances of Ixtla's death, he kills the warriors who lied to the Emperor.

_____________________ 12. Popo grieves for Ixtla.

_____________________ 13. Therefore, Popo instructs the warriors to build two pyramids.

_____________________ 14. Popo stands atop the second pyramid, holding a burning torch.

_____________________ 15. Over time, the pyramids became mountains.

"Popocatepetl and Ixtlaccihuatl" by Juliet Piggott Wood
Literary Analysis: Legends and Facts

A **legend** is a traditional story about the past. A legend generally starts out as a story based on **fact**—something that can be proved true. Over the course of many generations, however, the story is retold and transformed into fiction. It becomes a legend.

Every culture has its own legends to immortalize real people who were famous in their time. Most legends include these elements:

- a larger-than-life hero or heroine
- fantastic events
- roots, or a basis, in historical facts
- actions and events that reflect the culture that created the legend

A powerful Aztec emperor wants to pass his kingdom on to his daughter, Ixtlaccihuatl, or Ixtla. Ixtla studies hard so that she will be worthy of this role. She loves Popocatepetl, or Popo, a brave and strong warrior in the service of the emperor. The emperor, Ixtla, and Popo are three larger-than-life characters who will form the basis of the legend.

DIRECTIONS: *Read each excerpt from "Popocatepetl and Ixtlaccihuatl." On the line, identify the element or elements of a legend that the passage reflects, and briefly explain how you recognized the element.*

1. The pass through which the Spaniards came to the ancient Tenochtitlan is still there, as are the volcanoes on each side of that pass. Their names have not been changed. The one to the north is Ixtlaccihuatl and the one on the south of the pass is Popocatepetl.

   Element of legend: ____

   Explanation: ____

2. There was once an Aztec Emperor in Tenochtitlan. He was very powerful. Some thought he was wise as well, whilst other doubted his wisdom.

   Element of legend: ____

   Explanation: ____

3. As time went on natural leaders emerged and, of these, undoubtedly Popo was the best. Finally it was he, brandishing his club and shield, who led the great charge of running warriors across the valley, with their enemies fleeing before them.

   Element of legend: ____

   Explanation: ____

4. So Popocatepetl stood there, holding the torch in memory of Ixtlaccihuatl, for the rest of his days.

   The snows came and, as the years went by, the pyramids of stone became high white-capped mountains.

   Element of legend: ____

   Explanation: ____

"Popocatepetl and Ixtlaccihuatl" by Juliet Piggott Wood
Vocabulary Builder

Word List

decreed   unanimous   routed

A. DIRECTIONS: *Read each item, and think about the meaning of the underlined word from the Word List. Then, answer the question, and explain your answer.*

1. The Emperor <u>decreed</u> that the triumphant warrior would marry his daughter. What kind of statement did the Emperor make?

   ____

2. The story would have ended happily if the warriors' support for Popo had been <u>unanimous</u>. What would have been different?

   ____

   ____

3. The warriors, led by Popo, <u>routed</u> the enemy. Did the battles continue?

   ____

B. DIRECTIONS: *Write the letter of the word that means the same or about the same as the word from the Word List.*

____ 1. decreed
    A. refused   **C.** ordered
    B. challenged   **D.** answered

____ 2. unanimous
    A. scattered   **C.** disappointed
    B. compared   **D.** undisputed

____ 3. routed
    A. cheered   **C.** slotted
    B. defeated   **D.** selected

"Popocatepetl and Ixtlaccihuatl" by Juliet Piggott Wood
Support for **Writing a Description**

Use this chart to take notes as you prepare to write a **description** of Ixtla. Refer to the legend to determine what Ixtla is like. Write down as many details as you can to describe the various aspects of her character. Include verbs and adjectives that appeal to the five senses: sight, touch, taste, smell, and hearing.

Ixtla

Physical appearance:
Attitude and disposition (what Ixtla is like):
How she acts (what Ixtla does):

Now, use your notes to write a draft of a description of the character of Ixtla. Be sure to use vivid verbs and adjectives that will make your description interesting to your readers. Use words that appeal to the senses of sight, touch, taste, smell, and hearing.

245

"Tenochtitlan: Inside the Aztec Capital" by Jacqueline Dineen
"Popocatepetl and Ixtlaccihuatl" by Juliet Piggott Wood
Build Language Skills: Vocabulary

Denotation and Connotation

A word's **denotation** is the literal meaning, the meaning that appears in a dictionary. A word's **connotations** are the meanings of the word apart from its exact definition; they are the ideas that are associated with the word. (Often a dictionary will provide some clues to a word's connotations, as well.)

Consider the verbs *alter* and *transform,* for example. Both words carry the denotation of "to change." Note that *alter* has the connotation of a slight change, one that does not affect the basic identity of the thing that is changing. *Transform,* however, has the connotation of a major change, such that the basic identity of the thing changes radically.

When you read, paying attention to connotations can help you figure out a work's deeper meaning.

A. DIRECTIONS: *Study each pair of synonyms and their denotation. If you are unsure of the words' connotations, consult a dictionary. Then, complete the sentences that follow by writing the correct synonym.*

resolute, obstinate: determined

1. Ixtla was _______________ in her commitment to the Emperor's wishes.
2. The Emperor was _______________ in his wish that his daughter not marry.

   excited, agitated: stirred up; aroused

3. When Ixtla heard that Popo had died, she became _______________.
4. When the warriors routed the enemy, they were happy and _______________.

Academic Vocabulary Practice

B. DIRECTIONS: *Read each sentence, and think about the meaning of the underlined Academic Vocabulary word. Then, answer the question, and explain your answer.*

1. What might be an <u>effect</u> of a long-term drought?

   ____

2. How might a drought <u>affect</u> a region?

   ____

3. What might be the <u>consequence</u> of contracting a virus?

   ____

4. What might <u>occur</u> if warring nations call for a truce?

   ____

5. Why might you <u>alter</u> the route you take to school?

   ____

"Tenochtitlan: Inside the Aztec Capital" by Jacqueline Dineen
"Popocatepetl and Ixtlaccihuatl" by Juliet Piggott Wood

Build Language Skills: Grammar

Commas and Semicolons

A **comma** (,) is used in the following ways:

Function	Example
to separate two independent clauses that are joined by a conjunction	One mountain is called Popocatepetl, and the other one is called Ixtlaccihuatl.
to separate three or more words, phrases, or clauses in a series	There were goblets for pulque and other drinks, graters for grinding chills, and storage pots of various designs.
after an introductory word, phrase, or clause	Unfortunately, some warriors were jealous of Popo. On an island in a swampy lake, the Aztecs built a city. As the city grew, more and more land was drained.

The **semicolon** (;) looks like a period above a comma. It has two main uses:

Function	Example
to join independent clauses that are not joined by a conjunction	One mountain is called Popocatepetl; the other one is called Ixtlaccihuatl.
to separate items in a series when one or more of the items itself contains a comma	The three main characters in the legend are the Emperor; his daughter, Ixtla; and Popo, a warrior.

A. PRACTICE: *Each sentence is missing one or more commas or semicolons. Rewrite each sentence with the correct punctuation.*

1. The family consisted of a couple their married children and their grandchildren.

____

2. Aztec houses were very plain everyone slept on mats of reeds.

____

B. Writing Application: *Write two sentences about the Aztecs. In one, use one or more semicolons, and in the other, use one or more commas.*

____

____

____

____

"Perseus" by Alice Low
"Percy-Us Brings the Gawgon's Head" by Lloyd Alexander
Literary Analysis: Comparing Treatment of Epic Conventions

An **epic** is a story or long poem about the adventures of a larger-than-life hero. The hero's parents are often gods or members of a royal family. Epic tales usually focus on the hero's bravery, strength, and success in battle or adventure. In addition to telling the story of a hero, an epic is a portrait of the culture that produced it. The following **epic conventions** are traditional characteristics of this form of literature:

- An epic involves a dangerous journey, or *quest*, that the hero must take.
- Gods or powerful characters help the hero.
- The setting of an epic is broad, covering several nations or even the universe.
- The style is serious and formal.

Because epics have become an important part of the literature of different cultures, they often inspire the works of later generations. The new works may vary widely. For example, one modern author based an ambitious novel on the ancient Greek epic the *Odyssey*, while another has used the epic to tell a humorous tale. As you read "Perseus" and "Percy-Us Brings the Gawgon's Head," determine which story is closer to the original epic and which was written to make you chuckle.

DIRECTIONS: *Use the following chart to compare "Perseus" and "Percy-Us Brings the Gawgon's Head." If the information to answer a question does not appear in the selection,* write *information not mentioned.*

Questions	"Perseus"	"Percy-Us Brings the Gawgon's Head"
1. What is the setting?		
2. Who is the hero?		
3. Who are the hero's parents?		
4. What dangerous journey must the hero undertake?		
5. Who helps the hero in his quest?		
6. What is the creature like that the hero must face?		
7. What does each hero accomplish?		
8. Which story is closer to the original? Which is humorous?		

"Perseus" by Alice Low
"Percy-Us Brings the Gawgon's Head" by Lloyd Alexander
Vocabulary Builder

Word List

cowered	hideous	pursuit	knack	reveling	pathetic	petrified

A. DIRECTIONS: *Think about the meaning of each italicized word from the Word List. Then, explain whether the sentence makes sense. If it does not make sense, write a new sentence. In the new sentence, use the italicized word correctly.*

1. Everyone admired the *hideous* dress.

   Explanation: ____

   New sentence: ____

2. My family visited a *petrified* forest to see trees that had turned to rock.

   Explanation: ____

   New sentence: ____

3. The children were in *pursuit* of their mother as they waited on the front porch.

   Explanation: ____

   New sentence: ____

4. The dog *cowered* under the table during the fierce thunderstorm.

   Explanation: ____

   New sentence: ____

B. DIRECTIONS: *Write the letter of the word or group of words whose meaning is* most opposite *that of the vocabulary word.*

____ 1. knack
   A. noise
   B. lack of noise
   C. talent
   D. lack of talent

____ 2. pathetic
   A. admirable
   B. pitiful
   C. foolish
   D. tolerant

____ 3. reveling
   A. exposing
   B. waiting
   C. mourning
   D. hiding

Unit 6 Resources: Themes in the Oral Tradition

249

"Perseus" by Alice Low
"Percy-Us Brings the Gawgon's Head" by Lloyd Alexander
Support for Writing to Compare Literary Works

Use this graphic organizer to take notes for an **essay** in which you compare and contrast the heroes Perseus and Percy-Us.

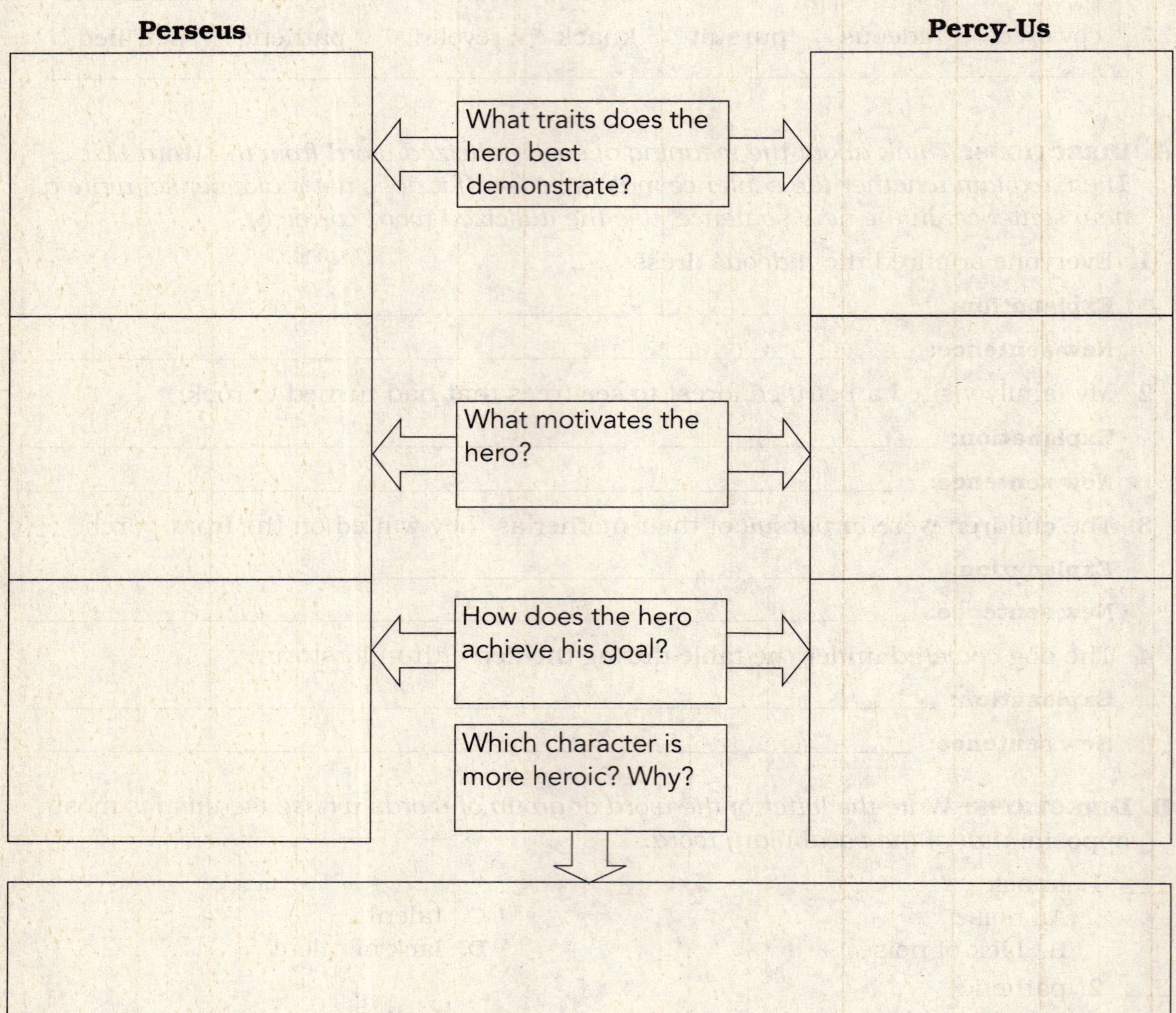

Now, use your notes to write an essay comparing and contrasting the heroes Perseus and Percy-Us.

"Sun and Moon in a Box" by Richard Erdoes and Alfonso Ortiz
Reading: Use Prior Knowledge to Compare and Contrast

A **comparison** tells how two or more things are alike. A **contrast** tells how two or more things are different. When you **compare and contrast,** you recognize similarities and differences. You can often understand an unfamiliar concept by **using your prior knowledge to compare and contrast.** For example, you may understand an ancient culture better if you look for ways in which it is similar to and different from your own culture. You also might find similarities and differences between a story told long ago and one that is popular today. To compare and contrast stories, ask questions such as "What does this event bring to mind?" or "Does this character make me think of someone I know or have read about?"

DIRECTIONS: *Read each passage from "Sun and Moon in a Box." In the second column of the chart, write a question that will help you compare or contrast the passage to something else you have read or to something or someone you know or know about. In the third column, write the answer to your question. The first item has been completed as an example.*

Passage from "Sun and Moon in a Box"	Question Based on My Prior Knowledge	Comparison or Contrast
1. Coyote and Eagle were hunting. Eagle caught rabbits. Coyote caught nothing but grasshoppers. Coyote said, "Friend Eagle, my chief, we make a great hunting pair."	How are these characters like Wile E. Coyote and Road Runner in the cartoons I used to watch?	Road Runner is a bird, but not an eagle, and Wile E. Coyote tries to catch him. Here, the coyote and the eagle seem to be friends.
2. Whenever [the Kachinas] wanted light they opened the lid and let the sun peek out. Then, it was day. When they wanted less light, they opened the box just a little for the moon to look out.		
3. After a while Coyote called Eagle, "My chief, let me have the box. I am ashamed to let you do all the carrying." "No," said Eagle, "You are not reliable. You might be curious and open the box."		
4. [Coyote] sat down and opened the box. In a flash, . . . icy winds made all living things shiver. Then, before Coyote could put the lid back, . . . snow fell down from heaven and covered the plains and the mountains.		

"Sun and Moon in a Box" by Richard Erdoes and Alfonso Ortiz

Literary Analysis: Cultural Context

Stories such as fables, folk tales, and myths are influenced by cultural context. **Cultural context** is the background, customs, and beliefs of the people who originally told them. Knowing the cultural context of a work will help you understand and appreciate it. You can keep track of the cultural context of a work by considering these elements: the *title* of the selection, the *time* in which it takes place, the *place* in which it takes place, the *customs* of the characters, the *beliefs* that are expressed or suggested.

Consider this passage from "Sun and Moon in a Box":

> Now, at this time, the earth was still soft and new. There was as yet no sun and no moon.

The passage tells you that the folk tale is set in the distant past, before Earth looked as it does today and before there was a sun and a moon. From the cultural context, you can infer that the people who told the tale believed there was a time when Earth existed, but the sun and the moon as yet did not.

DIRECTIONS: *Read each passage from "Sun and Moon in a Box." In the second column of the chart, indicate which element of the cultural context—*time, place, customs, *or* beliefs—*the passage illustrates. Then, explain your choice. Tell why you think the example shows the element you have chosen.*

Passage from "Sun and Moon in a Box"	Element of Cultural Context and Explanation
1. [Eagle and Coyote] went toward the west. They came to a deep canyon.	
2. Whenever [the Kachinas] wanted light they opened the lid and let the sun peek out. . . . When they wanted less light, they opened the box just a little for the moon to look out.	
3. "Let us steal the box," said Coyote. "No, that would be wrong," said Eagle. "Let us just borrow it."	
4. Eagle grabbed the box and . . . Coyote ran after him on the ground. After a while Coyote called Eagle: "My chief, let me have the box. I am ashamed to let you do all the carrying."	

252

"Sun and Moon in a Box" by Richard Erdoes and Alfonso Ortiz
Vocabulary Builder

Word List

reliable	relented	curb

A. DIRECTIONS: *For each item below, think about the meaning of the underlined word from the Word List. Then, answer the question and explain your answer.*

1. Zach lent a book to his most <u>reliable</u> classmate, Tyler. Was Tyler likely to return the book?

   ____

   ____

2. For days, the children pleaded with their parents to let them keep the stray dog, and, at last, their parents <u>relented</u>. Did the family keep the dog?

   ____

   ____

3. As summer vacation approached and Ashley looked forward to going away, she could not stop herself from making lists and plans. Was she able to <u>curb</u> her excitement?

   ____

   ____

B. DIRECTIONS: *Indicate whether each statement is* true *or* false. *Then, explain your answer.*

1. A car that starts only half the time is *reliable*.

   T / F: ______ **Explanation:** ____

   ____

2. A teacher who refuses her students' pleas to make a test easier has *relented*.

   T / F: ______ **Explanation:** ____

   ____

3. Someone who can keep a secret is able to *curb* the desire to tell his or her best friend everything.

   T / F: ______ **Explanation:** ____

   ____

Name _______________________________________ Date ___________________

"Sun and Moon in a Box" by Richard Erdoes and Alfonso Ortiz

Support for Writing a Plot Summary

Use this chart to take notes for a **plot summary** of "Sun and Moon in a Box."

Plot Summary of "Sun and Moon in a Box"

<table>
<tr><td colspan="3">Setting:

</td></tr>
<tr><td colspan="2">Major character Eagle:

</td><td>Major character Coyote:

</td></tr>
<tr><td>Main event from beginning of folk tale:

</td><td>Main event from middle of folk tale:

</td><td>Main event from end of folk tale:

</td></tr>
<tr><td colspan="3">Final outcome:

</td></tr>
</table>

Now, use your notes to write your **plot summary.** Be sure to include all the information called for on the chart.

"How the Snake Got Poison" by Zora Neale Hurston
Reading: Use Prior Knowledge to Compare and Contrast

A **comparison** tells how two or more things are alike. A **contrast** tells how two or more things are different. When you **compare and contrast,** you recognize similarities and differences. You can often understand an unfamiliar concept by **using your prior knowledge to compare and contrast.** For example, you may understand an ancient culture better if you look for ways in which it is similar to and different from your own culture. You also might find similarities and differences between a story told long ago and one that is popular today. To compare and contrast stories, ask questions such as "What does this event bring to mind?" or "Does this character make me think of someone I know or have read about?"

DIRECTIONS: *Read each passage from "How the Snake Got Poison." In the second column of the chart, write a question that will help you compare or contrast the passage to something else you have read or to something or someone you know or know about. In the third column, write the answer to your question. The first item has been completed as an example.*

Passage from "How the Snake Got Poison"	Question Based on My Prior Knowledge	Comparison or Contrast
1. "Ah ain't so many, God, you put me down here on my belly in de dust and everything trods upon me and kills off my generations. Ah ain't got no kind of protection at all."	How does this snake compare with Nag and Nagaina in the story "Rikki-tikki-tavi"?	Like this snake, Nag and Nagaina can talk. They also have a problem protecting themselves and their unborn children.
2. "God, please do somethin' 'bout dat snake. He' layin' in de bushes there wid poison in his mouf and he's strikin' everything dat shakes de bushes. He's killin' up our generations."		
3. "Lawd, you know Ah'm down here in de dust. Ah ain't got no claws to fight wid, and Ah ain't got no feets to git me out de way. All Ah kin see is feets comin' to tromple me. Ah can't tell who my enemy is. . . ."		
4. "Well, snake, I don't want yo' generations all stomped out and I don't want you killin' everything else dat moves. Here take dis bell and tie it to yo' tail."		

"How the Snake Got Poison" by Zora Neale Hurston
Literary Analysis: Cultural Context

Stories such as fables, folk tales, and myths are influenced by cultural context. **Cultural context** is the background, customs, and beliefs of the people who originally told them. Knowing the cultural context of a work will help you understand and appreciate it. You can keep track of the cultural context of a work by considering these elements: the *title* of the selection, the *time* in which it takes place, the *place* in which it takes place, the *customs* of the characters, the *beliefs* that are expressed or suggested.

Consider this passage from "How the Snake Got Poison":

Well, when God made de snake he put him in de bushes to ornament de ground.

The passage tells you that the folk tale is set in the distant past. From the cultural context, you can infer that the people who told the tale held beliefs about the purpose of the snake in nature.

DIRECTIONS: *These passages from "How the Snake Got Poison" illustrate the folk tale's cultural context by suggesting beliefs held by the people who told the tale. In the second column of the chart, tell what belief the passage illustrates.*

Passage from "How the Snake Got Poison"	Suggested Belief
1. God . . . said, "Ah didn't mean for nothin' to be stompin' you snakes lak dat. You got to have some kind of a protection. Here, take dis poison and put it in yo' mouf and when they tromps on you, protect yo'self."	
2. "Snake, . . . Ah didn't mean for you to be hittin' and killin' everything dat shake de bush. I give you dat poison and tole you to protect yo'self when they tromples on you. But you kil-lin' everything dat moves."	
3. "Here take dis bell and tie it to yo' tail. When you hear feets comin' you ring yo' bell and if it's yo' friend, he'll be keerful. If it's yo' enemy, it's you and him."	

"How the Snake Got Poison" by Zora Neale Hurston
Vocabulary Builder

Word List

ornament   immensity

A. DIRECTIONS: *For each item below, think about the meaning of the underlined word from the Word List. Then, answer the question and explain your answer.*

1. If you leave garbage cans in front of your house all week, will they <u>ornament</u> your property?

   ____

   ____

2. The condor must have an <u>immensity</u> in which to fly. Can the condor survive in a small space?

   ____

   ____

B. DIRECTIONS: *Indicate whether each statement is* true *or* false. *Then, explain your answer.*

1. Colored lights and Chinese lanterns will *ornament* a backyard party.

   T / F: ______ **Explanation:** ____

   ____

2. An *immensity* can easily be fenced in.

   T / F: ______ **Explanation:** ____

   ____

C. DIRECTIONS: *Write the letter of the word that means the same or about the same as the vocabulary word.*

____ 1. ornament
    A. pollute   B. convince   C. decorate   D. detain

____ 2. immensity
    A. comedy   B. transition   C. tranquillity   D. vastness

"How the Snake Got Poison" by Zora Neale Hurston
Support for Writing a Plot Summary

Use this chart to take notes for a **plot summary** of "How the Snake Got Poison."

Plot Summary of "How the Snake Got Poison"

Setting:		

Major character God:	**Major character Snake:**

Main event from beginning of folk tale:	**Main event from middle of folk tale:**	**Main event from end of folk tale:**

Final outcome:

Now, use your notes to write your **plot summary.** Be sure to include all the information called for on the chart.

"Sun and Moon in a Box" by Richard Erdoes and Alfonso Ortiz
"How the Snake Got Poison" by Zora Neale Hurston
Build Language Skills: Vocabulary

Idioms

An **idiomatic expression** is one in which the meaning of the expression is different from the meaning of the individual words that make up the expression. Idioms and idiomatic expressions are commonly used. We are so accustomed to hearing them that we may forget that they do not make sense if we take them literally. For example, if you have difficulty coming up with something to say to someone you have just met, it may be suggested that you find a way to *break the ice*. The suggestion has nothing to do with ice fishing or any other winter activity. It simply means "find a way to start a conversation."

A. DIRECTIONS: *Rewrite each of the following sentences. In place of the underlined idiomatic expression, use a literal expression, one whose meaning does not differ from the meaning of the individual words that make it up. If you are unsure of the meaning of an idiom, look it up in a dictionary (under the most important word in the expression) or on the Internet.*

1. The rudeness of the person who bumped into me in the mall was so extreme that I was <u>seeing red</u> for the next hour.

   ____

   ____

2. Anthony <u>made no bones about</u> his desire to win the science-fair competition.

   ____

Academic Vocabulary Practice

B. DIRECTIONS: *Answer each question using the underlined Academic Vocabulary word. Be sure to include the vocabulary word in your answer.*

1. Why do scientists <u>analyze</u> the results of an experiment?

   ____

2. What <u>aspect</u> of snakes might you do research on?

   ____

3. Which <u>detail</u> in "Sun and Moon in a Box" or "How the Snake Got Poison" did you particularly like?

   ____

4. What is a <u>unique characteristic</u> of a snake?

   ____

"Sun and Moon in a Box" by Richard Erdoes and Alfonso Ortiz
"How the Snake Got Poison" by Zora Neale Hurston
Build Language Skills: Grammar

Capitalization

Capitalization is the use of uppercase letters (*A*, *B*, *C*, and so on). Capital letters signal the beginning of a sentence or a quotation and identify proper nouns and proper adjectives. **Proper nouns** include the names of people, geographical locations, specific events and time periods, organizations, languages, and religions. **Proper adjectives** are derived from proper nouns.

Use of Capital Letter	Example
Sentence beginning	The coyote was a bad swimmer. He nearly drowned.
Quotation	The snake said, "You know I'm down here in the dust."
Proper nouns	They traveled through the Southwest.
Proper adjectives	Coyote might have run as far as the Mexican border.

A. Practice: *Rewrite each sentence below. Use capitalization correctly.*

1. the character named coyote suggested that they steal the box.

   ____

2. the folk tale takes place in the american southwest, perhaps in present-day arizona or new mexico.

   ____

   ____

3. coyote said to eagle, "this is a wonderful thing."

   ____

4. "i do not trust you," eagle said many times. "you will open that box."

   ____

B. Writing Application: *Write a short episode telling what Coyote might have done after he let the sun and the moon escape from the box. Include at least one quotation, one proper noun, and one proper adjective. Use capitalization correctly.*

____

____

____

____

____

"The People Could Fly" by Virginia Hamilton
Reading: Use a Venn Diagram to Compare and Contrast

When you **compare and contrast,** you recognize similarities and differences. You can compare and contrast elements in a literary work by **using a Venn diagram** to examine character traits, situations, and ideas. First, reread the text to locate the details you will compare. Then, write the details on a diagram like the ones shown below. Recording these details will help you understand the similarities and differences in a literary work.

DIRECTIONS: *Fill in the Venn diagrams as directed to make comparisons about elements of "The People Could Fly."*

1. Compare Toby and Sarah. Write characteristics of Toby in the left-hand oval and characteristics of Sarah in the right-hand oval. Write characteristics that they share in the overlapping part of the two ovals.

Toby   **Both**   **Sarah**

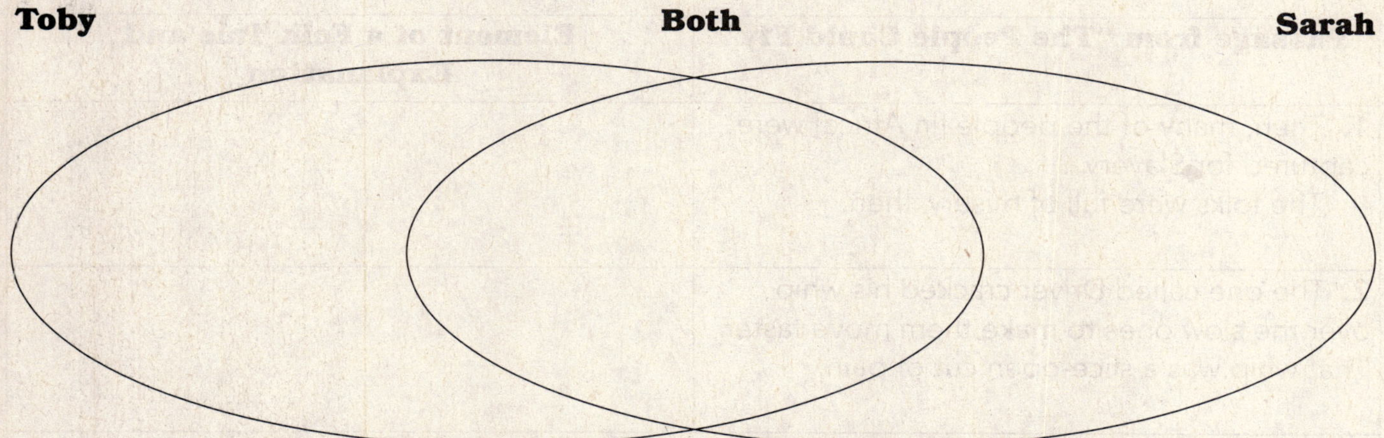

2. Compare the enslaved people with the Overseer and Driver. Write characteristics of the enslaved people in the left-hand oval and characteristics of the Overseer and Driver in the right-hand oval. Write characteristics that they share in the overlapping part of the two ovals.

Enslaved People   **Both**   **Overseer and Driver**

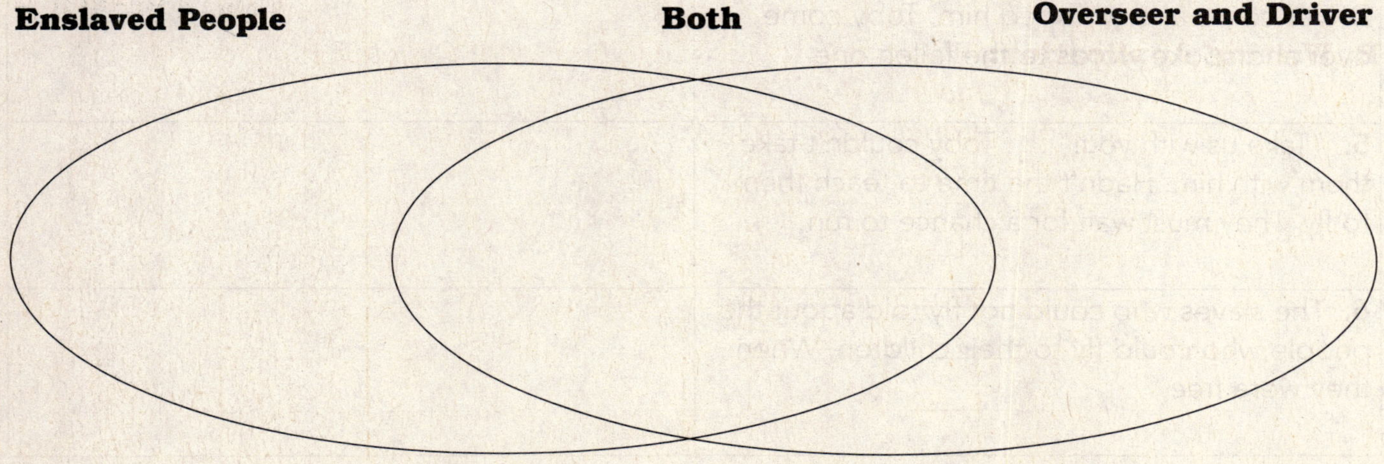

"The People Could Fly" by Virginia Hamilton
Literary Analysis: Folk Tale

A **folk tale** is a story that is composed orally and then passed from person to person by word of mouth. Although folk tales originate in this **oral tradition,** many of them are eventually collected and written down. Similar folk tales are told by different cultures throughout the world. Such folk tales have common character types, plot elements, and themes. Folk tales often teach a lesson about life and present a clear separation between good and evil. Folk tales are part of the oral tradition that also includes fairy tales, legends, myths, fables, tall tales, and ghost stories.

DIRECTIONS: *Read each passage from "The People Could Fly." In the second column of the chart, indicate whether the passage* teaches a lesson about life *or whether it* clearly presents good, clearly presents evil, *or presents a clear distinction between the two. Then, explain your choice. Tell why you think the example shows the element you have chosen.*

Passage from "The People Could Fly"	Element of a Folk Tale and Explanation
1. Then, many of the people [in Africa] were captured for Slavery. . . . The folks were full of misery, then.	
2. The one called Driver cracked his whip over the slow ones to make them move faster. That whip was a slice-open cut of pain.	
3. The . . . woman fell to the earth. The old man that was there, Toby, came and helped her to her feet.	
4. A young man slave fell from the heat. The Driver come and whipped him. Toby come over and spoke words to the fallen one.	
5. "Take us with you!" . . . Toby couldn't take them with him. Hadn't the time to teach them to fly. They must wait for a chance to run.	
6. The slaves who could not fly told about the people who could fly to their children. When they were free.	

Unit 6 Resources: Themes in the Oral Tradition

"The People Could Fly" by Virginia Hamilton
Vocabulary Builder

Word List

scorned	croon	shuffle

A. DIRECTIONS: *For each item below, think about the meaning of the underlined word from the Word List. Then, answer the question, and explain your answer.*

1. The workers were so <u>scorned</u> by the company owner that they protested. Were they right to protest?

   ____

2. The popular singer will <u>croon</u> the audience's favorite song. What kind of song will the singer perform?

   ____

3. The clowns <u>shuffle</u> across the stage. How are they moving?

   ____

B. DIRECTIONS: *Indicate whether each statement is* true *or* false. *Then, explain your answer.*

1. A well-loved teacher is one who is very much *scorned*.

   T / F: ______ **Explanation:** ____

   ____

2. A singer is likely to *croon* a love song.

   T / F: ______ **Explanation:** ____

   ____

3. A person taking a power walk is likely to *shuffle*.

   T / F: ______ **Explanation:** ____

   ____

C. DIRECTIONS: *Write the letter of the word or group of words that means* the opposite of *the vocabulary word.*

_____ 1. scorned
   A. commanded   B. resigned   C. appreciated   D. hired

_____ 2. croon
   A. sing softly   B. speak quietly   C. speak haltingly   D. sing loudly

Unit 6 Resources: Themes in the Oral Tradition

Name ____ Date _______________________

"The People Could Fly" by Virginia Hamilton
Support for Writing a Review

Use this chart to take notes for a **review** of "The People Could Fly."

Notes for Review of "The People Could Fly" by Virginia Hamilton

Element of the Tale	My Opinion of the Element	Details from the Tale That Support My Opinion
Characters		
Description		
Dialogue		
Plot		

Now, write a draft of your review. Tell readers whether or not you think they will enjoy "The People Could Fly." Remember to support your opinions with details from the tale.

"**All Stories Are Anansi's**" by Harold Courlander
Reading: Use a Venn Diagram to Compare and Contrast

When you **compare and contrast,** you recognize similarities and differences. You can compare and contrast elements in a literary work by **using a Venn diagram** to examine character traits, situations, and ideas. First, reread the text to locate the details you will compare. Then, write the details on a diagram like the ones shown below. Recording these details will help you understand the similarities and differences in a literary work.

DIRECTIONS: *Fill in the Venn diagrams as directed to make comparisons about elements of "All Stories Are Anansi's."*

1. Compare Anansi and Onini, the great python. Write characteristics of Anansi in the left-hand oval and characteristics of Onini in the right-hand oval. Write characteristics that they share in the overlapping part of the two ovals.

Anansi   **Both**   **Onini**

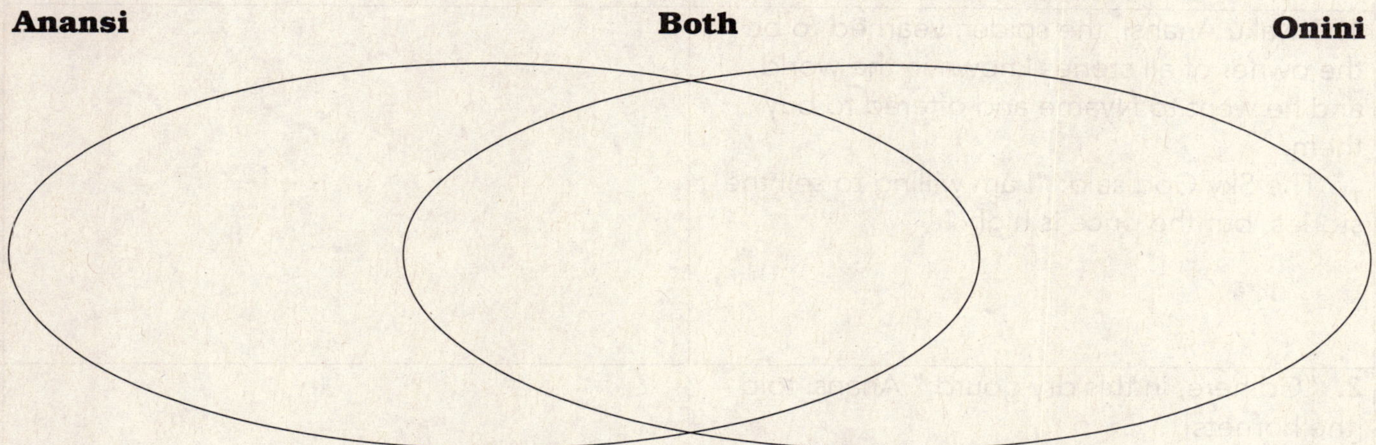

2. Compare Mmoboro, the hornets, with Osebo, the leopard. Write characteristics of the hornets in the left-hand oval and characteristics of the leopard in the right-hand oval. Write characteristics that they share in the overlapping part of the two ovals.

Hornets   **Both**   **Leopard**

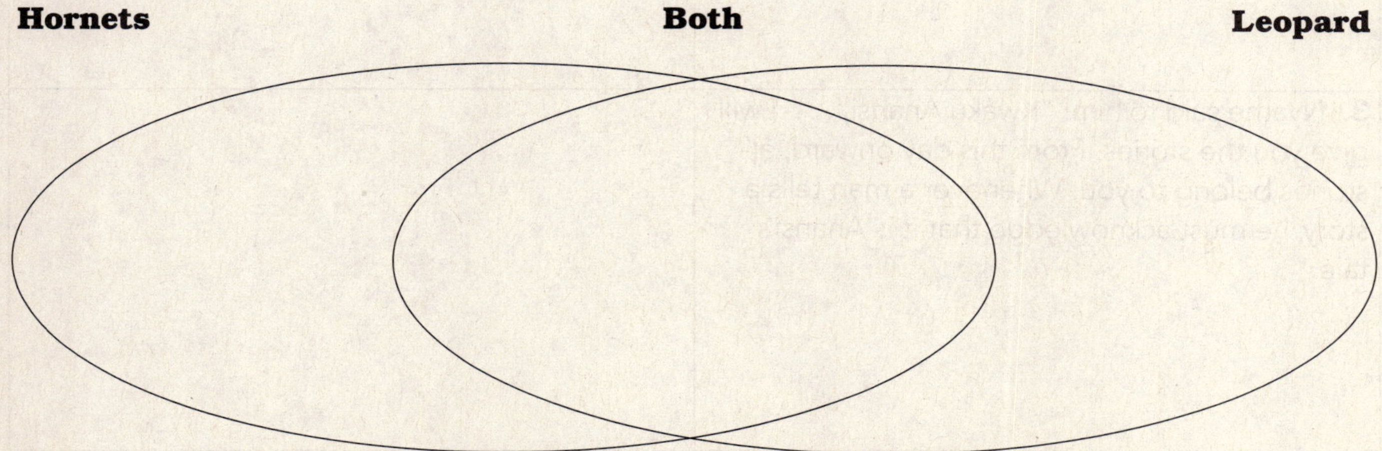

"All Stories Are Anansi's" by Harold Courlander
Literary Analysis: Folk Tale

A **folk tale** is a story that is composed orally and then passed from person to person by word of mouth. Although folk tales originate in this **oral tradition,** many of them are eventually collected and written down. Similar folk tales are told by different cultures throughout the world. Such folk tales have common character types, plot elements, and themes. Folk tales often teach a lesson about life and present a clear separation between good and evil. Folk tales are part of the oral tradition that also includes fairy tales, legends, myths, fables, tall tales, and ghost stories.

DIRECTIONS: *Read each passage from "All Stories Are Anansi's." In the second column of the chart, indicate what value or lesson about life the passage teaches. Then, explain your choice.*

Passage from "All Stories Are Anansi's"	Value or Lesson About Life and Explanation
1. Kwaku Anansi, the spider, yearned to be the owner of all stories known in the world, and he went to Nyame and offered to buy them. The Sky God said: "I am willing to sell the stories, but the price is high."	
2. "Go here, in this dry gourd," Anansi told [the hornets]. . . . When the last of them had entered, Anansi plugged the hole with a ball of grass, saying: "Oh, yes, but you are really foolish people!"	
3. Nyame said to him: "Kwaku Anansi, . . . I will give you the stories. From this day onward, all stories belong to you. Whenever a man tells a story, he must acknowledge that it is Anansi's tale."	

Name _______________________________________ Date _______________________

"All Stories Are Anansi's" by Harold Courlander
Vocabulary Builder

Word List

| yearned | gourd | acknowledge |

A. DIRECTIONS: *For each item below, think about the meaning of the underlined word from the Word List. Then, answer the question, and explain your answer.*

1. The hornets probably <u>yearned</u> to play a trick on Anansi. Did they want very much to get back at him?

   ____

2. A <u>gourd</u> was put on the table when dinner was served. For what would the gourd be used?

   ____

3. Will you <u>acknowledge</u> Anansi as the owner of every story you tell?

   ____

B. DIRECTIONS: *Indicate whether each statement is* true *or* false. *Then, explain your answer.*

1. You *yearn* for something you do not want.

   T / F: _______ **Explanation:** _________________________________

   ____

2. It would be appropriate to serve water in a *gourd*.

   T / F: _______ **Explanation:** _________________________________

   ____

3. You can *acknowledge* someone by ignoring him or her.

   T / F: _______ **Explanation:** _________________________________

   ____

C. DIRECTIONS: *Write the letter of the word that means* the same or about the same as *the vocabulary word.*

____ 1. yearned
    A. rejected   B. questioned   C. desired   D. ignored

____ 2. gourd
    A. cup   B. fork   C. platter   D. knife

____ 3. acknowledge
    A. taunt   B. challenge   C. credit   D. dismiss

"**All Stories Are Anansi's**" by Harold Courlander
Support for Writing a Review

Use this chart to take notes for a **review** of "All Stories Are Anansi's."

Notes for Review of "All Stories Are Anansi's" by Harold Courlander

Element of the Tale	My Opinion of the Element	Details From the Tale That Support My Opinion
Characters		
Description		
Dialogue		
Plot		

Now, write a draft of your review. Tell readers whether or not you think they will enjoy "All Stories Are Anansi's." Remember to support your opinions with details from the tale.

"The People Could Fly" by Virginia Hamilton
"All Stories Are Anansi's" by Harold Courlander
Build Language Skills: Vocabulary

Idioms

An **idiomatic expression** is one in which the meaning of the expression is different from the meaning of the individual words that make up the expression. We are so accustomed to hearing idioms and idiomatic expressions that we may forget that they do not make sense if we take them literally. For example, in "The People Could Fly," Sarah is so worn out that she cannot sing to her baby. The narrator says, "She had no heart to croon to it." That does not mean that Sarah's heart has been removed. It means she does not have the will or the spirit to comfort the child.

A. DIRECTIONS: *Use the context to figure out the meaning of the underlined idiom in each sentence. Then, rewrite the sentence, using a* literal *expression for the idiom. A literal expression is one whose meaning does* not *differ from the meaning of the individual words that make it up.*

1. The story of the family who lost all their possessions in a flood <u>broke my heart</u>.

   ____

2. Tom took his teacher's advice <u>to heart</u> and immediately began studying harder.

   ____

Academic Vocabulary Practice

B. DIRECTIONS: *Is each sentence* true *or* false? *Circle* T *or* F; *then, explain your answer.*

1. When you *analyze* a problem, you express a generalization about it.

   T / F: ________   **Explanation:** _________________________________

   ____

2. Suspense is not a *characteristic* of mystery stories.

   T / F: ________   **Explanation:** _________________________________

3. An *aspect* of folk tales is the common character type.

   T / F: ________   **Explanation:** _________________________________

   ____

4. A *detail* may be important or unimportant.

   T / F: ________   **Explanation:** _________________________________

   ____

5. A *unique* work of art is probably just like a lot of other works of art.

   T / F: ________   **Explanation:** _________________________________

   ____

"The People Could Fly" by Virginia Hamilton
"All Stories Are Anansi's" by Harold Courlander
Build Language Skills: Grammar

Abbreviations

An **abbreviation** is a shortened form of a word or phrase. Most abbreviations end with a period, but many do not, and some may be written either with or without a period. Most dictionaries have entries for abbreviations, so look them up if you are not sure of the correct form. Note which abbreviations are written with periods, which ones are not, and which ones appear in capital letters in these lists:

Titles of persons: Mr. Ms. Mrs.

Days of the week: Sun. Mon. Tues. Wed. Thurs. Fri. Sat. Sun.

Months of the year: Jan. Feb. Mar. Apr. Aug. Sept. Oct. Nov. Dec.

Times of day: a.m. p.m.

Street designations: Ave. Blvd. Pl. St.

State postal abbreviations: AL AK AZ AR CA CO CT DE FL GA HI ID IL IN IA KS KY LA ME MD MA MI MN MS MO MT NE NV NH NJ NM NY NC ND OH OK OR PA RI SC SD TN TX UT VT VA WA WV WI WY

Organizations: NAACP UN YMCA

Units of measure: in. ft. yd. lb. qt. gal. *but* mm cm m mg g ml dl l

A. PRACTICE: *Rewrite each sentence below, and abbreviate the words in italics.*

1. James lives at 115 Elm *Street*, Pleasant Valley, *Nebraska*.

   ____

2. The gardener said that if your yard measures 50 *feet* (16.6 *yards*) by 40 *feet* (13.3 *yards*), you will need 2 *pounds* of fertilizer.

   ____

   ____

3. *Mister* Raymond works for the *United Nations*.

   ____

B. Writing Application: *Compose an e-mail message to a friend. Tell about something you have done recently. Use at least five abbreviations. If you are not sure of the correct form, look up the abbreviation in a dictionary.*

____

____

____

____

____

"The Fox Outwits the Crow" by William Cleary
"The Fox and the Crow" by Aesop
Literary Analysis: Comparing Tone

The **tone** of a literary work is the writer's attitude toward his or her subject and characters. The tone can often be described by a single adjective, such as *formal, playful,* or *respectful.* Factors that contribute to the tone include word choice, details, sentence structure, rhythm, and rhyme.

The poem "The Fox Outwits the Crow" and the fable "The Fox and the Crow" have similar characters, settings, and plots, but the authors who wrote them have different attitudes toward their subject. To determine the tone of each selection, notice the words and phrases that the authors use to express their ideas.

DIRECTIONS: *Compare the tone of the two selections about the fox and the crow by completing this chart. Choose one adjective to describe each passage. Use* serious, formal, informal, *or* playful. *Then, answer the question that follows.*

"The Fox Outwits the Crow"	Adjective	"The Fox and the Crow"	Adjective
1. One day a young Crow snatched a fat piece of cheese.		A Fox once saw a Crow fly off with a piece of cheese in its beak.	
2. A Fox . . . got a whiff of the cheese, / The best of his favorite hors d'oeuvres		"That's for me, as I am a Fox," said master Reynard.	
3. Hey, you glamorous thing, / Does your voice match your beautiful curves?		"I feel sure your voice must surpass that of other birds, just as your figure does."	
4. She opened her mouth—and the cheese tumbled out, /		The moment she opened her mouth the . . . cheese fell to the ground . . .	
5. Which the Fox gobbled up full of malice		only to be snapped up by Master Fox.	
6. While he chuckled to think how that dim-witted Crow		"That will do," said he. "That was all I wanted."	
7. Could believe she was MARIA CALLAS		"In exchange for your cheese I will give you . . . advice for the future—"	

8. What is each author's attitude toward his subject and his characters?

____

"The Fox Outwits the Crow" by William Cleary
"The Fox and the Crow" by Aesop
Vocabulary Builder

Word List

whiff	hors d'oeuvres	malice	glossy	surpass	flatterers

A. DIRECTIONS: *Circle* T *if the statement is true and* F *if the statement is false. Then, explain your answer.*

1. A true bloodhound can follow someone's trail after getting only a *whiff* of the person's odor.

   T / F ____

2. *Flatterers* are honest and sincere.

   T / F ____

3. Something that is *glossy* has a rough finish.

   T / F ____

4. Most people would feel *malice* toward someone who has harmed them.

   T / F ____

5. *Hors d'oeuvres* are served after the main course.

   T / F ____

6. For a person to *surpass* expectations, he or she must do better than expected.

   T / F ____

B. DIRECTIONS: *For each pair of words in CAPITAL LETTERS, write the letter of the pair of words that best expresses a similar relationship.*

____ 1. OUTDO : SURPASS ::
    A. lose : win   C. work : play
    B. talk : remember   D. throw : toss

____ 2. WHIFF : SCENT ::
    A. sight : hearing   C. love : adoration
    B. good : bad   D. eyes : nose

____ 3. MALICE : GOODWILL ::
    A. stroll : walk   C. large : humongous
    B. painter : artist   D. blame : praise

"The Fox Outwits the Crow" by William Cleary
"The Fox and the Crow" by Aesop

Support for Writing to Compare Reactions to Tone

Use this graphic organizer to take notes for an essay that compares your reaction to the author's tone in "The Fox Outwits the Crow" with your reaction to the author's tone in "The Fox and the Crow."

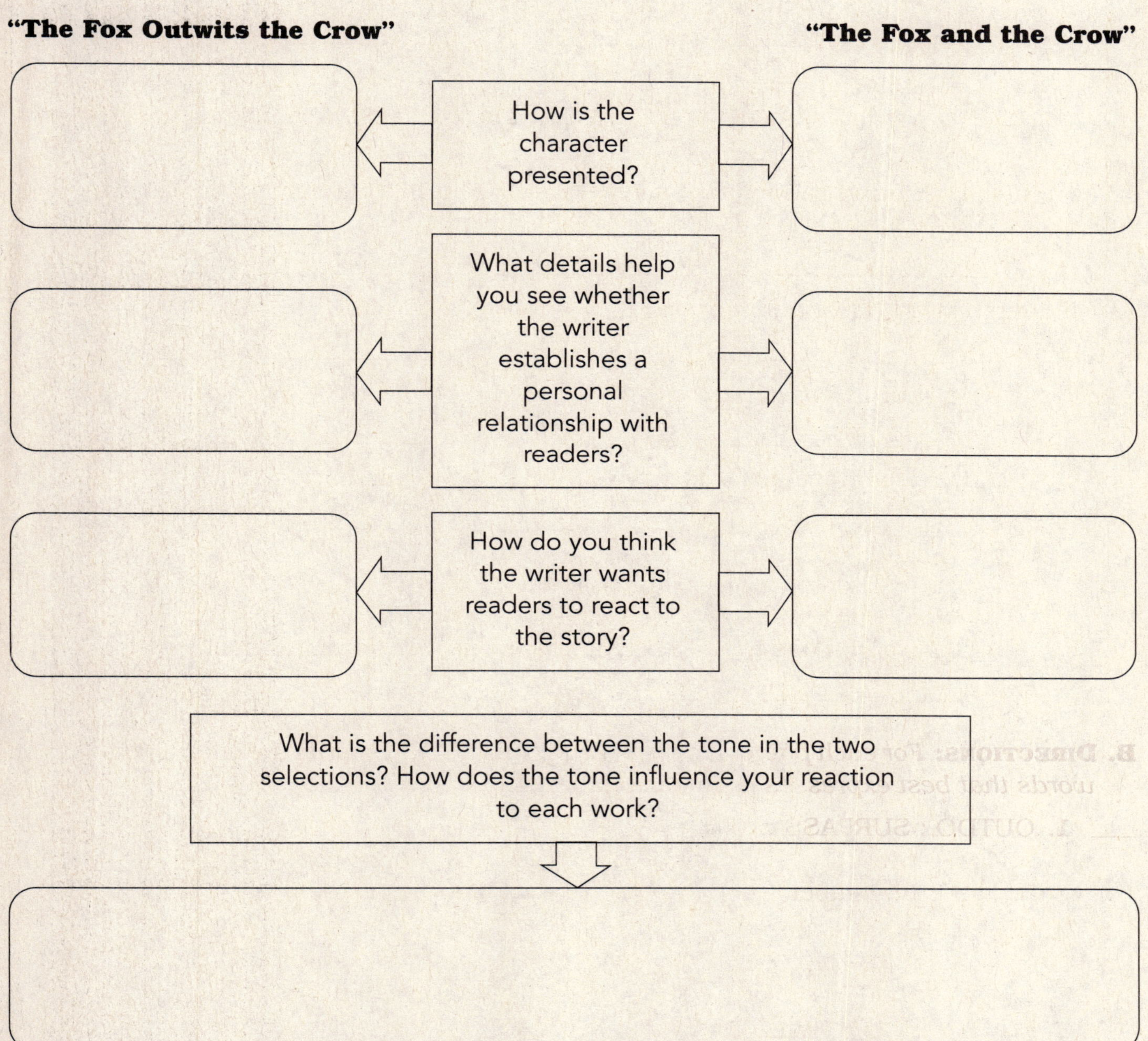

Now, use your notes to write an essay in which you compare your reaction to the tone of "The Fox Outwits the Crow" with your reaction to the tone of "The Fox and the Crow."